The Risk of War

THE ETHNOGRAPHY
OF POLITICAL VIOLENCE

Tobias Kelly, *Series Editor*

A complete list of books in the series
is available from the publisher.

THE RISK
OF WAR

Everyday Sociality
in the Republic of Macedonia

Vasiliki P. Neofotistos

PENN

UNIVERSITY OF PENNSYLVANIA PRESS

PHILADELPHIA

Published by
University of Pennsylvania Press
Philadelphia, Pennsylvania 19104-4112
www.upenn.edu/pennpress

Printed in the United States of America on acid-free paper
10 9 8 7 6 5 4 3 2 1

Library of Congress Cataloging-in-Publication Data
Neofotistos, Vasiliki P.
The risk of war : everyday sociality in the Republic of Macedonia /
Vasiliki P. Neofotistos. — 1st. ed.
    p.   cm. — (The ethnography of political violence)
Includes bibliographical references and index.
ISBN 978-0-8122-4399-4 (hardcover : alk. paper)
    1. Macedonia (Republic)—Ethnic relations—Political aspects. 2. Macedonia
(Republic)—Social conditions. 3. Macedonia (Republic)—Politics and
government—1992– I. Title. II. Series: Ethnography of political violence.
DR2253.N46   2012
949.7603—dc23   2011044322

για τη Νανού καί τον Μπάκο

CONTENTS

Introduction

On 16 February 2001, members of a journalistic team working for the Macedonian TV station A1 claimed that they had been kidnapped by armed Albanian men, some in black uniforms, for a few hours. By all accounts this event took place in the Albanian-populated village of Tanuševci in northern Macedonia, just across the border from UN-administered Kosovo (see Figure 1).[1] The crew had traveled to Tanuševci to check the veracity of information regarding the alleged existence of a Kosovo Liberation Army, or KLA (in Albanian, Ushtria Çlirimtare e Kosovës, UÇK) training camp in the village and film a report.[2] (The KLA, an Albanian insurgent group that fought against Serbian forces in the adjoining Kosovo in the 1990s with a view to Kosovo's independence, was officially disbanded under NATO supervision in June 1999.[3]) The armed men allegedly confiscated the crew's equipment and cell phones, and told the journalists the village had been "liberated" by the hitherto totally unknown, except perhaps to NATO and Macedonian intelligence, Albanian National Liberation Army, or NLA (in Albanian, Ushtria Çlirimtare Kombëtare, UÇK) and that Macedonians were not welcome there, indicating that the village was no longer under the jurisdiction of the Macedonian state.[4] Media sources proclaimed that after the journalists were released, a Macedonian Border Patrol unit entered the village and clashed with the armed group. After an approximately hour-long gun battle, the armed group reportedly withdrew into Kosovo on the other side of the border.

These are the beginnings of the 2001 armed conflict between Macedonian government forces and the Albanian NLA in the Republic of Macedonia. According to the NLA, the goal of the insurgency was to secure greater rights for Albanians in Macedonia, who make up 25.17 percent of the overall population of the country.[5] The decision to take up arms was allegedly motivated by the failure of the Macedonian state, ten years after independence, to pass the laws necessary to carry certain provisions of the founding Constitution into effect and hence provide the Albanian community with

Figure 1. Map of Macedonia. Based on a UN map, UN Cartographic Section.

the rights it reportedly deserved and demanded throughout the 1990s, including the establishment of an Albanian-speaking state-sponsored university and increase in the number of Albanian employees in the public sector. Macedonian officials, on the other hand, branded the NLA as a terrorist organization and the insurgency as a provocation against the territorial integrity of the Macedonian state.

During the conflict, a plan for "peaceful" resolution, involving the exchange of populations and territories between Albania and Macedonia, was leaked to the press reportedly by the Macedonian Academy of Sciences and Arts. The plan proposed that Macedonia should give northwestern territory, where the Albanian population is most densely populated, to Kosovo, and also give Debar to Albania in return for territories with Macedonian majorities in southeastern Albania.[6] The proposal was left undenounced by Ljubčo Georgievski, Macedonian prime minister and leader of the nationalist Internal Macedonian Revolutionary Organization-Democratic Party of National Unity (VMRO-DPMNE), and by Stojan Andov, speaker of Parliament and member of the Liberal Party of Macedonia (LPM, a junior partner in the government coalition). For fear that the conflict in Macedonia would escalate into a civil war and spread throughout the Balkans, international mediators from NATO and the European Union stepped in to help manage the crisis. Fighting between the two armies stopped a mere five miles from the capital city of Skopje before it ended on 13 August 2001 with the signing of the internationally brokered Ohrid Framework Agreement (otherwise known as the Framework Agreement; see Appendix for full text). The Agreement provided the basis for constitutional amendments, meant to clarify what was inadequately addressed in the founding Constitution and improve the overall status of the Albanian community in the country as well as that of other minorities (cf. Nikolovska and Siljanovska-Davkova 2001, Vankovska 2007).[7]

The conflict heightened feelings of insecurity among Macedonia's population, and nobody inside or outside the country knew what to expect. There were speculations that Macedonia would be engulfed in civil war, be partitioned, or become a UN protectorate. In what follows, I provide an ethnographic account of the ways middle- and working-class Muslim Albanians and Orthodox Macedonians in Macedonia's capital practiced daily life at a time when fear and uncertainty regarding their existence and the viability of the state were intense and widespread. I do not want to give the wrong impression that members of other communities in the country, such as Roms, Turks, and Vlahs, were unaffected by the crisis.[8] Rather, I focus in particular on the Albanian and Macedonian communities, which are chiefly Sunni Muslim (and speak the Gheg dialect of Albanian) and Orthodox respectively, because they are the numerically largest in Macedonia.[9] I consider the following questions. What impact did the 2001 conflict have on everyday life? How did social actors who did not engage in armed combat construct social reality at the time? How did they position themselves vis-à-vis people of different ethnonational backgrounds? In addressing these questions, I explore the ways middle- and working-class Macedonians and Albanians in Skopje made sense of violence and tried to restore a sense of order and stability in the midst of uncertainty and political turmoil.

The 2001 Conflict as a Success Story

The 2001 armed conflict was neither the first nor the last crisis in Macedonia. After the country emerged from the dissolution of Yugoslavia as an independent nation-state in 1991, numerous key events occurred (see Chapter 1) that not only disrupted everyday life but also brought about new modes of socio-political action and redefined sociopolitical categories of belonging—what Veena Das has called "critical events" (1995: 6).

Compared to previous events, however, the crisis of 2001 was unique in terms of its duration and intensity, and also its social and political ramifications for Macedonia's future. The conflict lasted six months, claimed a few hundred lives on both the Macedonian and Albanian sides, and generated hundreds of internally displaced persons. Fighting was limited to mountainous areas in the northwestern parts of the country bordering on Kosovo, where a segment of the Albanian population is heavily concentrated, and did not spread to areas that border on Albania and have large concentrations of Albanians, such as the western town of Debar, the southwestern town of Struga, and the villages in between and farther east. With the benefit of hindsight, we can say that the 2001 conflict was a foundational moment in contemporary Macedonian history in the sense that it ushered in unprecedented structural change—it was what political scientists term a "critical juncture" (see Calder 2008). For example, the Constitution was amended, state funds were provided for university level education in Albanian, local self-government was strengthened by incorporating Albanians, and in units of local self-government where at least 20 percent of the population spoke a language other than Macedonian that language and its alphabet became official in addition to Macedonian and the Cyrillic alphabet (see Appendix). Nonetheless, while the conflict was unfolding, nobody in Macedonia or abroad could tell if all-out war would be averted or a new power structure be established.

Following the signing of the Ohrid Agreement in August 2001, Macedonia was declared a success story by politicians in Macedonia, EU officials, the international media, and Western nongovernmental organizations. Talk proliferated about how Macedonia's political leadership with the diplomatic assistance of the EU and the U.S. had averted yet another war in the Balkans. These assessments miss a crucial factor, namely the way social actors "on the ground," including members of the Albanian community for whom the conflict was allegedly fought, positioned themselves in relation to the insurgency and to each other during interpersonal and intergroup interactions. Even the most detailed study to date of the events that comprised the 2001 crisis, *Macedonia: Warlords and Rebels in the Balkans* (2004) by journalist John Philips, does not offer much insight into the interpersonal dynamics among civilians with different ethnonational backgrounds. Additional works to which I extend the same critique include *Diary of an Uncivil War: The Violent Aftermath of the Kosovo Conflict* (2002) by journalist Scott Taylor,

Macedonian Unfinished Crisis: Challenges in the Process of Democratization and Stabilization (2003) by political scientist Veton Latifi, and *Walking on the Edge: Consolidating Multiethnic Macedonia, 1989–2004* (2006) by political scientist Židas Daskalovski.

Besides not possessing the efficacy of ethnographic analysis that is grounded in the details of everyday life, such accounts of the 2001 crisis have also been wittingly or unwittingly complicit in perpetuating a simplistic and, in my experience, inaccurate image of Macedonia as "the very exemplar of an ethnically divided society" (Hislope 2007: 154). The Macedonia I experienced prior to the eruption of the insurgency, similar to what Bringa observes in prewar Bosnia (Bringa 1995: 3), was characterized simultaneously by "coexistence and conflict, tolerance and prejudice, suspicion and friendship." Unlike the case for Bosnia (see Maček 2009), armed violence did not reach a massive scale and everyday forms of sociality in the capital were not shattered during the period of hostilities. I do not mean to deny or minimize the role local and foreign officials and organizations played in averting civil war and safeguarding territorial integrity—as several scholars have shown (for example, Ackermann 2003; Kaufman 1996; Petroska-Beška 1996; Sokalski 2003), the international factor has played an important role in keeping the peace. Nonetheless, any attempt toward a holistic understanding of violence (and also peace) in Macedonia cannot afford to exclude the dynamics of intergroup contact in everyday life. Such dynamics, I argue, reveal how social actors can respond with resilience and wit to disruptive and threatening changes in the social structure and help to avert full-scale war.

Making Sense of Recurring Violence

Sporadic outbursts of both internal and external political upheaval and unrest, followed by periods of seeming calm, have characterized the history of post-independence Macedonia (Chapter 1). In this ethnography, I treat the 2001 crisis as a moment in a series of events that have created instability and unpredictability throughout Macedonia's history, and analyze it as a "diagnostic event," an occurrence that, as Sally Falk Moore has argued, sheds light on "substantial areas of normative indeterminacy" (1987: 729) and "reveals ongoing contests and conflicts and competition and the efforts to prevent, suppress, or repress these" (730). Treated this way, the 2001 crisis is diagnostic of the flux of continual and ongoing sociopolitical arrangements and rearrangements in Macedonia and, more specifically, of intense political struggles, couched in ethnonational terms, over the allocation of power in the newly founded state. Furthermore, I use the 2001 armed conflict as a window onto some of the tensions and contestations on the level of everyday life.

Much anthropological work throws into relief the processes through which social actors make their social world meaningful and construct social reality within the context of violence and war (for example, Aretxaga 1997; Das 2007; Feldman 1991; Greenhouse et al. 2002; Nordstrom 1997; Strathern et al. 2005). My ethnography adds to this body of work through a focus on the ways people (re)position themselves and others in the social fabric during a period characterized by heightened political instability. The practices and performances explored in this book revolve around the eschewal of one single and absolute meaning concerning the nature of social reality, and help to highlight and promote indeterminacy, a condition that Moore (1978: 47) describes as "elements in [social] situations which are . . . matters of open or multiple option." What I wish to underline here is the flexibility and creativity with which social actors are able to address dangerous contingencies and navigate turbulent times. Such a stance carries, it seems to me, important implications for the avoidance of all-out war.

An additional goal of this book is to contribute to anthropological studies of former Yugoslavia, whose main focus has been on exploring the conditions of war between neighbors and the effects of war on the lives of individuals (see, among others, Gagnon 2004; Halpern and Kideckel 2000; Bringa 1995). My account of events and daily life during the 2001 conflict aims to help us better understand how Macedonia thus far has managed, despite high political volatility and ethnonationalist rivalries, to escape civil bloodshed. The enhancement of understanding, I suggest, lies in the consideration of interpersonal dynamics of intergroup contact under circumstances of armed violence. As Susanna Trnka (2008: 15) eloquently notes in her analysis of the 2000 nationalist coup in Fiji, comprehension of how people ascribe meaning to violence and negotiate these meanings during interpersonal, intergroup interactions remains somewhat fragmentary. In agreement with scholars who address this point at issue (for example, Maček 2009, Nordstrom 1997, Trnka 2008), I direct attention to the interpersonal exchanges in which middle- and working-class Macedonians and Albanians in Skopje engaged to negotiate around the unfolding conflict and face the unpredictable in 2001. In so doing, I also add to the growing ethnographic literature on Macedonia whose predominant focus is on the ethnic Macedonian community (for example, Brown 2003; Friedman et al. 2010; Thiessen 2007; Roudometof 2000).

Methodological Questions

Learning to converse in both Macedonian and Albanian was a requisite for my ethnographic research among members of the Macedonian and Albanian communities in Macedonia. I took Macedonian language classes in graduate school in the United States and private, intensive Albanian-language lessons for about ten months shortly after my arrival in Macedonia to commence fieldwork in the spring of 2000. My entrance into Macedonian society was greatly facilitated by the parents of my Macedonian language tutor, who became my adoptive aunt and uncle and helped me network among their relatives, friends, and neighbors. I conducted research in Skopje from March 2000 to August 2001, when the NLA insurgency came to an end. My decision to live and work in the capital city, home to nearly a fourth of the country's total population of nearly two million, was solely based on my personal preference for living in large urban areas.

I took up residence in the ethnically heterogeneous administrative district (*naselba*) of Čair (from Turkish *çayir*, "field") for the following reasons. In the first place, the district had (and still has) some of the highest concentrations of Albanians in Skopje, and so it seemed to me an ideal entryway into the Albanian community.[10] The colorfulness of the district was a further attraction. When compared to other districts in Skopje, Čair has a tremendous variety of people from various ethnic and religious backgrounds (the area is inhabited by, among others, Albanians, Turks, Macedonians, Roms, Bosnians, Serbs, and Vlahs) and of sounds and scents. Men play cards or chess outdoors, or frequent the teashops that abound in the area. Small groups of women in Islamic headscarves (*shamija*) and long, loose over-garments resembling coatdresses (generally referred to as *mantila*) stroll along dusty paths to the houses of relatives for Turkish tea and coffee. While walking just a few blocks, one can hear all the languages of Macedonia spoken by passersby. The call to prayer from minarets puncturing the skyline mingles with the noise of traffic and the voices of children playing carefree in the narrow streets in residential neighborhoods.

An additional reason why I chose to live in Čair had to do with the strong admonitions that some of my Macedonian friends who did not live in that district, and with whom I became acquainted during my exploratory fieldwork in the summer of 1999, gave me against going, let alone living, there. Reportedly, Čair was "dirty" (*prljav*) and different from the "clean" (*čisti*) parts of the city. These designations are commonly used to describe areas in northwestern Skopje that are heavily Albanian-populated and areas in southeastern

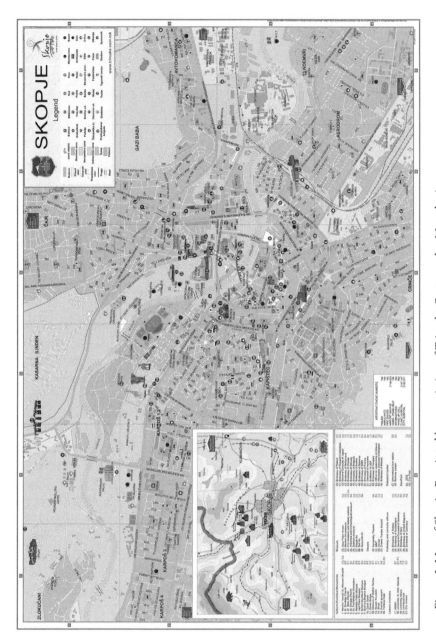

Figure 2. Map of Skopje. Reprinted by permission of Trimaks Cartography, Macedonia.

Skopje that are predominantly Macedonian-populated, respectively. The Vardar River, which rises in the mountains near Gostivar and flows through Skopje, is perceived as a symbolic boundary between the so-called Macedonian and Albanian parts of the city, and was historically the boundary between Skopje's older and newer parts, which were built after the city was struck by an earthquake in 1963 (see Figure 2). Also, "dirty" areas are allegedly inhabited by criminals dealing in drugs, women and guns, while "clean" areas by harmless and friendly people. Intrigued by such classifications, and recalling Mary Douglas's (1966) observation that concepts of pollution are often used to describe threats to the social order, I decided that upon my return to Macedonia in the spring of 2000 I would live in Čair and learn Albanian in order to be able to expand my research into, and establish my legitimacy as an ethnographer within, the Albanian community. Although it raised some eyebrows at first, my decision did not alienate me from those Macedonians who lived outside my chosen neighborhood.

While I lived and worked with members of the Macedonian and Albanian communities within the geographic bounds of Čair, I accompanied my research participants on their outings to the wider city and also recorded narratives about intergroup interactions outside my neighborhood. The present work thus centers around social networks: it concerns middle- and working-class Macedonian and Albanian men and women who interacted with each other either because they were neighbors in Čair, worked together inside or outside the neighborhood, originated from long-established urban families (see Ellis 2003) and kept in touch despite geographic separation or the passage of time, or because they accidentally encountered each other in cafés, state institutions, or the streets of Skopje.

Becoming "Ours"

During my first exploratory visit to Skopje in summer 1999, one of the people with whom I struck up a conversation was Pance, a Macedonian car mechanic in his late forties. Pance was washing his battered-looking Zastava car in his small front yard when I stopped a few feet away from his house, located in a neighborhood of Čair, to study my Skopje city map in hopes that I would get my bearings. As soon as he realized that I was lost, Pance eagerly interrupted his task to give me directions back to the main street. Before too long, as often happened during my fieldwork, I was asked about my place of origin and my work, and responded that I was an ethnographer interested in relations between Macedonians and Albanians after the collapse of socialism. "We've lived together well for years and years now," Pance immediately commented and nervously resumed his car-washing task. I felt a quiver in my stomach when he shot a glance at me and said sternly, "Relations between Macedonians and Albanians are good until people like *you* start asking questions; it is then that we have problems!" I awkwardly explained that it was not my intention to stir up trouble, but Pance did not seem to want to listen to what I had to say—instead, he became engrossed in his task. My attempts to speak with Pance again in the days that followed yielded no results. Every time that I passed by his house and he happened to be sitting in his yard, he hastily greeted me hello and immediately disappeared inside.

My scholarly interest in interethnic relations between Macedonians and Albanians in post-independence Macedonia, especially after the NLA insurgency erupted in February 2001 and I narrowed my central research focus to the practice of everyday life during the period of the armed conflict, caused great unease in the Macedonian community. Many Macedonians with whom I worked, similar to Pance, argued that any research about interethnic relations in the country was "irrelevant" (*bez vrska*) because the state had always provided for its citizens in a fair and just manner. Those who welcomed my presence in the country suggested that my eighteen-month research stay was too short a time for an outsider to grasp the intricacies of local politics. Some Macedonians recommended that I extend my stay in Macedonia in order to comprehend fully the allegedly malevolent Albanian psyche and become able to discern the Albanian irredentist aspirations behind the rhetoric of "greater rights."

Many Albanians, too, voiced reservations about meeting and speaking with me for reasons relating to the position of the larger Albanian collectivity within Macedonian society. More specifically, as members of a community whose political leaders, as I discuss in Chapter 1, have organized large-scale initiatives to challenge the distribution of power in the Macedonian state, Albanians generally worried whether speaking with me would get them into trouble with state authorities. When, for example, in April 2000 Risto, a Macedonian elementary school teacher and neighbor of my Macedonian adoptive aunt and uncle, called his Albanian colleague Mustafa to ask if Mustafa would be willing to speak with me, Mustafa asked Risto if my intended visit was politically motivated and the conversation would be politically exploited. My entry into the Albanian community in Cair was made possible thanks to Risto's guarantee of my scholarly interests and the friendliness of Mustafa and his wife Bahrie, a high-school teacher who subsequently became my private language tutor.

Even though at first they were suspicious of my research motives, and as so often happens in fieldwork (for example, Bonilla and Glazer 1970; Sluka 1990; Dudwick 2000: 24) assumed that I was a foreign spy, Macedonians and Albanians gradually accepted me into their communities as "ours" (naša/e jona in Macedonian/Albanian) for different reasons. Many members of the Macedonian community, despite the still (as of this writing) unresolved controversy between Greece and Macedonia over the name of the Republic (see Danforth 1995) and despite the 1992 and 1994 Greek trade embargoes against Macedonia, tended to react enthusiastically when they heard from mutual friends that my parents were Greek and I had grown up in Greece: "You are from Greece?! Oh, but then you are ours!" The aspects of my personal background on which they focused to identify me as "ours" (naša) were threefold. Similar to them, I was Orthodox Christian, could converse fluently in Macedonian (hence many Macedonians with whom I spoke assumed that I originated from the geographical area of Greece that is called Macedonia, where Macedonian-language speakers reside), and had personal ties to the Balkan region, thereby allegedly sharing the same Balkan mentality (appreciation for family and friends, an inherent understanding of how to enjoy life, and warm temperament).[11] For many members of the Albanian community, these aspects of my background were utterly insignificant; instead, my birthplace and current country of residence, the United States, combined with my commitment to conversing with them in Albanian and my having taken up residence in a neighborhood of Čair despite many Macedonians' admonitions to the contrary, rendered me "ours" (e jona). The emphasis that my Albanian research participants placed on American-ness can be understood in the context of America's key role in the 1999 NATO bombing campaign against Serbia—a campaign that gave rise to the widespread belief in the Albanian community in Macedonia and Kosovo that anyone from the United States supported, by default, Albanian political interests.[12] The different features of my personal biography on which Macedonians and Albanians chose to focus were common knowledge among everyone who helped me network across ethnonational borders. Macedonians thus introduced me to Albanians as an ethnographer from America, while Albanians introduced me to Macedonians as an ethnographer of Greek origin.

The Layout of This Book

This ethnography is organized into six main chapters. In Chapter 1, I show how the dissolution of Yugoslavia and the emergence of Macedonia as an independent nation-state ushered in a period of profound political instability and uncertainty about the future. During the 1990s, Macedonia and its people lived through a series of critical events. I identify these events and their Albanian protagonists, namely, the Albanian boycott of the population census in Yugoslavia in April 1991; the boycott of the referendum on Macedonian independence in September 1991 and the conduct among the Albanian community of a referendum on political and territorial autonomy for Albanians in Macedonia in January 1992; the shooting incident involving police in Bit Pazar (where the largest open-air market in Skopje is held) that left three Albanian men and one Macedonian woman dead in November 1992; the extraordinary census in the summer of 1994; the public opening of the Albanian-speaking Tetovo University in December 1994; and the demonstrations in the town of Gostivar in July 1997. I also discuss these events as politically organized attempts to change the distribution of power between the two dominant ethnonational groups and (re)define the categories and meanings of political membership in post-independence Macedonia.

Chapter 2 focuses on the eruption of the 2001 armed conflict, the most severe political crisis in the history of Macedonia thus far. I consider the sudden, phantom-like emergence of the Albanian NLA in January 2001 and the uncertainty that shrouded the existence of the organization. I also examine the suggestive links between the NLA and the Kosovo Liberation Army, and the history of the fluidity of the northern Macedonian borderland, where the NLA insurgency broke out in February 2001. Moreover, I discuss how helicopter noise and television images broadcast during the insurgency stirred among the population in Skopje memories of recent conflicts in the Balkans and gave rise to the experience of the uncanny.

In Chapter 3, I examine how the spread of the NLA's control over territory in northwestern Macedonia and the escalation of armed hostilities between the Macedonian armed forces and the NLA sent reverberations of anxiety through the Macedonian and Albanian communities in Skopje and created fear that an all-out war could erupt anytime. Exploring conflicting rumors, including rumors about the participation of Muslim mujahideen fighters in the NLA, I consider the generation of profound uncertainty and confusion over what was reality and what was illusion. I also discuss how joke telling helped social actors in Skopje create a sense of control over their own lives. Furthermore, I examine how international involvement in the crisis helped to generate heightened feelings of vulnerability in the Macedonian community, and how Macedonian- and Albanian-language media constructed different social realities.

In Chapter 4, I analyze performances of civility, whereby Macedonian and Albanian men and women who shared professional ties, or long-standing ties of friendship or neighborliness, appeared during interpersonal interactions unaligned with any side in the conflict. Examining the use of the prevailing truism "politics is a whore" and the discourse of nostalgia for Tito's socialism, together with the widespread practice of hospitality, I consider how some social actors tended to promote a harmonious and agreeable social world and mutually sustain congenial assumptions regarding the trumping significance of common humanness.

Chapter 5 concerns the attempts of some members of the Macedonian collectivity to introduce an element of stability into the social order by establishing a fixed set of relationships of power during interpersonal, intergroup interactions. More specifically, I analyze how Macedonian men and women respectively engaged in efforts to establish male/ethnonational dominance and satisfy preoccupations relating to the protection of children from imminent danger. I show how such attempts remained inconclusive.

In Chapter 6, I explore enactments of respectable and "modern" Albanian selfhood. These performances, which many Albanian residents of Skopje recognized as such and hence as acts that were meaningful to them, were geared toward claiming respect from members of the Macedonian community, and charted possibilities for belonging to a society where anti-Albanian prejudice had no place. The social performances under discussion illuminated non-armed tactics to address the status of Albanians in Macedonian society.

In the Epilogue I consider how, more than a decade after the end of the 2001 turmoil, uncertainty about the future continues to permeate everyday life and Macedonia remains at risk of political instability.

CHAPTER 1

Critical Events

The 2001 armed conflict did not mark the first time that post-independence Macedonia and its people were confronted with high political instability, deriving from Macedonian and Albanian political struggles over the distribution of power in Macedonian society. During the 1990s, a series of critical events (in Veena Das's use of the term; see 1995: 6), which disrupted everyday life and brought about new modes of sociopolitical action, took place. In what follows, I identify these key events and discuss each one of them as politically organized attempts to (re)define the categories and meanings of membership in post-1991 Macedonia: the 1991 Albanian boycott of the population census in Yugoslavia; the boycott of the referendum on Macedonian independence; the 1992 conduct among the Albanian community of a referendum on the political and territorial autonomy of Albanians in Macedonia; the 1992 deadly shooting in Bit Pazar; the 1994 extraordinary census; the 1994 public opening of the Albanian-speaking Tetovo University; and, the 1997 demonstrations in Gostivar.

Before delving into the main discussion, I first need to address sociopolitical developments during the socialist period, which set the stage for critical events to unfold in Macedonia after the dissolution of federal Yugoslavia.

The Socialist Period

The People's Republic of Macedonia (proclaimed the Socialist Republic of Macedonia in the 1974 Constitution) was one of the smallest and most multiethnic republics of the Federal People's Republic of Yugoslavia. According to the 1971 census (see Friedman 1996: 90), it had 1,647,308 inhabitants: 69.3 percent Macedonians, 17 percent Albanians, 6.6 percent Turks, 2.8 percent

Serbs, 1.5 percent Roms, 0.6 percent Vlahs, 0.2 Bulgarians, 0.2 percent Yu-goslav, 0.1 percent Muslims, and 1.7 percent "other" (for the disconnect be-tween declared nationality and declared mother tongue, see Friedman 2003). Importantly, Macedonia played a marginal role or, as Rossos puts it, was a "junior partner" (2008: 235) in the Yugoslav federation: it was economically underdeveloped and the poorest republic of all, largely rural, and lacked strong political leadership that could lobby for Macedonian national inter-ests, such as the establishment of a Macedonian national church and the protection of Macedonians' rights in Greece and Bulgaria, or influence gov-ernment policy.[1]

External pressures, too, encouraged and sustained a climate of insecurity in socialist Macedonia: Bulgaria, Serbia and Greece continued a long tradi-tion, firmly rooted in the late nineteenth and early twentieth centuries (see, for example, Brown 2003; Irvine and Gal 2000; Wilkinson 1951), of advanc-ing competing nationalist claims and denying the existence of the Macedo-nian language, church and identity, respectively. More specifically, Bulgaria continued to dispute the existence of the Macedonian language and view it as a "degenerate dialect" of Bulgarian (Friedman 1985: 34) as evidenced in *The Unity of the Bulgarian Language in the Past and Today*, originally published in Bulgarian in 1978 and translated and circulated as an off-print in English, French, German, and Russian by the Bulgarian Academy of Sciences (1980). Moreover, the Serbian patriarchate denied the existence of the Macedonian Orthodox Church after the Macedonian clergy proclaimed the Church's auto-cephaly on 18 July 1967. Although the Communist government continuously urged the two national churches to settle their dispute and thus help diffuse political tensions between Serbia and Macedonia, the Serbian Church has been unwilling to revise its stance, arguing that the Macedonian Orthodox Church has not emerged in compliance with ecclesiastical rules, that is, from agreement among all Orthodox churches (see also Risteski 2009). As Brown notes (1998: 75), the refusal of the Serbian Orthodox Church to recognize the Macedonian one implies a dispute over the disposition of church property in Macedonia prior to 1967, when—between 1919 and 1941—Serbia controlled the territorial area where present-day Macedonia lies. Furthermore, deny-ing the multi-ethnicity and multiculturalism of the northern Greek prov-ince of Macedonia (see Karakasidou 1993, 1997; see also Rossos 1991), the Greek state launched systematic efforts to undermine a separate Macedonian identity and develop a Macedonian cultural identity that was fundamentally Greek in character (see Mackridge and Yannakakis 1997). As a result, many Macedonian speakers who lived in Greece's northern province of Macedonia fled, or were expelled from, Greece during the Greek Civil War (1946–49) and moved into refugee camps and orphanages before setting up homes across eastern Europe (see Monova 2002a). These political refugees, widely known in Macedonia as *deca begalci*, "refugee children," were also deprived of their properties and Greek citizenship.[2] Strict measures against use of the Macedonian language were adopted (Kostopoulos 2000) and, what is more, Greek nationalist politicians and scholars, to whom Karakasidou (1994) refers as "sacred scholars" vindicating the Greek nationalist cause, established exclusivist claims to the name "Macedonia" and posited that the Republic of Macedonia was an invention of Yugoslav leader Josip Broz Tito (see, for example, Andriotes 1957, 1960; Christides 1949; Kofos 1964; Martis 1983).

Equally important, the situation of the Albanian minority in the first Yugoslavia (1918–41) helped engender and sustain among the Albanian population a lingering attitude of mistrust toward Yugoslav authority and prepared the ground for sharp political antagonisms between Macedonians and Albanians in the 1990s. Specifically, the Serb-dominated government in Belgrade implemented a severe policy of Albanian persecution (see Bisaku et al. 1997: 361–99). Some of the key elements of this policy are listed in a memorandum entitled "The Expulsion of the Albanians" and presented by Serbian university professor Vaso Čubrilović in March 1937 to the Communist leadership in Belgrade (see Elsie 1997: 400–424):

> The mass evacuation of the Albanians from their triangle is the only effective course we can take. . . . The first prerequisite is the creation of a suitable psychosis. . . . We must first of all win over the clergy and men of influence through money and threats. . . . The law must be enforced to the letter so as to make staying intolerable for the Albanians: fines, imprisonment, ruthless application of all police regulations, such as the prohibition of smuggling, cutting forests, damaging agriculture, leaving dogs unchained, compulsory labour and any other measure that an experienced police force can contrive. . . . Private initiative, too, can greatly assist in this direction. We should distribute weapons to our colonists, as need be. . . . Local riots can be incited. . . . There remains one more method Serbia employed with great practical effect after 1878, that is, secretly razing Albanian villages and urban settlements to the ground. (409–10)

As a result of this anti-Albanian policy, about 45,000 people left Kosovo and over 50,000 Albanians were imprisoned during the interwar period (von

Kohl and Libal 1997: 32). Furthermore, in the aftermath of the break between Tito and Stalin in June 1948, Albania's communist ruler Enver Hoxha, who was a close ally of Tito during World War II, declared his loyalty to Stalin. The Yugoslav Secret Police stepped up their hunt for Albanians throughout Yugoslavia, especially Kosovo, on suspicion that agents from Albania had infiltrated the country seeking to undermine and destabilize Tito's regime in order to unite Kosovo and Albania. After decades of persecution, and starting in 1953 when Yugoslavia signed a treaty of peaceful relations with Turkey, more than 200,000 Muslims, mostly the Şehirli and Kasabali (the Turkish-speaking Muslim urban dwellers of Macedonia; see Ellis 2003) and also Albanians, Turks, Bosnians, and Roms, declared themselves to be Turks and migrated to Turkey (50).

In 1968, two years after the discharge of Aleksandar Ranković, Yugoslav minister of interior with the overall responsibility for the severe anti-Albanian security policy in the 1950s and 1960s, Albanian demonstrations took place in Prishtina that called for Kosovo to be made a republic. Such demands arose from widespread feelings among Albanians that they were second-class citizens in former Yugoslavia because they had not been granted their own republic despite their numbers (5.0 and 6.4 percent of the population of former Yugoslavia in 1961 and 1971, respectively) being larger than, for instance, Montenegrins (2.8 and 2.5 percent; see Woodward 1995a: 32). The demonstrations in Kosovo sparked similar demonstrations across the border in the Macedonian town of Tetovo that demanded the heavily Albanian-populated areas of western and northern Macedonia unite with Kosovo in one Republic. Authorities clamped down on the demonstrations in both Prishtina and Tetovo, adding to widespread Albanian dissatisfaction with the tactics of the Yugoslav regime. Albanian political activism raised fears among Macedonians that Albanians in Macedonia were determined to pursue their own ethnonational objectives, jeopardizing the territorial integrity of Macedonia.

The tense political atmosphere was aggravated by the structural characteristics of Yugoslavia's political system. In particular, the Yugoslav system placed emphasis on rights rather than interests and the federal government in Belgrade was the one to guarantee and protect these rights on the basis of national equality. This arrangement, among other things, put in a disadvantageous position people who did not belong to the majority nation in any given republic because the government in Belgrade in practice did not implement equal rights. Language policy is an eloquent case in point. As Kovačec notes (1992), only the languages of constituent nations (*narodi*)—that is to say, Macedonian, Serbo-Croatian, and Slovenian—were official at the national level while the languages spoken by nonconstituent nations in the former Yugoslavia were official at a smaller, local level. Additionally, the implementation of the principle of proportional representation of constituent nations, otherwise known as *ključ* or "(national) key," in personnel policy produced divisiveness instead of unity. Different groups had different access to socioeconomic power and political privileges and tended to view each other's resources as a threat to their own wellbeing (see Woodward 1995b). After all, as Verdery (1993) has shown, the very organization of socialism built up national consciousness and amplified the importance of the national idea (also see Vucinich 1969).

In the wake of the ethnic violence of World War II, Tito's commitment to the ideology of "brotherhood and unity" and the principle of national equality managed to keep the threat of Yugoslavia's disintegration at bay. But after his death in May 1980, uncertainty prevailed regarding the long-term viability of Yugoslavia. On 23–25 March 1981 during student demonstrations in Prishtina, which had begun a few days earlier demanding better food in the school cafeteria and improved living conditions in the dormitories, some of the protesters called for republic status for Kosovo, a demand viewed as a prelude to demands for the right to secede. Although right to secession was not actually guaranteed in the Yugoslav Constitution, republic status was widely perceived as necessary to any attempt at secession. Macedonian authorities feared the spread of Albanian nationalist sentiment and introduced repressive measures against the local Albanian population, such as the closing of the Albanian-language program of the Pedagogical Academy in Skopje (where Albanians trained to become teachers) in 1985, dismissal of Albanian teachers, cancellation of classes held in Albanian that lacked "sufficient" enrollment of Albanian pupils, jail sentences, decrease in numbers of Albanian employees in state administration, and official refusal to register baby names that were taken as an index of support for Albanian nationalism (for example, Rilind, from *rilindje* or "renaissance"; Flamur or "Flag"; or Enver because it was the name of Albania's ruler) (see Poulton 1995: 128–30). Albanians in Macedonia engaged in demonstrations against such measures while requesting greater political rights throughout the 1980s.

The deteriorating economic situation and increasing unemployment in the 1980s generated a widespread sense of social and economic uncertainty and unease, compounded by political insecurity, in all of Yugoslavia. Acceptance of the stringent conditions imposed by the International Monetary Fund (IMF) regarding debt repayment brought about salary freezes, a drastic cut in imports, severe cuts in federal government subsidies, and currency devaluation (see Woodward 1995b). Nationalist politicians advocated for the social and economic rights of their ethnonationalist communities over others and eventually made demands for political rights and territory, including independence from the federation. The struggles over power in the Yugoslav republics in the late 1980s and early 1990s are eloquently captured in the pronouncement from Yugoslav political theorist Vladimir Gligorov, "Why should I be a minority in your state when you can be a minority in mine?" (cited in Woodward 1995a: xvi). Gradually but steadily nationalist leaders gained prominence, especially between 1985 and 1989 when the international order of the Cold War began to collapse and federal Yugoslavia was plunged into greater instability and uncertainty regarding its existence.

The spread of nationalism and the collapse of the one-party system in Yugoslavia ushered in a new period of extreme uncertainty regarding Macedonia's future. Macedonia held its first multiparty elections in November 1990. Most political parties were founded on an ethnonational basis with the aim of advancing the interests of "their" constituents, thus encouraging voters to cast ballots along ethnonational lines. After three rounds of balloting, and unlike in other Yugoslav republics where nationalists won a majority of electoral votes, no party won outright in Macedonia. A new government that encompassed old Communist Party members as well as reformist communists and nationalists took power.[3] As the Yugoslav federal army attacked Slovenia and Croatia (both of which declared independence from Yugoslavia in June 1991) on the grounds of protecting the territorial integrity of Yugoslavia, Macedonia was left with two options: it could join in some federated arrangement with a Yugoslavia whose ultimate shape was unclear at that time; or it could declare full sovereignty and independence. The Macedonian government determined to hold a referendum on independence in September 1991 and let the people decide.

Boycott of the 1991 Yugoslav Census

In the meantime, the opportunity for Albanians to express overtly their discontent over decades of political marginalization in Yugoslavia arose during 1–15 April 1991 when a population census took place. In an atmosphere of pervasive distrust, and suspicious that Yugoslav authorities were going to manipulate the results of the census and misrepresent the percentage of the Albanian population in order to marginalize the Albanian group, leaders of the two largest Albanian political parties at the time, namely, the Party for Democratic Prosperity (PDP/PPD) and the People's Democratic Party (NDP/PDP), issued a call for a boycott of the census.[4] Their call was widely answered, and the boycott was observed in Kosovo and also in the municipalities (*opštini*) of Debar, Gostivar, Kičevo, Kumanovo, Ohrid, Skopje, Struga, Tetovo, and Titov Veles (see Antonovska et al. 1996, cited in Friedman 1996). Statisticians used (among other things) the latest available census data, 1981, according to which Albanians amounted to 377,208 or 19.8 percent of the total population of Macedonia (Friedman 1996: 90), and thus attempted to estimate the numbers of Albanians in areas where the census was boycotted.

Albanian politicians also launched an international media campaign asserting that the Albanian community had been deliberately miscounted and that Albanians made up 40 percent of the overall population in Macedonia, thereby making demands for the creation of two distinct majorities (Macedonian and Albanian) and leaving all other ethnic groups in the country out of a potential redistribution of political power. For its part, the Macedonian government contended that Albanians were only about 15 or 20 percent at the most. According to Friedman (1996: 89), Albanian political leaders were not the only ones claiming such large numbers: Serbs, Turks, Roms, Greeks, Egyptians, Bulgarians, and Vlahs released figures that when added altogether exceeded the total number of inhabitants in the Republic, even without taking account of Macedonians. Identity politics, as Kertzer and Arel remind us (2002: 30), "is a numbers game, or more precisely a battle over relative proportions, both within the state and within particular territories of the larger state. Groups fear a change of proportion disadvantageous to themselves, as this often directly affects how political and economic power are allocated" (see also Anderson 1998).

According to the preliminary results of the 1991 Yugoslav census, announced in November 1991, Albanians at 441,987 were the second largest group, 21.7 percent of the entire population of Macedonia (Friedman 1996: 90). Emotions in the country run high as Albanian political leaders challenged the results. Steadfast efforts to promote internationally the image of Albanians as an unfairly marginalized group in Macedonia, nonetheless, met with success: the international community, as I discuss in greater detail later in this chapter, called for an extraordinary census to be monitored by international observers.

Boycott of the Referendum on Macedonian Independence

Besides boycotting the population census in Yugoslavia, Albanians also boycotted the official referendum on Macedonian independence on 8 September

1991 and held a separate referendum on 11–12 January 1992 to decide on the political and territorial autonomy for Albanians in Macedonia. Despite government warnings that such a referendum would be considered illegal, it was conducted publicly at more than 500 polling stations (Ramet 2002: 189); 74 percent of approximately 280,000 Albanians, or 92 percent of eligible voters, favored autonomy (Ackermann 2000: 61). Albanian politicians used the overwhelming popular support for autonomy as political leverage to try and secure greater political and cultural rights for the Albanian community, thus fueling within the Macedonian community even greater resentment of Albanians. Three months later, in April 1992, a group of Albanian radicals proclaimed the establishment of the "Republic of Illirida" in the area surrounding the town of Struga.[5] This proclamation took place only a few kilometers south of the Macedonian-populated village of Vevčani, whose approximately two thousand inhabitants in early 1992 voted in a referendum to proclaim their own "Republic of Vevčani." As a political move, the Albanian proclamation was thus designed not only to further highlight the independent spirit of Albanians but also to underscore the scope of dissatisfaction with central authority.

Meantime, with about three quarters of the voters in favor of independence, the Macedonian Assembly adopted the Founding Constitution in November 1991.[6] The Preamble of the Constitution defined Macedonia as "a national state of the Macedonian people [narod], in which full equality as citizens and permanent coexistence with the Macedonian people is provided for Albanians, Turks, Vlahs, Romanies and other nationalities [nacionalnosti] living in the Republic of Macedonia." From the viewpoint of Macedonian lawmakers, the phrasing "together with the Macedonian people" in the Preamble was a guarantee for equal human (that is, individual) but not equal political rights for all communities living in the country. The category narod, or people/ethnically defined nation, was institutionalized as a meaningful category at the inception of federal Yugoslavia in 1944 and, despite several revisions of the Yugoslav Constitution, indicated until the dissolution of Yugoslavia that each constituent republic (except Bosnia-Herzegovina) belonged to the majority nation rather than to the entire body of citizens in each republic—a phenomenon Robert Hayden describes as "constitutional nationalism" (1992) and associates with the eruption of conflict in Yugoslavia (see Hayden 1999).[7] As Vlaisavljević (2002: 204) notes in his discussion of South Slav ethnie, Tito's slogan bratstvo i jedinstvo, or "brotherhood and unity," really referred to ethnic communities that were already recognized. Following the Yugoslav tradition, Macedonian lawmakers instituted a sharp distinction between the Macedonian *narod*, as the "real Macedonians" who deserved full political membership in their state, and other *nacionalnosti*, who did not have the *narod* status and could not qualify for proportional representation on national and regional public bodies and for the rights to self-determination and self-governance.

In other words, Macedonian statehood was determined from the outset in ethnonational terms like most other statehoods in the region and, more generally, in Europe (see, for example, Brubaker 1996). Central to this definition was a heightened urgency to protect the recently emergent nation-state against potential threats to stability and sovereignty by generating a hierarchical structure whereby Macedonians were connected to other, non-Macedonian groups in the country in a dominant relation of encompassment and non-ethnic Macedonians were connected to Macedonians in a subordinate relation of incorporation (see also Neofotistos 2004). In reserving the right to regulate all affairs pertaining to the nation-state, Macedonians retained a status similar to that of any ethnic majority in any European nation-state, thus allowing for the political marginalization of numerically smaller communities. As Brown (2003: 247) notes, Macedonian national thinking and the prominence it assigns to Slavic solidarity owes much to models of folk solidarity that can be traced back to the German national revival movement in the early nineteenth century. After all, the question "to whom does the state belong?" has played a pivotal role in determining the character of most European nation-states. Nonetheless, as Brown has shown, Macedonia's lived sociopolitical reality has been especially susceptible to "the violence of ideas" (247) regarding its multicultural future—ideas that, as I am about to explain, were materialized into action in the years following independence.

Regional Reactions

To get a comprehensive picture of the unstable terrain that social actors in post-1991 Macedonia have had to navigate, it is important at this point to take a step back and consider the regional reactions to Macedonia's proclamation of independence on 20 November 1991. Thus, the Bulgarian government recognized the Macedonian state, but continued to deny the existence of a distinct Macedonian nation and, as of this writing, still claims as Bulgarians Macedonians who live in Macedonia, many thousands of Macedonians in Albania, Greece, and the Gorans of Kosovo and Albania.[8] Additionally, the Bulgarian government still views the Macedonian language as a dialect of

Bulgarian (Mahon 2004; Shea 1997: 351–55) and denies the existence of its own Macedonian minority. Moreover, Serbia continued to deny the existence of the Macedonian Orthodox Church.

Furthermore, the name dispute between Greece and Macedonia intensified (see also Brown 2003: 35–36; Cowan 2000; Danforth 1995). Greece refused to recognize Macedonia on the grounds that the use of the name "Macedonia" was an attempt to steal Greece's history and cultural heritage and might be accompanied by aspirations against Greece's territorial integrity. Greek nationalists claimed more loudly and aggressively than prior to 1991 that modern Macedonians had no right to their name because, unlike Greeks (according to them), they were not descended from ancient Macedonians and Alexander the Great. In a conciliatory move, the Macedonian Parliament in January 1992 ratified Constitutional Amendment I, according to which Macedonia has no territorial pretensions toward any neighboring state and the borders of Macedonia can only be changed in accordance with generally accepted international norms, and Amendment II, according to which Macedonia will not interfere in the sovereign rights or internal affairs of other states. Be that as it may, European Community (EC, now EU, European Union) members did not challenge Greece's position and did not extend recognition to Macedonia. They thus ignored the advisory opinion of the Badinter Arbitration Commission, a group of jurists set up by the EC in November 1991, whereby Macedonia (and not Croatia, on which recognition was nonetheless later conferred) met the Commission's conditions for EC recognition.[9] In consequence, Macedonia could not establish diplomatic relations with the EC and its member states (Weller 1992: 588) and, what is more, was ineligible for much-needed financial assistance from international organizations, including the IMF and the World Bank.

The imposition of Greek embargoes exacerbated the already dire socioeconomic situation in Macedonia. In February 1992, Antonis Samaras, minister of foreign affairs in the right-wing government of Constantine Mitsotakis, played a leading role in achieving the imposition on Macedonia of an unofficial and covert trade embargo that became official in August of the same year (see Michas 2002: 42–57). In February 1994, after Macedonia had been admitted to the UN under the provisional name "The former Yugoslav Republic of Macedonia" (FYROM) and listed under "T" (for "The"), the new socialist government of Andreas Papandreou pursued an equally hard line against Macedonia: it took overt retaliatory action over the Republic's selection of a symbol from the ancient Macedonian past (what is widely known in Greece as the 16-ray sun or star of Vergina) for the Republic's flag by imposing a nineteen-month official trade embargo on its northern neighbor (see Brown 1994, 2000).[10] The embargo generated severe criticisms by Greece's partners in the European Union and by United Nations members (Shea 1997: 278–310) until Greece signed a UN-brokered interim agreement with Macedonia in September 1995 and lifted the embargo in November.[11] During the same year, Greece registered with the World Intellectual Property Organization (WIPO), a specialized agency of the UN, the 16-, 12-, and 8-ray "sun/star of Vergina" as state emblems. The dispute over the name "Macedonia," as of this writing, remains unresolved and continues to strain relations between the two neighboring countries.

Such adverse reactions to Macedonia's independence have undermined Macedonia's legitimacy as a sovereign state in the international arena and blocked the country's full, economic and political, integration into the world economy and community. As such, they have exacerbated instability and uncertainty regarding the future of Macedonia and its people.

The Bit Pazar Shooting in 1992

After the proclamation of Macedonia's independence, the government passed in October 1992 a law whereby residents of the Republic could obtain Macedonian citizenship if they provided proof that they had at least fifteen years of continuous residence, or Macedonian ancestry from both parents, or proof that they were born in Macedonia. These requirements were a clear break with practices in the former Yugoslavia, where people were citizens of both the Yugoslav federation and the constituent Republic in which they resided. Unlike other Republics, where immigration was regulated and supervised (see Gaber and Joveska 2004), Macedonia allowed the uncontrolled settlement of immigrants without regard to naturalization and citizenship laws and procedures. Albanians without documented proof of their residence in Macedonia prior to the collapse of Yugoslavia could not satisfy the above-mentioned criteria and were not eligible to hold a Macedonian passport, receive health care, or be hired in state institutions. For many Albanians in Macedonia, the 1991 Founding Constitution and the above-mentioned law both reified Macedonian hostility since Tito's death in 1980 and brought home to them the potential for the perpetuation of marginalization suffered in Yugoslavia in the 1980s.

Against this background of increasing acrimony, the following critical event unfolded. On 6 November 1992, the police cracked down on smug-

Figure 3. Entrance to Bit Pazar. Photo by author.

gling activities in Bit Pazar (the largest open market in Skopje) and confusion
arose regarding what happened next. According to one version of what happened (see Friedman 1998: 190–91), an Albanian teenager who was selling
smuggled cigarettes in the Pazar attempted to escape Macedonian police inspection by running away, fell over, and began crying out that he was beaten
by the police. A different version of events (see Brown 2001: 423) claimed

that the police took the Albanian teenager to the nearby hospital, that the boy had been maltreated or killed, and that an angry crowd gathered outside the hospital and started banging on the doors trying to enter the building. Other accounts (see Woodward 1995a: 342) suggested that several Albanians were arrested during the police crackdown in the market and news reports circulated that a young Albanian man had been beaten to death in a police station. Confusion over what had happened helped to spark a demonstration during which there was shooting and three Albanian men and one Macedonian woman were killed.

The Bit Pazar incident marked a crisis in Macedonian-Albanian relations for two reasons. First, it highlighted that the threat of the eruption of armed violence in Macedonia, especially at the time when there was a bloody war going on in Bosnia-Herzegovina, was after all a very palpable possibility. As such, it generated anxiety about the future and raised doubts among Macedonians about Albanians' loyalty to the state. Second, the incident undermined efforts to project the image of Macedonia as a stable and strong state and gain wider recognition abroad under the constitutional name "Republic of Macedonia." Only a handful of countries at first recognized the newly emerged state under that name, while Greece, Bulgaria, and Serbia, as mentioned earlier, disputed Macedonian identity, language, and Church respectively. The clash in Bit Pazar therefore left little to no room for redress of the crisis of legitimacy with which Macedonia was faced in the international arena.

Despite such adverse sociopolitical conditions, the governance of Macedonian president Kiro Gligorov, together with the participation of Albanian politicians Abdurrahman Aliti and Hisen Ramadani, exerted a moderating influence. Under Gligorov's leadership, the Serbs withdrew peacefully and a UN preventive deployment mission (United Nations Protection Force, or UNPROFOR, which in 1995 was replaced by the United Nations Preventive Deployment Force, or UNPREDEP) was dispatched in 1993 to avert the spillover of the Yugoslav wars into Macedonia, safeguard Macedonia's territorial integrity, and appease increasing concerns over interethnic relations. The presence of the UNPROFOR, together with the work of local and international nongovernmental organizations, played a significant role in warding off the threat of war in the early years of Macedonia's independence (see Ackermann 2003; Petroska-Beška 1996; Burg 1996; Williams 2000). The popular phrase *oaza na mir*, "oasis of peace," was often used by the local and international media to compare Macedonia with the warring former Yugoslav Republics and describe it as a success of preventive deployment—the first of its kind ever undertaken.

The cooperation among various political parties, including those that were ethnically identified, also seemed to give a promising message regarding the decrease in ethnonational tension. The coalition government between 1992 and 1994, for example, initiated the commencement of deliberations over the rights of the Albanian community in Macedonia, specifically over university education, the use of Albanian, and state employment. But the character of such cooperation cannot be fully understood unless it is noted that during the early years of Macedonia's independence Albanian politicians aligned themselves with Greece, which vehemently disputed the existence of Macedonian national identity and effectively threatened (and, as of this writing, still threatens) the international recognition of Macedonia under its constitutional name (Republic of Macedonia). In so doing, Albanian politicians and their constituents were largely perceived as part of the threat to Macedonia's identity. This political maneuver was meant to exercise indirectly political pressure on Macedonian politicians and thus achieve a bi-national state in which Albanians would be recognized as a *narod* and become a constitutive nation together with Macedonians.

The Extraordinary Census of 1994

In light of the boycotts of the 1991 census and independence referendum and strong Albanian allegations of discrimination and claims that the Albanian community constituted up to forty percent of the population, the Council of Europe and the European Union feared for Macedonia's political stability and funded a new, nationwide official census from 21 June to 5 July 1994. A team from the International Census Observation Mission (ICOM), consisting mostly of statisticians and bureaucrats (see Friedman 1996: 92), was appointed by the above-mentioned European organizations. The objectives of the team were to monitor the census and establish the real numbers for the Albanian community in Macedonia. The census provided a site where larger tensions, which as Friedman notes had been accumulating since the riots in Kosovo in 1981 but had not been a distinctive or permanent attribute of Macedonian life, became reified as a Macedonian-Albanian conflict.

Albanian political leaders threatened a major boycott again of the census, but drew back from the threat because of European pressure (Woodward 1995a: 477n32). Nonetheless, they found reasons in irregularities in the procedures of the census, including the fact that the Ministry of Internal Affairs

(MVR) had not distributed all citizenship documents in time for the census (Friedman 1996: 92–100), to contest the census results, which showed 442,914 Albanians, 22.9 percent of the country's population. Even though problems regarding the distribution of citizenship documents had taken place throughout Macedonia, and the ICOM had approved the results, Albanian politicians accused the Ministry of Interior of purposefully stalling citizenship procedures, and claimed a higher proportion of Albanians in the total population of Macedonia on the grounds that Albanians who had resided in the country prior to the collapse of Yugoslavia but had no documented proof of their residence, as well as Albanians who had escaped ethnic persecution in Kosovo in the 1990s but whose status in Macedonia had not been regulated, could not be counted in the census. A fierce controversy over population numbers thus reemerged, with Albanian claims that a large number of Albanians had resided in the country for many years, and Macedonian counterclaims that a large number of Albanians were recent newcomers to the state and, hence, did not count as Macedonian citizens.[12]

An additional point of contention involved the equation of language with nationality (Friedman 1996: 97–99), and consequently the negation of multilingual practices in Macedonia and the construction of a social reality that was characterized by the reification of group identity. Indeed, as Kertzer and Arel have argued (2002), censuses play a key role in constructing one version of social reality rather than another. Anderson's comment (1991: 166) is also apropos here: "The fiction of the census is that everyone is in it, and that everyone has one—and only one—extremely clear place. No fractions." Thus, as Friedman shows (1996), Albanian-speaking Roms and Vlahs in southwestern Macedonia were counted as ethnic Albanians, Muslim speakers of Macedonian who identified Islam with Albanian or Turkish ethnicity declared their nationality as Albanian or Turkish, and Christian speakers of Albanian who identified Orthodox Christianity with Macedonian ethnicity declared their nationality as Macedonian. The definition of categories in the 1994 census then provided fertile ground for further heated dispute between Albanian and Macedonian politicians over census results.

The Establishment of Tetovo University in 1995

Besides nursing grievances about allegedly deliberate official unwillingness to account accurately for the proportion of Albanians in the total Macedonian population, members of the Albanian community have also been resentful of the lack of adequate opportunities for public university education in Albanian. In the years immediately following the 1985 closing down of the Albanian-language program at the Pedagogical Academy in Skopje, attendance at Prishtina University in neighboring Kosovo (where higher education in Albanian had been available since the founding of the University in February 1970) became more than ever before a primary choice for many Macedonian Albanians. Subsequent to Macedonia's independence in 1991, however, Albanian students encountered difficulties traveling to Prishtina. Szajkowski (2000: 254), for example, mentions "long queues and regular harassment" at the border between Macedonia and the Federal Republic of Yugoslavia (which included Kosovo). Studies show disproportionately low enrollment rates for Albanians attending higher education institutions in Macedonia (specifically, Sts. Cyril and Methodius University in Skopje and St. Clement of Ohrid University in Bitola) in the early 1990s. Between 1992 and 1993, Reka notes (2008: 63), Albanians constituted 2.3 percent of the student body, while in 1993, only 38 Albanians compared to 2,022 Macedonians graduated from Macedonian universities (Brunnbauer 2004: 588).

Difficulties in attending Prishtina University prompted Albanian demands that the Macedonian government reinstate the two-year Albanian-language program, and also pass laws that would regulate the conditions of establishment of an Albanian-speaking university and carry into effect constitutional provisions related to the guarantee of the autonomy of universities in Macedonia (Article 69 of the Constitution). Macedonian foot-dragging, however, delayed educational reforms. Equally important, political developments in Kosovo in the early 1990s (see Kostovicova 2005) played a key role in the debate on education policy in Macedonia. Specifically, the Serbian Parliament's adoption of certain laws in the spring of 1990, whereby Serbian authorities had the right to intervene in all of Kosovo's institutions and enterprises, led to the dismissal and resignation of Albanian teachers, professors, managers, and employees, creating a large pool of unemployed Albanians. It is against this background that Albanian activists took matters into their own hands. In the midst of political controversy and despite a ban from the Macedonian Ministry of Interior, they used private funds to open in December 1994 the so-called Tetovo University (Universiteti i Tetovës) in the village of Mala Rečica near the town of Tetovo, where Albanian students could receive university education in Albanian exclusively. The public opening of the University took place at the headquarters of PDP/PPD in Tetovo on 17 December; attendees included Albanian Members of Parliament, representatives from all Albanian political parties in Macedonia, and Albanian of-

ficials from municipalities in Western Macedonia. Fadil Suleimani, a former
professor at Prishtina University who left Kosovo after the implementation
of Serbian education laws in 1990 and became rector of Tetovo University,
stated at a press conference (Shea 1997: 258): "The University in Tetovo has
been founded. This university will contribute to the wellbeing of all the nations in Macedonia. Everyone should rejoice, not only the Albanians." For
his part, Macedonian minister of interior Ljubomir Frčkoski described the
opening of the Tetovo University as a "private party" and a "blown up bal-
loon" and, evoking Article 48 of the Constitution that granted members of the
nationalities the right to instruction in their language only in primary and secondary (not tertiary) education, proclaimed the establishment of an Albanian-
speaking university in Macedonia unconstitutional and hence illegal.

In an attempt to redress Albanian grievances, the Macedonian government
promised to hire university professors to teach courses in Albanian (Shea 1997:
259–60), and announced plans for a four-year Albanian-language program
at the Pedagogical Faculty of Sts. Cyril and Methodius University in Skopje.
These promises did not placate Arben Xhaferi, who had recently arrived from
Kosovo after he was dismissed from his position as senior editor at the state-
run TV station in Prishtina, or Fadil Suleimani. Political controversy over the
opening of the University, which Suleimani announced on Albania's Radio
Tirana in February 1995 (260), thus continued. Macedonians insisted that
the university was illegal, and that its construction and operation were violations of state sovereignty; Albanians argued that the lack of adequate educational opportunities in Albanian at the tertiary level constituted violation of
the human rights of the Albanian-speaking population in the country, more
specifically the right to mother tongue education, protected by international
law (see, for example, Pentassuglia 2002). Meanwhile, Albanians appealed to
the international community yet again to increase their political leverage and
bargaining power against Macedonians. During his visit to the United States,
where he signed an agreement on bilateral cooperation between the University of Tetovo and George Washington University, Suleimani met with deputy
secretary of state Richard Holbrooke to discuss the tensions surrounding the
establishment of the university and the alleged state discrimination against
the Albanian community in Macedonia.

On 15 February 1995 the opening ceremony of the University of Tetovo
took place. Guests included, among others, officials from the Organization for
Security and Co-operation in Europe (OSCE), former U.S. representative and
leader of the U.S. Albanian lobby Joseph DioGuardi (R-N.Y.), and representative of George Washington University (and Serb dissident) Mihajlo Mihajlov

(Shea 1997: 260). Albanian political actors in Macedonia, except for ministers in the government, were also among those who attended the ceremony. There was no police presence at the official opening, and the event ended peacefully. Violence, however, broke out on 17 February, when police and bulldozers were sent in to the university facilities while classes were in session and Albanian demonstrators stood in the way. During the clashes between the police and the crowd that day, nineteen people were seriously injured and one Albanian man, Emini Abdulselam, died. Albanian politicians intervened and managed to persuade the crowd to disperse peacefully and the police troops to withdraw, ameliorating the situation temporarily. Tensions reignited, however, after Albanian local leaders, including Fadil Suleimani, were arrested and sentenced for their involvement in the demonstration. In particular, after the funeral for Abdulselam, attended by over 10,000 people in Mala Rečica and monitored from the surrounding hills by UNPROFOR (1997: 263), a large crowd of Albanians headed for the police station in Tetovo. In this heightened political atmosphere, the crowd demanded that Suleimani be released; after reassurances by Albanian deputy Sali Ramadani that the release of all arrested Albanians would be negotiated, the crowd dispersed.

The crisis became all the more acute as rumors circulated regarding Serbian involvement in the incident. When Serbian symbols were found on walls of the Tetovo University buildings, the villagers in Mala Rečica accused the police of having sprayed the symbols, but the Ministry of Interior denied the charge (263). At the same time, the Macedonian daily *Nova Makedonija* claimed that Fadil Suleimani was an agent for the Serb secret intelligence service whose aim was to divert the attention of the international community from Kosovo to Macedonia, thereby enhancing the image of Serbia as a peacemaker and encouraging the UN to lift the sanctions the Security Council had imposed against Serbia in May 1992 (265).[13] Dosta Dimovska, Macedonian vice president of the opposition party VMRO-DPMNE, asserted that the incident in Tetovo was part of president Kiro Gligorov's plans to grant territorial and political autonomy to Albanians in Macedonia as a way of easing Albanian-Serbian tensions in Kosovo and give the remaining part of Macedonia to Serbia (269).

The establishment of Tetovo University thus emerges as an integral part of the tapestry of critical events in the history of independent Macedonia. Not only did it carry the potential for the spread of armed violence in the country; it also revealed forceful Albanian resolution to institutionalize new educational practices, geared toward the creation of a bi-national state. Brown argues (2000: 131) that the events in Tetovo "were the pursuit of politics by other means," thereby bringing to mind Clausewitz's famous dictum regarding war—that war is a continuation of politics by other means. We can indeed argue that the events in Tetovo were a different kind of war. Although armed violence did not engulf the country, any sense of "normalcy" in everyday life was lost, as it is in war conditions (see Nordstrom 1997: 131). The actions of Albanians helped set in motion unprecedented events that bore witness to an excess of affect in Macedonian political culture. In 1997, for example, the Macedonian Parliament passed a law approving the use of the Albanian language at the Pedagogical Faculty of Sts. Cyril and Methodius University in Skopje. The law provoked student demonstrations featuring signs that read, among other things, "Albanians to the gas chambers [*za Šiptari* (the derogatory term for 'Albanians') *gasna komora*] and "Macedonia for the Macedonians" (*Makedonija za Makedoncite*) (see ICG 1997: 11). Students also held a hunger strike demanding unsuccessfully that the law be repealed.[14] As I discuss in the next section, the events in Tetovo also ushered in a new era in Macedonia's political history whereby Albanians enacted what they claimed to be human rights in the public arena (see also Slyomovics 2005) while forthrightly defying and vociferously opposing through collective protest action definitions of Macedonia as the state of the Macedonian *narod*.

It should also be mentioned that the international community played a role in advancing Albanian-language education in Macedonia. In April 2000, OSCE high commissioner on national minorities Max Van der Stoel submitted a proposal to the Macedonian government for the establishment of a multilingual university, the "Southeast European University" (Univerzitet na Jugoistočna Evropa in Macedonian, Universiteti i Evropës Juglindore in Albanian—popularly known as Štulov Univerzitet '[van der] Stoel's University' in Macedonian), in Tetovo. The university would offer classes in Albanian, English, and Macedonian, and would be funded through donations from some European foundations and the Council of Europe for the first four years of its operation. The Parliament passed legislation to ratify the proposal that summer, and construction of the university premises was scheduled to begin in late 2000 on land donated by the government; the university officially opened in November 2001 and has operated since then. The same legislation also granted private foundation status to the Tetovo University, and in January 2004 further legislation was passed to recognize the university as a state institution of higher learning under the name "The State University of Tetovo" (Državen Univerzitet vo Tetovo in Macedonian, Universiteti Shtetëror i Tetovës in Albanian).

Demonstrations in Gostivar in 1997

After the February 1997 municipal elections several Albanian candidates from Arben Xhaferi's Democratic Party of Albanians (DPA/PDSH), a merger between the Party for Democratic Prosperity of the Albanians (PDP-A/PPD-Sh, the radical faction of the Party for Democratic Prosperity, PDP/PPD, that split off in February 1994 to form its own party) and the smaller radical People's Democratic Party (NDP/PDP), took office. The Gostivar City Council, led by newly elected DPA/PDSH mayor Rufi Osmani, decided that it would fly the Albanian and Turkish national flags next to the Macedonian flag in front of the town hall, declaring that those flags represented the ethno-demographic composition of the Gostivar municipality in western Macedonia. In so doing, Osmani and the Council sought to effectuate the right to fly the Albanian national flag—a right that the Yugoslav regime had granted Kosovar Albanians as a measure of appeasement in the wake of the 1968 demonstrations in Prishtina (see Elsie 1997). Meantime, a constitutional court ruling was passed in May 1997 whereby flying foreign flags (including the flags of Albania and Turkey) in public was a violation of Macedonian state sovereignty. Osmani called on Albanians in Gostivar to "protect their flag with their blood," thus stepping up the rhetorical attack against central state authorities, and demonstrations were organized to defend flying the Albanian flag outside municipal state buildings (ICG 1997: 13).

While the controversy over the flag issue remained unresolved, the collapse of the Albanian state under the Berisha government and the looting of military stockpiles in neighboring Albania in spring 1997 (see Vickers and Pettifer 1997) cast a gloomy shadow over Macedonia. For fear that it might have to contend with a massive influx of refugees from Albania—an influx that could aggravate ethnonational tensions and overtax the state's meager resources—Macedonia put its military on high alert. Even though a refugee wave did not materialize and the political situation in Albania gradually began to stabilize after elections took place at the end of the summer, the Gligorov administration remained concerned over the possibilities of arms smuggling, which would strengthen Albanian radicals in Macedonia, and armed incidents in the areas bordering Albania.

It is against this background of anxiety springing from the political climate in the country and the region that tensions came to a head. In July 1997, riots broke out after Macedonian police forces removed the Albanian and Turkish flags that had been hoisted over the town hall in Gostivar. A small number of Albanians were killed and several others were wounded

in the clashes with the police, and local media and international organizations, including Human Rights Watch, recorded instances where the police used excessive force.[15] Rufi Osmani, together with four hundred others
who were mainly DPA activists (Poulton 1995: 189), were arrested. Osmani was sentenced to almost fourteen years imprisonment on the charge
of "inciting national, racial and religious hatred" (Brown 2000: 132), but
his sentence was reduced to seven years after the court allowed the appeal in February 1998. Bomb explosions occurred outside the municipal
buildings in Gostivar and Tetovo in December 1997 and outside police
stations in Skopje and Tetovo in May 1998. The Macedonian police attributed responsibility for these explosions to the Kosovo Liberation Army
(KLA), the Albanian insurgent group fighting for Kosovo's independence
beginning in April 1996.[16] Suspicions proliferated that KLA cells operated
in Macedonia, recruiting volunteers for the independence struggle in Kosovo and inciting Albanian separatism in Macedonia. Additionally, demonstrations, during which protesters called for Osmani's release and also
declared support for the Albanian struggle for independence in Kosovo,
took place in May 1998.

More so than previous critical events unfolding in independent Macedonia, the demonstrations and the flying of the Albanian flag in Gostivar
spurred much debate over the use of symbols in the Macedonian state—
and as such, as Brown (2000: 132) argues, "can be read as indication[s] of
a broadening of the zone of engagement between ethnically differentiable
populations in Macedonia." From the official Albanian viewpoint, the Albanian flag was primarily not a symbol of the Albanian state, but rather
a symbol of the unity of the Albanian nation (*kombi shqiptar*), dispersed
throughout the Balkans and the rest of the world.[17] The Albanian flag, in
other words, was portrayed as a symbol of *cultural* difference and autonomy, not political autonomy (see also Perry 1988). Albanian politicians also
pointed to the constitution of the Macedonian state to suggest the legitimacy of their claims. Rufi Osmani, for example, argued that the Gostivar
City Council based its decision to fly the Albanian flag on article 48 of the
Macedonian constitution, according to which "members of nationalities
have a right freely to express, foster, and develop their identity and national
attributes" (HRW 1998: 7). In a context whereby culture was presented as
a right to which Albanians were entitled, the reaction of Macedonian authorities against the flying of the Albanian national flag in Gostivar was
portrayed as a violation of constitutional rights and also as indicative of
state discrimination against Albanians.

As Bhabha reminds us (1990b: 292), the "slippage into analogous, even metonymic, categories, like the people, minorities, or 'cultural difference' that continually overlap in the act of writing the nation" marks "the ambivalence of the nation as a narrative strategy—and an apparatus of power." Put differently (3–4), "the nation, as a form of cultural elaboration (in the Gramscian sense), is an agency of ambivalent narration that holds culture at its most productive position, as a force for 'subordination, fracturing, diffusing, reproducing, as much as producing, creating, forcing, guiding'" (emphases removed from original). It is precisely this kind of ambivalence embedded in the term "nation" in its usage by Albanian politicians that provided fertile ground for contestation: Macedonian politicians and the general public argued that Albanian claims of cultural autonomy and freedom to exercise cultural rights were not precisely defined. Rather, according to them, such claims were allegedly grounded in political aspirations for political autonomy and the creation of Greater Albania, an Albanian national state that would include northwestern Macedonia and Kosovo. Against the background of the use of the universal concepts of rights and rights violations as a strategy to redraw geographical boundaries after the collapse of socialism in the Balkans (see Woodward 1995a; Cowan et al. 2001), the Albanian discourse of entitlement to rights, specifically the right to culture, was also viewed as a strategy to attract and gain international sympathy for the Albanian nationalist cause.

The viability of the Macedonian state seemed to be, perhaps more than ever before, at risk, and so the crisis in Gostivar renewed the need for international monitoring. To underline the importance of preserving stability in Macedonia, the UN Security Council in July 1998 extended through February 1999 the mandate of the UN Preventive Deployment Force (UNPREDEP) to monitor the border areas between Macedonia and the Federal Republic of Yugoslavia and Macedonia and Albania. In an inauspicious turn of events, in January 1999 Macedonia became the only European state besides the Vatican City State to recognize Taiwan as an independent state; in late February China used its veto power in the UN Security Council to block a proposal to extend the mandate of UNPREDEP.[18] The UNPREDEP withdrawal from Macedonia coincided with the escalation of conflict in neighboring Kosovo, and the ensuing NATO bombing campaign against Yugoslavia raised security concerns. A nervous peace was nonetheless maintained in Macedonia—but it was not long before it was ruptured again.

CHAPTER 2

The Eruption of the 2001 Conflict

A few weeks prior to the eruption of the NLA insurgency in the village of Tanuševci, on 22 January 2001, one Macedonian policeman was killed and three others were wounded in an attack on the police station in the predominantly Albanian-populated village of Tearce, near the border with the UN-administered province of Kosovo in southern Serbia. The NLA claimed responsibility for the attack in a communiqué, entitled "Communiqué no 4," sent 23 January by telefax from a cell-phone number in Germany to *Dnevnik*, one of the most widely read Macedonian-language newspapers in Macedonia.[1] The communiqué, published in Albanian on the front page of *Dnevnik* and translated into Macedonian, read as follows:[2]

> On 22 January a special team unit of the National Liberation Army supported by a group of observers with automatic rifles and hand grenade launchers attacked the Macedonian police station [in Tearce]. In the attack the opponent forces were quickly paralyzed and they did not resist while the other Macedonian forces from the other directions did not approach in time the location of the event. The attack was limited and was a proclamation to the Macedonian occupiers and their Albanophone [*Albanofonskite*] collaborators. The uniform of the Macedonian occupiers will be further attacked until the Albanian people are liberated. The policemen are called upon to return to their families so that they do not give their lives in vain for the illusory Macedonian plans for domination over the Albanian majority.

The lethal grenade attack in Tearce marked the first time the NLA made publicly known its political agenda regarding the purported liberation of the Albanian people. In subsequent communiqués, statements of its spokesperson

Ali Ahmeti, and commanders' interviews circulated in the national and international media until the conflict came to a close in August 2001, the NLA asserted that it favored the preservation of Macedonia's territorial integrity and respected NATO's interests in Macedonia, and also described its objectives in Macedonia: status of constituent nation for Albanians, institutionalization of Albanian as the second official language, and equal participation of Albanians in state administration (see Ackermann 2001). To justify its use of armed violence, the organization referred to a so-called "reign of terror" whereby the Macedonian state had allegedly been denying for ten years since independence in 1991 the granting of greater rights to the Albanian community (Rusi 2002: 20).

In the meantime, uncertainty and confusion arose over the very existence of the organization. Specifically, minister of internal affairs Dosta Dimovska disclaimed any knowledge of the existence of an organization by the name National Liberation Army and asserted that the fax number in Germany from which the communiqué had been sent to *Dnevnik* was nonexistent. Former director of the Intelligence Agency of Macedonia Aleksa Stamenkovski, however, asserted that while in office he had information that the NLA had been established at the same time as the Albanian Liberation Army of Preševo, Medvedja, and Bujanovac (Albanian Ushtria Çlirimtare e Preshevës, Medvegjës dhe Bujanocit, UÇPMB), and former minister of internal affairs Pavle Trajanov stated that the two organizations operated in Yugoslavia.[3] Named after the three predominantly Albanian-populated districts in Preševo Valley, a five-kilometer-wide buffer zone in southern Serbia north of Macedonia, UÇPMB was an Albanian insurgent group that announced its existence in early 2000 and operated in the valley.[4] UÇPMB also enjoyed the support of some former Kosovo Liberation Army (KLA) men, who anticipated an eventual exchange of territories (see Judah 2002: ix) between Serbia and a future independent Kosovo.[5]

Macedonian prime minister Ljupčo Georgievski and his Albanian ruling coalition partner Arben Xhaferi, leaders of VMRO-DPMNE and DPA/PDSH respectively, mentioned during media appearances that they unequivocally condemned the bomb attacks. Nonetheless, inconclusive talk about whether the NLA *really* existed lent political life in Macedonia a strange, phantasmagoric quality, as if nobody could tell the difference between fact and fiction, real and unreal. The contours of the political landscape had suddenly become hazy, and it was unclear who the actors on the political stage really were, where they had really come from, and what intentions they really had. This spectral character of everyday life, what Aretxaga in her work on political violence in the Basque country calls the specter of the "really real" that always eludes us (2005: 227–28), persisted over the ensuing months.

The phantom-like—sudden, seemingly random and out-of-nowhere—emergence of an organization that carried the name National Liberation Army generated widespread anxiety over the palpable possibility of further violence breaking out at any time. Anxiety became even more intense when four days later, on 26 January 2001, another bomb attack took place—this time on the Skopje-Kičevo train. In a fax sent to the Albanian TV station Era, the NLA assumed responsibility for the attack. The fax was sent on paper that bore the emblem of the former KLA, providing ground for strong suspicion as to whether the NLA and the former KLA were one and the same, especially given that the two organizations bore the same acronym, UÇK (Ushtria Çlirimtare Kombëtare for the NLA; Ushtria Çlirimtare e Kosovës for the KLA) (Latifi 2001). These suggestive yet unconfirmed links between the NLA and guerrilla forces operating in neighboring Kosovo illuminated the porousness of Macedonia's northern border.

As the specter of the violent acts committed by the NLA loomed large, many Macedonians and Albanians in their everyday conversations with me and with people of ethnonational backgrounds similar to theirs chose the trope of knowledge to organize and make sense of their everyday worlds. "It is known who they are!" was a remark that I often heard my Macedonian friends and neighbors make with adamant certainty about the origin of the perpetrators. Sometimes irritated by my asking to elaborate on what they meant, as if annoyed by my assumed inability to discern real truth, my Macedonian research participants blamed the fragile situation in Macedonia on Albanian extremists from Macedonia and Kosovo. For them, a long history of Albanian vocal dissatisfaction with Yugoslav and Macedonian policies helped to make understandable the predicament at hand. Albanians with whom I worked tended to express their perplexion and dismay about the NLA attacks. Many retorted, "Who knows who they are?" Yet others claimed that they knew the primary perpetrators were disgruntled Albanians for whom the Macedonian government's treatment of Albanians throughout the 1990s echoed the Serbian treatment of Albanians in Yugoslavia—and as such was a symptom of allegedly Slavic assault against Albanian ethnonational identity. Claims to knowledge and to lack of knowledge illuminate the role divergent constructions of history and memory can play in imbuing key political events with diverse meanings. Such claims also reveal thirst for knowledge about what was really happening, and could be viewed as efforts to mitigate harmful effects of violence such as anxiety and fear.

The public's attention to the news of the bomb attacks on the police station and the train slowly faded, especially after the government arrested four individuals and announced at the end of the month that the perpetrators were radicals who had acted independently and were unconnected to the KLA or any other organization (Latifi 2001). After a while, the topic of the bomb attacks did not come up in everyday conversation—and yet there was a growing sense of profound discomfort, a feeling of deep unease at the possibility of having to endure further instability.

The Breakout of the NLA insurgency

Many people were shocked when news about the NLA abduction of the A1 television crew, the purported liberation of Tanuševci, and the ensuing gun battle between the NLA and a Macedonian border patrol unit in the village circulated through television and radio reporting on the evening of 16 February 2001. Not many of my research participants had heard of Tanuševci before the village made national news; sitting on a mountainous plateau, the village is accessible via a road that is unpaved, winding, and steep in places.

The shock effect, transmitted through television and newspaper images of the remote village, was bound up with the history of the northern Macedonian borderland. Tanuševci originally was the summer grazing village of Vitinje, now in Kosovo (Churcher 2002: 3). Between 1929 and 1941, Tanuševci and Vitinje were part of the Vardar banovina (Vardar province), consisting of the Yugoslav part of Macedonia and parts of Serbia and Kosovo; between 1941 and 1944 they were incorporated into Italian-controlled Albania. During the socialist period, the 260-kilometer border was administrative and unmarked (Roudometof 2002: 214). After Yugoslavia's disintegration and Macedonia's independence, the government of the Federal Republic of Yugoslavia continued to consider the border administrative, but in Macedonia it was considered international. The lack of agreement over the character of the border generated tension between the two countries. Nonetheless, the border between Tanuševci and the region of Kosovo remained nonexistent in practice: Tanuševci residents habitually drove the narrow, unpaved dirt roads leading into Kosovo for common activities, such as shopping or going to the doctor, and returned home without any disturbance. When I last visited Tanuševci in 2008, the road trip through the region was still bumpy and exhausting.

Starting in 2000 the legitimate and seemingly innocuous activity of border-crossing into Kosovo turned dangerous when, according to journal-

Figure 4. Close view of Tanuševci, 2008. Photo by author.

istic reports, the village became a transit point for smuggling arms into the Preševo Valley to support UÇPMB activities.[6] The lawlessness in the northern borderland, where there were not enough resources to police the border, became embodied in the reportedly black uniforms worn by the NLA members involved in the Tanuševci incident. Only the former self-proclaimed KLA "military police," which conducted activities such as abductions, interrogations, detentions, and executions of Serb, Albanian, and Romani civilians during the Kosovo war (see Krieger 2001: 235), wore all-black uniforms. These Kosovo Albanian paramilitary units had also set up their own "Military Court," where people were arraigned on charges of violating the civilian-military "book of regulations of the KLA." Similar to what occurred from the mid–1980s onward in Colombia (see Taussig 2003), the culture of terror in Kosovo in the late 1990s was much based on the operation of paramilitaries and their relentless production of fear and uncertainty regarding who would be targeted next and why.

The news about the black uniforms of the abductors in Tanuševci all of a sudden awakened the general populace in Macedonia to the possibility that the culture of terror had become revitalized despite the presence of the UN mission in Kosovo (UNMIK), and was seeping into Macedonia through the porous, contested, and inadequately patrolled northern border with Kosovo. To appease growing public anxiety, defense minister Ljuben Paunovski said the following in an interview on 18 February on television station A1: "The Defense Ministry has full control of the territory of Macedonia. The fact that the Macedonian Army is the most stable factor in the region of the northern and western border, which is a part of a very unstable region, proves that."[7] In spite of government assurance that the situation was under control, there was growing unease over Macedonian national security. As the two-day regional summit on the South East European Cooperation Process started in Skopje on 22 February, more than a hundred Albanians in Tanuševci prepared to evacuate the village by tractor and cross into Kosovo (IWPR 2001). Meantime, the Macedonian army was on high alert in the immediate vicinity of Tanuševci, and six hundred police commandos were dispatched to the region as soon as the summit ended. Importantly (as I explain shortly), a border demarcation agreement between Macedonia and the Federal Republic of Yugoslavia (consisting of Serbia, including Kosovo, and Montenegro), signed at the Skopje summit on 23 February to promote regional cooperation, was rejected by members of the Albanian opposition party PDP/PPD, who argued that it was immoral to exclude Kosovo's political leaders and UNMIK from the negotiations, and also by two MPs of the soon-to-be formed Albanian National Democratic Party (NDP/PDK), led by Kastriot Haxhirexha.[8] The agreement was also rejected by the Democratic Alliance of Kosovo, Kosovo's main political party, on similar grounds.

Small-scale skirmishes and shootings in Tanuševci between the NLA and the Macedonian border patrol unit continued through February and reached a climax on 26 February, when a two-hour gun battle in the village was reported in the news. During the battle, Macedonian Special Forces were deployed to Tanuševci, thus generating widespread public suspicion about the severity of the situation. Special Forces officers reported that two hundred black uniformed invaders were waiting to enter Macedonia from the region of Kosovo (Phillips 2004: 11). The next day, 27 February, *Dnevnik* reported on a grave prediction in the *New York Times* that "for Kosovars, the battle moves to the border of Macedonia" (Gall 2001). Adding to the feeling of doom and gloom, national and international media reported on complaints from Albanians in Tanuševci, alleging maltreatment by the Macedonian Special Forces dispatched to the area. Menduh Thaçi, DPA/PDSH deputy leader, urged the democratic resolution of the incidents at Tanuševci and warned "if that should fail, it is well known how it [the situation] should be solved" (ICG

2001: 5). For his part, Imer Imeri, PDP/PPD party leader, alleged that "ethnic cleansing" was taking place at Tanuševci.

In this atmosphere of heightened uncertainty about what was really going on and what might transpire in the future, Macedonians and Albanians generally tended to stay home and watch the evening news on various television channels just in case new information, such as the origin of the NLA and statements from politicians, became publicly available. I vividly recall the calmness with which my Albanian language teacher Bahrie and I sat in Bahrie's living room, sipping Turkish tea and chatting after our afternoon Albanian classes ended—a calmness that was disrupted around the time for the evening news. That was when, remote control in one hand, a cup of tea in the other, Bahrie flipped through all the channels with maddening persistence. Indeed, an unusual, sharp awareness of time gripped the people with whom I worked. Many were keen on making social plans before or occasionally after the main evening news bulletins were broadcast between six and eight o'clock. Those who were not home to watch the evening news somehow just knew when it was on. For example, in the midst of complaining over coffee about some of her colleagues at the bank where she worked, my friend Ana suddenly looked at her watch and announced stoically that we just had missed the news. References to violence started to seep into daily conversations and worry began to permeate slowly but steadily the lives of people in the capital.

Intensification of the Conflict and the Elusive NLA

Shortly after the Macedonian Parliament ratified the border demarcation agreement between Macedonia and the Federal Republic of Yugoslavia on 1 March, violent confrontations between the NLA and Macedonian Special Forces escalated in Tanuševci. On the morning of Sunday 4 March, two Macedonian soldiers who were leading a convoy of foreign observers into Tanuševci were killed when their jeep drove over an anti-vehicle mine. A third was picked off by a sniper and died shortly thereafter. Immediately following the killings, a dozen U.S. KFOR army Humvees crowded the streets of Debelde, a village a couple of steep and rocky ridges away from Tanuševci and directly across the border from Kosovo, while two helicopters and an unmanned drone spy plane hovered directly above Debelde.[9]

No NLA insurgents were found in Tanuševci when the Macedonian army moved into the village to conduct a limited military operation on 5 March.

The army destroyed six sniper nests, two machine-gun nests, and eight fortifications—all indications that the NLA had been in the village but had apparently abandoned its positions before the arrival of the Macedonian army.[10] Shortly thereafter, the NLA dispatched a new communiqué, stating: "We feel obliged to send a contingent of our troops to Tanuševci to protect the civilian population after they increased the number of Macedonian army representatives" (ICG 2001: 6).

In hopes of pinning down the elusive NLA insurgents, the KFOR military presence intensified on the side of the border with Kosovo. According to U.S. military reports, by mid-afternoon 5 March, U.S. troops assigned to KFOR had cordoned off the village of Mijak, which lies between Debelde and Tanuševci inside Kosovo, and sealed off the border with Macedonia.[11] On 6 March, the Macedonian army and police launched an attack on Tanuševci in which around one hundred and fifty armed NLA insurgents retreated into Kosovo and some were captured and detained by Alliance troops. According to a KFOR spokesman, Alliance troops had seen many border-crossers from Macedonia into Kosovo enter local buildings in black uniforms and leave wearing civilian clothes, thereby escaping capture.[12] In the following days, U.S. KFOR forces in Mijak shot two NLA insurgents seemingly preparing to fire their guns at a patrol and managed to capture two men before the insurgents were seen moving into Macedonia.[13]

The NLA thus became increasingly daring: it was now killing Macedonian soldiers, publicly announcing that it would step up its military presence in Tanuševci, aiming guns at U.S. forces (the same forces that a couple of years before had inspired awe in the Albanian community for helping overthrow the Milošević regime in Yugoslavia), erasing distinctions between civilian and military, and escaping destruction. The organization underscored its blatant disregard for state authority on 9 March, when its members attacked a police convoy including Albanian deputy minister of interior Refet Elmazi, Macedonian state secretary at the Ministry of Interior Ljube Boskovski, and police general Aleksandar Dončev between the villages of Gosince and Brest, east of Tanuševci. The convoy was under siege by the NLA for 20 hours before back-up police forces came to the rescue.

The Emergence of the Uncanny

On the first day of Kurban Bajram, Monday 5 March, the sidewalks of Čair were bustling with women in long over-garments and headscarves, young children, and men on their way to visit relatives and wish them many happy returns of the day. Taxis and cars filled with people were driving through my neighborhood. People traveling to visit relatives in different parts of the city crammed into buses. All in all nothing in Čair betrayed trouble or anxiety. In the afternoon of that day, I too visited some of my Albanian friends to pay my respects. When I arrived at the house of my language teacher, no other visitors were present. Bahrie and I were thus able to indulge in conversation uninterruptedly, without her having to attend to the needs of other guests. It was not long before the recent developments in Tanuševci dominated the discussion. Over Turkish tea and snacks, Bahrie told me she was too afraid to sleep after the news about the killing of the Macedonian soldiers had spread the evening before. Expressing her worry about the deteriorating situation, she said, "I am afraid not for myself, but for the others," referring to her three sons who were in their early twenties and hence eligible for conscription into the Macedonian army.

Bahrie's fear arose from the uncanny noise of the helicopter transporting the dead bodies of the three Macedonian soldiers from Tanuševci to the Ilinden barracks, in an area of Skopje not too far from Čair. The staccato of helicopter blades cleaving the air stirred memories of helicopters flying over Skopje en route to bomb Serbia, and generated a feeling of undefined, imminent danger. In her own words:

> The helicopter flying across the sky yesterday reminded me of the NATO helicopters that exactly two years ago, again on the eve of Kurban Bajram, flew over the territory of Macedonia to bombard Serbia. It was very scary, the whole house was trembling. The loud noise that the helicopter made shocked me.

The violence of shock, the gripping anxiety generated by the noise of helicopter rotors, was not a one-time occurrence. As the conflict gradually escalated and violence spread across the northwest, attack helicopters often appeared out of nowhere and flew at low altitude over the northwestern areas of Skopje, including Čair, en route to conflict zones. During the day, the sudden rattling noise interrupted conversations, disrupted activities, and directed people's gaze to the sky. In the night, like a bad dream that comes back to haunt you, the noise disturbed people's sleep. Many Macedonians and Albanians recounted to their relatives, friends, colleagues, and neighbors where they were, whom they were with, what they were doing, how their houses trembled, and how shocked they were when a helicopter flew over Skopje. The sound triggered recollections of the peacekeeping presence of UNPROFOR and UNPREDEP, whose helicopter pad was located opposite the Ilinden barracks, and of the wars in the 1990s.[14] In many accounts, helicopters featured as omens of impending evil. Shortly after a military chopper passed over our heads, for example, a middle-aged friend with whom I was taking a walk looked up at the sky and told me that war had been trickling from Croatia and Bosnia down to Kosovo and had probably arrived in Macedonia.

This "peculiar commingling of the familiar and unfamiliar," as Royle succinctly describes the uncanny (2003: 1), also arose from the images of death and destruction—coffins containing Macedonian soldiers' bodies, people crying at funerals, bomb-shelled houses, burnt animal carcasses and so on— that appeared on television news during the conflict. People often associated these images with pictures of human suffering in wartime Bosnia, articulating the uncertain possibilities that the situation in Macedonia might deteriorate and Macedonia might become (or perhaps was already?) the next Bosnia. Time distinctions between past, present, and future thus collapsed: the 2001 conflict became thoroughly imbued with a sense of déjà vu and the possibility of detrimental effects on the wellbeing of the people of Macedonia. Such experiences of anxiety and strangeness, whereby one could not tell for sure what was really going on from what one imagined was happening, persisted throughout the conflict and formed the backdrop for social interaction across ethnonational lines.

CHAPTER 3

Living in a Confusing World

Peace Rallies

Against a background of escalating violence in the northwest of the country, the Democratic Party of Albanians, the junior partner in the Macedonian government coalition, organized on 13 March a peace rally in Skopje. I attended the rally together with thousands of other people, many of whom were Albanians and held placards reading *pravda i mir* ("justice and peace" in Macedonian) and double-sided signs with the word *paqe* ("peace" in Albanian) on one side and the two-headed black eagle, which is Albania's national emblem and also the emblem of the KLA and the NLA, on the other.[1]

Many Macedonians with whom I worked—even some of those who had walked alongside Albanians chanting "Peace!"—viewed the rally with skepticism and distrust. For them, Albanian calls for peace and rights echoed the cry for greater rights that reverberated across Albanian demonstrations in the towns of Tetovo and Gostivar in the late 1990s (see Chapter 1). The rally was thus considered to be yet another forum for the rearticulation, this time under the guise of peace seeking, of demands that had a purely political character and aimed at destroying the Macedonian state's national character. Interestingly enough then, for members of the Macedonian community the peace rally brought to life the stereotypical vision of the Albanian "Other"— the enemy par excellence, the militant extremist in the guise of the nonviolent peace demonstrator whose ultimate aim had always been to annihilate the Macedonian national Self.

The distinctions between "militants" and "democrats," and "peaceful" and "violent" Albanians became even more blurred for many Macedonians in the aftermath of a second rally that took place the following day, on 14 March in Tetovo—the third largest city (after Skopje and Bitola) and also the

Figure 5. View of Tetovo from Baltepe Hill. Photo credit: Alirami Jashari.

center of Albanian political life in Macedonia. The mass meeting was organized by three Albanian nongovernmental organizations (NGOs), namely,
the Organization of Albanian Women, the Civil Rights Forum, and the Association of Political Prisoners, under the slogan "Stop Macedonian government terror against Albanians." These NGOs had until then been moderate
and, according to Latifi (2003: 92), enjoyed close ties to the Albanian opposition party PDP/PPD and the then newly formed National Democratic Party
(NDP/PDK) led by Kastriot Haxhirexha. Shortly before the rally began, and
as television crews were getting ready to cover the event and a large crowd of
demonstrators was gathering in the main city square, NLA insurgents seized
Tetovo Kale (the Ottoman fortress atop the Baltepe hill, above the center of
Tetovo) and started shooting in the air, thereby opening a new fighting front
on the outskirts of Macedonia's third largest city.[2] The crowd's reaction, recorded by television cameras and shown on TV, was to chant "UÇK, UÇK"
every time the machine guns spat fire in the hill.

The open and public expression of support for the NLA during the Tetovo
rally, especially when considered together with the events discussed below,
shocked public opinion in Macedonia and aroused within the Macedonian
community anxiety and uncertainty regarding the political loyalties of the
Albanian population in the country.

The Tetovo Factor

Immediately following the opening of a new front twenty-five miles west of the capital on the forested hills above Tetovo, Macedonian government troops with machine guns and sniper rifles moved with urgent haste into the city and established a stronghold near the football stadium in the eastern districts. In a move meant to show that he would not tolerate the slightest possibility of a conflict of interest, the ethnic Macedonian Minister of Interior dismissed the Albanian police commander in Tetovo and replaced him with an ethnic Macedonian officer.[3] The government imposed a night curfew on Tetovo on 18 March, and thereafter the same spectacle, playing on television screens nationwide and featured in international media, unfolded with uncanny precision: from dusk to dawn, government troops would fire thousands of mortar rounds and shells into the surrounding rebel-controlled hills, and city garbage collectors working early morning shifts would shove the cartridges into plastic sacks (Phillips 2004: 86), as if cleaning and preparing the stage for the same sinister performance the next evening.

The uncontrollability and unpredictability of unfolding events in Tetovo continued to cause much anxiety among the populace. The Macedonian Parliament, including the Albanian parties in power (PDSH) and in opposition (PPD), condemned the so-called armed group of extremists and called for foreign military help. The NLA actions were also condemned by the leaders of Albanian political parties in neighboring Kosovo, and by NATO secretary general and chairman of the North Atlantic Council George Robertson, who stated the following: "We are determined that we will starve [sic] this limited number of localized extremists from being able to carry out their mischief and we will take what measures are necessary on the military front" (Jeffries 2002: 261).

Tanks and infantry units moved into the city in preparation for a full-scale offensive against the NLA, which was now controlling the villages nestled in the forested hills overlooking Tetovo. On March 20, the government postponed the planned offensive and gave the NLA a twenty-four-hour ultimatum to leave Macedonia. Just hours before the ultimatum expired, Ali Ahmeti, self-identified NLA political leader, appeared on neighboring Kosovo's RTK television to announce a unilateral ceasefire and call for talks with the Macedonian government.[4] Macedonian president Boris Trajkovski rejected the NLA call for talks, and EU high representative for common foreign and security policy Javier Solana backed up the government's decision by saying it would be a mistake to negotiate with so-called "terrorists."[5] In the meantime, to escape hostilities, thousands of people in the mountainous villages surrounding Tetovo evacuated their homes and fled to other parts of the country, European countries such as Germany and Switzerland, and Kosovo and Turkey, where they had relatives—mainly Albanian *gastarbeiter* (guest workers).

The national drama rose to a crescendo when around noon on 22 March a soldier in full combat gear—combat boots, camouflage uniform, flak vest, helmet, and rifle—raised a lollipop-shaped traffic baton at a roadblock near a machine-gun post and stopped a white Maruti Suzuki car with two male passengers (father and son, as it became known afterward) driving into town. Complying with the soldier's request, a middle-aged man in the passenger seat got out of the car and presented his driver's license while the elderly driver, who was wearing a tight round brimless skullcap (a visible marker of Muslim identity and, given that the majority of Muslims in Macedonia are Albanian, largely associated with Albanians), walked to the back of the car and opened the trunk for inspection. The middle-aged passenger suddenly reached into his right pocket and pulled out a small-sized object that fit into the palm of his hand. The soldier then started shouting and beating the man with the traffic baton at the same time as a second soldier in combat gear began firing his rifle, smashing the side windows of the car. In the midst of this mayhem, the passenger broke free from the policeman, bent his knees, and lifted at chest level his right hand with which he was still holding the small object. Several soldiers in the immediate vicinity shouted to the policeman to run for cover and shot at the man and his companion, killing both men almost instantaneously.

The incident occurred in front of a large group of domestic and international journalists, who were in Tetovo covering the confrontation between the NLA and government troops, and was captured on film. Reports of the incident and photographs from the film sequence circulated in the print and electronic media only to give rise to conflicting interpretations regarding what had actually happened. The Macedonian government and media claimed that the police had acted in self-defense because the man was holding a grenade and was about to throw it at a nearby stronghold of the Macedonian troops. The newspaper *Dnevnik*, for example, published a story titled "Two Terrorists Killed with Bombs in Their Hands," and reported that "For the time being the security forces react only to provocations."[6] In his eyewitness account of the incident, journalist John Phillips also describes the object as a grenade (2004: 86) and confirms these claims. Members of the Albanian community in Tetovo (89) and the Albanian media, however, claimed the police had acted aggressively against innocent Albanian civilians. The newspaper *Flaka*, for instance, reported that "Father and son were killed by members of the ARM [Armija na Republika Makedonija, Army of the Republic of Macedonia]," and referred to the killings as "a crime" that took place "in unclear circumstances."[7] Speculation also circulated in the Albanian community that the object in question was a cell phone—not a grenade.

Irrespective of whether the claims regarding killing of menacing Albanians in self-defense/ execution of innocent Albanians by the police were true or false, the lethal shootings in Tetovo made palpable for Macedonians and Albanians the possibility that these claims could materialize at any time, and thus intensified the climate of fear and uncertainty in which everyone was living. Additionally, the divergent constructions of the shootings shed light on an emerging and growing rift between the Macedonian- and Albanian-language media.

The shelling of NLA guerrilla targets on the hillside villages near Tetovo was followed on 25 March by a full-scale military offensive. The Macedonian army used tanks, heavy artillery, infantry units, and helicopter gunships to drive the NLA out of its strategic positions around the town and in the region of northern Macedonia, close to the border with Kosovo. George Robertson and Javier Solana, who traveled to Macedonia to encourage political dialogue on inter-ethnic relations in view of the impending signing of the stabilization and association agreement between Macedonia and the EU, praised the government for its "proportionate" military response to the NLA.[8] Macedonian forces gained control of the Tetovo Kale and the hill above the center of Tetovo, but the offensive came at a cost: it resulted in a couple of Albanian casualties, the killing of a British journalist, and extensive damage to civilian property owned by Albanians in villages not only within the country but also in the village of Krivenik in neighboring Kosovo. The offensive was met with sharp criticism from Albanians in Tetovo who accused the state of using terrorism against some of its own citizens (see also Phillips 2004: 97). Macedonian government officials promised compensation for civilian damage, but disclaimed responsibility for the killings, asserting that NLA insurgents had disguised themselves as Macedonian soldiers and shelled Albanian civilians in a deliberate attempt to bring the Macedonian army into disrepute.[9]

Reverberations of Anxiety

Who, after all, was the aggressor and who was the victim? Was the NLA or the Macedonian state the terrorist committing acts of aggression? Profound uncertainty about the nature of reality and fears for one's safety and the safety of loved ones in Tetovo sent reverberations of anxiety through the Macedonian and Albanian communities in Skopje. The dramatic character of the unfolding events in northern Macedonia—the competing armies, mortar shells fired into the air over the main square in Tetovo, destruction and disarray, the spread of armed conflict from the outskirts of Tetovo to the region of Kumanovo (northeast of Skopje) in late April and to the village of Aračinovo (five miles from Skopje) in early June—made for a compelling spectacle. Many of my Macedonian and Albanian research participants stayed home and watched television news religiously in the evenings, especially at the outset of the conflict. After dusk, the clubs and cafés downtown were frequented by an unusually small number of customers. The streets in my neighborhood eerily stopped echoing with the clamor of children's voices whenever the media publicized interpretations of events, such as the killings of soldiers or the opening of a new front closer to the capital, that shocked the public.

A strong undercurrent of anxiety began to widen, gaining further force as the conflict spread, and broke through to the surface in some of my research participants' comments and actions concerning my presence in the country throughout the duration of the conflict. These comments and actions revealed how people in Skopje construed a social reality of intense uncertainty and fear that serious trouble could happen to anyone, anytime, anywhere—a reality akin to what Slavenka Drakulić describes in *The Balkan Express* (1993), a novel about the Balkan wars in the 1990s, as "parallel reality." To give a few indicative examples, an Albanian neighbor asked me to call him anytime, day or night, and let him know if the U.S. embassy in Skopje planned to evacuate American citizens from Macedonia so that he and his family would escape to Kosovo. Another Albanian friend, certain I had insights into the conflict, took his wife and two children to visit relatives in the town of Prizren in Kosovo when I left Skopje for a few days in June 2001 to visit my family in Athens, and returned home to Skopje soon after I was back in town. The families of my Albanian landlady and language teacher suggested that the situation in the country might be too scary for me to live alone and invited me to stay with them. My Macedonian adoptive family and some of my female friends who lived with their families in predominantly Macedonian-populated neighborhoods also invited me to move in with them and argued that I probably put myself in harm's way, especially while the conflict was unfolding, by living in a predominantly Albanian-populated neighborhood. Some of my Macedonian friends suggested that if the police were to stop me in Bit Pazar or in the streets of Čair and ask to see my identification papers I say that I was in the country visiting Macedonian relatives and tell nothing about my research and Albanian language learning in order to avoid potentially coming across as an NLA sympathizer.

Rumors

High levels of anxiety were also reflected in conflicting and indeterminate rumors. Sparked by current events and fueled by a haunting fear of war, rumors circulated and spread among people through kin and nonkin (friendship and neighborly) networks throughout the conflict. Rumors especially proliferated while an emergency session of Parliament, called on 16 March by Parliament speaker Stojan Andov to discuss the security situation in the country, lasted for three days and took place behind closed doors. The session prompted speculation among political experts and laypeople in Skopje that Prime Minister Georgievski proposed to the Assembly a declaration of a state of emergency or war and that the Macedonian opposition and Albanian parties voted against this proposal.

Rumors spiraled when, after the end of the emergency session of Parliament, authorities imposed an overnight curfew on Tetovo (from seven in the evening to six in the morning), and Georgievski announced the mobilization of 10,000 army reservists (what came to be known as "Wolves," "Tigers," "Lions," and "Scorpions," and were later speculated to be prison conscripts who knew each other from prison) in a televised address to the nation on 18 March.[10] In the afternoon of 21 March, for example, an ethnic Macedonian policeman was shot dead in the Albanian quarter of Čairčanka, a few blocks from where I lived. While Macedonian and Albanian media reported that a deadly shooting had taken place and that the perpetrators were still at large, unverified news spread throughout the city by word of mouth that the perpetrators had been NLA insurgents who managed to escape arrest because some Albanian family in Čair had hidden them. This rumor helped foster suspicion as it implied that members of the Albanian community had become active supporters of the NLA. At the same time, an alternative rumor circulated in the Albanian community in my neighborhood that the shooting had nothing to do with the NLA, but was a settling of accounts between the Albanian mafia and the policeman, who allegedly was a drug dealer and owed money to the mafia. Viewed through the prism of this rumor, the shooting incident in Čairčanka was rendered somewhat less ominous because it tapped into common knowledge regarding the criminal activities of mafia-type groups in Macedonia, and the Balkans more generally.[11] Both rumors sounded credible to those people who heard them (members of the Albanian community and people who had professional, personal or neighborly contacts within the Albanian community) but nobody knew for sure which account was true.

The circulation of rumor in Skopje, similar to that in zones of violence (Simons 1995), helped generate profound uncertainty and confusion over reality and illusion, what one should believe to be true or dismiss as false. Some of the media reported unconfirmed stories, thereby helping trigger rumors that spread across the country. The following story about Muslim mujahideen fighters' participation in the NLA is a telling case in point. The popular weekly political magazine *Start* in late March and mid-April published a couple of articles alleging, first, that Hezbollah was operating in Macedonia and that forty mujahideens had taken refuge in the area surrounding the Lipkovo village (in the region of Kumanovo in northwestern Macedonia), and second, that Macedonian citizens were involved in funneling money to pro-bin Laden operations.[12] While the rest of the media only picked up the stories that had run in *Start* subsequent to the signing of the Ohrid Framework Agreement (more specifically, in the aftermath of 9/11; see Icevska and Ajdini 2002), the news immediately captured the public imagination and provided a lens through which people sought to understand and interpret events during the conflict. When, for instance, news reports circulated in the media that some people in northwest Macedonia had been chased away from their homes by bearded men who fought in the ranks of the NLA, there was emotional torment and confusion among many Macedonians and Albanians with whom I worked over the meaning and significance of the beards. Speculations proliferated: did the wearing of beards, an Islamic practice in honor of the Prophet Mohammed, signify cold-blooded, foreign mujahideen terrorists who posed a grave threat to personal and national security? Did the practice perhaps signify less threatening Muslim men originating from the Balkans, or perhaps even Serbian chetnik paramilitaries who also wore beards?

Rumors concerning Serbia's purported involvement in the crisis in Macedonia and the alleged presence of foreign mujahideen fighters in the country spread widely. As is the case with rumor (Bhabha 1994: 200; Osborn 2008), they inspired panic, especially after details came to light about the gruesome event that came to be known as the Vejce massacre. On 28 April NLA insurgents killed eight Macedonian male commandos in the Macedonian Army Special Forces, also known as "Wolves" (Volci), in an ambush near the village of Vejce, nine miles north of Tetovo. According to the eyewitness account of the only Macedonian soldier who managed to escape the ambush, the assailants were bearded men. The killing shocked public opinion because the reportedly bearded assailants used knives to dig out the eyes and cut off the ears and genitals of the Macedonian soldiers while the soldiers were still alive, and raised once again haunting questions concerning the origin of the people who committed these atrocious acts.[13] The mutilation of the commandos' bodies, together with rumors about mujahideen groups operating in Macedonia, motivated people to action: in the city of Bitola (home of four of the commandos), Macedonians formed community self-defense groups; in Skopje, gunmen in a passing car opened fire on the Albanian Embassy and on an Albanian-owned pizzeria, killing an Albanian man; businesses and stores of Albanians and other Muslims in both cities were looted or burned.

As fighting between the two warring parties escalated and intensified, the prime minister announced in early May that consultations would be launched on whether to declare a state of war in Macedonia. Under international pressure, a parliamentary vote on the declaration of a state of war was postponed and a government of national unity led by Georgievski was established on 14 May, but fear nonetheless spread that the conflict might engulf the capital. Neighborhood incidents that were ostensibly unconnected to the unfolding conflict, and were not reported in the media, sparked rumors that made the possibility of widespread violence more palpable. Let me draw upon my personal experience and in an auto/ethnographic mode of inquiry capable of "plac[ing] the self within a social context" (Reed-Danahay 1997: 9), recount the following story to illustrate. I vividly remember how panic-stricken my next-door Macedonian neighbor was when on a May evening, as fighting intensified in the region of Kumanovo, she rang my doorbell to let me know that an armed man had come to my apartment looking for me. "I was on my way out of the apartment to go sit with the other women [on the park bench] downstairs when I saw a tall man ring your doorbell," Ljubica, a pensioner well into her sixties, said, palpitating with fright. I invited her inside, and she sat on the edge of the sofa and recounted how she had asked the man if he perhaps needed anything and how he had responded negatively before running off. Ljubica panted for breath as she continued: "He was carrying under his arm a small black case, small enough to hold a gun. Surely, he was [an] NLA [insurgent] and wanted to check if the apartment was unoccupied so that he could squat in it and make it an NLA bastion!"

Word that NLA insurgents wanted to occupy and establish headquarters in my rented apartment and then lay siege to the capital city quickly spread among my neighbors. People who lived on my floor seemed especially worried, and asked every time they saw me in the hallway or the stairwell if "he" had come back. Actually, the man did come back and ring my bell. Twice. The first time, I looked through the peephole in my front door only to stare at an eye drawing close to the peephole from the other side. I stumbled back a step and froze in my tracks, burdened by the debilitating effects of what struck me at that time as a rumor that had suddenly jumped into life. The second time around, having mustered up enough resolve, I unlocked and opened my front door. "Sorry" [*Izvini*], a man said to me in Macedonian and disappeared down the stairway before I had a chance to ask any questions. The following day when I told them what had happened, my neighbors seemed relieved at the news; word spread fast that the man was gone and there was nothing to worry about.

Rumors that the NLA had infiltrated Skopje became somaticized (see also Feldman 1995: 234) and physically jarring. People's bodies jolted at warfare sounds, such as bomb detonations and gunfire, that could occasionally be heard somewhere in the distance, especially at night. My Macedonian neighbor Dule, a man in his early twenties, narrated to me how his elderly mother had once awoken in the early hours of the morning to the muted sound of gunfire, and started shaking him, trying to wake him up—"Wake up, wake up, the NLA has come!" Even ordinary, everyday sounds became a grave cause for concern. For example, while she was having afternoon tea with her husband, and my Albanian landlady Fatmira and me, Melita, Fatmira's cousin, jumped up from the sofa at the sound of the doorbell. She placed her hand on her chest, and her whole body went rigid for a minute before she got up to open the door. "Ouf! It's you," she breathed a sigh of relief at the sight of Fisnik, Fatmira's husband. "I thought it was the NLA," she said with a tight, almost embarrassed smile, as she was closing the door behind her. "What NLA? There's nothing going on here!" Fisnik said in an authoritative voice, and Fatmira's smile grew broader.

Making a Joke Out of the Conflict

In the midst of such profound social and political confusion and upheaval, when the boundary between what we commonly call real and phantasmal was very thin, the people with whom I worked in Skopje improvised commentary on currents events that revealed the same "wry" sense of humor characterizing Macedonian responses to the disintegration of the Yugoslav federation in the early 1990s (Schwarz 1993: 115). To the best of my knowledge, Macedonians and Albanians did not make jokes directed against one another or against those who committed acts of violence during the conflict. A joke I often heard my Albanian friends make, especially young men who faced the possibilities of being summoned to serve as reservists in the Macedonian army and also asked to join the NLA, concerned the ambiguity of their dual identity as Macedonian citizens and members of the Albanian ethnonational community. Shortly after the insurgency spread to the outskirts of Tetovo, for example, Arton, the twenty-year-old son of my Albanian language teacher, told me that if he lived in Tetovo, he would wear a hat reading ARM on one side and UÇK on the other. "Then"—Arton started to laugh midway— "to walk down the city's main street, I'd wear the hat with the UÇK side facing the hills and the ARM side facing [the sandbagged barricades of] the Macedonians!"

Jokes also mocked the risk that ostensibly innocuous everyday activities carried. After the previously mentioned confrontation between Macedonian police and an Albanian man holding a hand grenade/cell phone had transpired in Tetovo, for example, I was out for coffee with some Albanian friends when my cell phone rang. "Wait, wait" my friend Armira cautioned as I was about to pull the phone out of my handbag. She took a swift look around and then said while trying hard to conceal a smile, "Well, good, there are no police, you can answer the phone!" Both Armira and her friends laughed loudly as I took the incoming call.

Other jokes focused on how the armed conflict interfered with social activities. On 22 June, Macedonian forces launched a heavy military offensive against the NLA, which now controlled the village of Aračinovo (near Skopje airport and just five miles from the center of the capital city). Shortly after the offensive ended, I visited my Macedonian adoptive parents who lived in a suburb on the outskirts of Skopje. Besides discussing current events, Borče and Jordanka recounted how on that Saturday evening when the offensive unfolded, Marko, the best man at their wedding (kum), and his wife Violeta had, just like every other Saturday, come over to play cards.[14] "What to tell you?" Jordanka began, "terrible, terrible, we could hear the detonations, the windows were shaking, terrible!" She sounded distraught, and so in an effort to distract her from unpleasant memories I asked how the card game was. "Well, fine [Pa, dobro]" she said dismissively, "we don't play cards for money, like that only, to keep company with each other [za društvo]."[15] She paused briefly, looked at her husband, and a slow smile broke across her face as she remembered, "At the end of the first hand, the kum said 'we won' and as soon as he uttered those words a loud detonation was heard. Oh dear [Lele], what to tell you! And the kum said 'we won and they [the Macedonian army] won, too!' How we laughed, we couldn't stop laughing!" Jordanka giggled. "The village is burning down, the grandmother is combing her hair!" (*seloto gori, babata se češla*) Borče invoked the proverbial saying and then he, too, chortled in amusement.[16]

Sometimes people laughed or made ironic comments when the absurdity of the situation became too gripping. On one occasion, for instance, as my landlady and I were in my apartment discussing over coffee the NLA and its potential objectives, my home phone rang. Fatmira leaned forward on the sofa, looked at me anxiously, and said in a serious voice that I should not answer the phone because the NLA could be on the other end of the line. I remember being struck at how improbable her suggestion sounded while at the same time contemplating the possibility she raised. For a brief moment, we sat in silence and stared at each other, leaving the phone unanswered— this silence can perhaps best be described as what Morris calls (1996: 28) "the silence of suffering": "Its silence reflects something not ultimately ungraspable but merely resistant to description." Then, as if all of a sudden she realized the impossibility of what she had said, Fatmira shook her head slightly from left to right in disbelief and gave an exclamation fairly common among Albanians, "Kuku!" which translates into English as "Oh dear!," as she ran her hand over her mouth. "Go ahead [*Ani*], answer the phone!" she said, letting out a short burst of laughter. On another occasion, upon seeing on the weather map on TV a blank line next to the temperature reading for Tetovo, a young Macedonian woman remarked sardonically that it was too hot in Tetovo.

Through joke-telling Macedonians and Albanians in Skopje, similar to people experiencing armed conflict elsewhere (Trnka 2008), were thus able to laugh in the face of adversity and emotional distress and hence diffuse, rather than increase, anxiety. At the same time, casual, wry-humored jokes enabled some people not only to situate themselves within the unstable political landscape in Macedonia (see Brown 1995) but, perhaps more important, to create with their actions a social order whereby they had, albeit temporarily, some sense of control over their lives.

Vulnerability

The inability of the Macedonian state to contain, let alone eradicate, the NLA insurgency, and the gradual but steady expansion of NLA control over northwest Macedonian territory intensified a sense of insecurity and uncertainty among everyone in Skopje. In the Macedonian community there was an especially heightened sense of vulnerability and related feelings of impending doom due to the widespread belief, supported by the international community's feeble stance toward Macedonia's worldwide recognition under its constitutional name (Republic of Macedonia, not FYROM), that the odds were stacking up against the Macedonian side in the conflict. Arguments that the international community (mainly representatives of NATO, EU, U.S., and OSCE) had adopted an outright pro-Albanian attitude and promoted the demands of the insurgents to the detriment of the Macedonian side played a crucial role in this regard. Such arguments were throughout the conflict advanced by Macedonian nationalist politicians and promoted in some Macedonian-language media in a bid to increase audience size. Two incidents concerning international involvement in the crisis, nonetheless, were instrumental in solidifying the perception that Macedonians' chances of winning the conflict grew slimmer and slimmer.

The first incident, in March 2001, concerned an alleged peace agreement that was reached among Ali Ahmeti, NLA political leader, Arben Xhaferi, leader of the Albanian party in power DPA/PDSH, and Imer Imeri, leader of the Albanian opposition party PDP/PPD—that is, without the participation of the Macedonian political leadership. According to media reports, the agreement contained a number of provisions favorable to Albanians, such as amendments to the constitution, recognition of Albanian as an official state language, and amnesty for the NLA insurgents.[17] Importantly, the agreement was allegedly facilitated by Robert Frowick, former American diplomat who had been appointed as Personal Representative for Macedonia of the OSCE Chairman-in-Office. Although Frowick denied direct contact with the NLA, and the U.S. and EU denounced any attempts at that time to negotiate with the insurgents, the belief that Albanians had succeeded in winning international sympathy took firm root within the Macedonian community and persisted until the end of the conflict in August.

The second incident concerned the mediating role EU security chief Javier Solana played in negotiating a ceasefire between Macedonian government forces and the NLA in late June 2001. Solana brokered the deal after the NLA occupied the village of Aračinovo and threatened to bomb strategic targets, namely, the Skopje international airport (which closed for a few days due to security concerns) and the country's only oil refinery, Okta AD, located near the airport, and thus not only wreak havoc in the country but also cut off valuable KFOR supply lines into Kosovo. The terms of the ceasefire included the evacuation of NLA forces, under NATO escort, from Aračinovo to the

NLA-controlled village of Nikushak, four miles farther north. Because the insurgents were allowed to evacuate without surrendering their weapons to NATO, the operation caused angry protests in front of the Parliament building: demonstrators demanded the resignation of the late President Boris Trajkovski and some of them chanted "gas chambers for Šiptari" (*za Šiptari gasna komora*). The operation also earned Javier Solana the nickname of *kavijar so lajno*, "caviar with crap"—a mocking play on his name.[18] Many Macedonians with whom I spoke viewed the incident as conclusive evidence of strong pro-Albanian bias in the international community and hence of imminent Macedonian defeat in the conflict.

This sense of vulnerability and impending doom in the Macedonian community deepened as thousands of Albanian women and children moved out of the country and waited out the conflict with relatives and acquaintances abroad, mainly in Kosovo. For their part, Albanian men tended to help their families relocate and to return to Skopje.[19] In our conversations, my Albanian male research participants gave varied explanations of their decision to return. Some argued that they wished to protect their families' properties in the event that the situation in Macedonia deteriorated and fighting engulfed the capital city of Skopje. Others, especially young Albanian men in their twenties and thirties, suggested that they did not want to lose face vis-à-vis co-ethnics who might view their departure as an indication of cowardice in the face of escalating hostility against the Albanian people. They seemed especially concerned over the lack of prestige they would suffer if they were to leave Macedonia during the conflict and return after the conflict to reap whatever advantages might have been gained in the meantime by Albanians who had stayed behind and made some contribution to the insurgency. Still others returned to join the NLA, an army composed of, among other participants, Albanians (mainly men but also several women) from Macedonia, Kosovo, Albania, and the Albanian diaspora. The men with whom I spoke were motivated by a wide range of factors, including family and peer camaraderie, nationalist aspirations of territorial separation, the possibility of improved status for Albanians in Macedonia, official and unofficial narratives of collective suffering and persecution, and a strong sense of national duty fostered in large part by popular patriotic songs about the Kosovo war and the KLA (see Sugarman 2010).[20]

Within the Macedonian community, then, the departure of Albanian women and children was met with fear not only because it made more real the sinister possibility that something might go wrong, but also because it exacerbated widespread feelings of entrapment and isolation that have taken root in Macedonia since the disintegration of Yugoslavia and the imposition of Greek political blockades and trade embargos. Although, similar to Albanians, they agonized over what lay ahead and worried about the safety of their loved ones and the protection of their property, Macedonians could not get away from the immediate political reality due to their lack of social networks in countries that did not require travel visas for Macedonian citizens. Joining relatives and friends in faraway countries where Macedonian diaspora communities are mainly concentrated (for example, the United States, Canada, or Australia) meant having to apply for a visa—a time-consuming, not to mention expensive for local standards process in Macedonia—and to spend a lot of money toward travel expenses. Additionally, the return of Albanian men was met with suspicion: many Macedonians entertained the possibility that Albanians might have returned to join the ranks of the NLA. Suspicions were reinforced by alleged eyewitness accounts, reported by the Macedonian-language media, whereby Macedonians in ethnically heterogeneous villages had seen some of their Albanian neighbors put on NLA uniforms and vanish into thin air.

Competing Realities

The coverage of the conflict by Macedonian- and Albanian-language state-government-controlled and independent media played an important role in crystallizing reality, as people came to know it.[21] Iso Rusi, editor-in-chief of the Albanian weekly *Lobi*, describes the media coverage of the conflict at the outset as "restrained" and "low key" (2003: 102–3) and notes that, as the conflict escalated, the media tended to promote fundamentally different and increasingly divisive reports. Rusi relates the use of inflammatory rhetoric and nationalistic stereotypes to the hardening of political attitudes and the appointment of hard-liners to key government positions, such as the Ministry of Internal Affairs and the Ministry of Defense. As Daskalovski (2009: 174) suggests, when compared with media coverage of the wars in Serbia, Croatia, and Bosnia-Herzegovina after the disintegration of Yugoslavia, the media in Macedonia during the 2001 conflict did not produce such high levels of hate-speech. At the same time, some local analysts (Icevska and Ajdini 2002) argue that the Macedonian- and Albanian-language media "operated in two parallel universes."

Perhaps the most notable example of the schism between the Macedonian- and Albanian-language media was the consistent use of the terms "terrorists" (*teroristi*) by the former and "fighters" (*luftëtarë*) by the latter to describe the NLA (Icevska and Ajdini 2002: 37). In the Macedonian-language media, additional references to the NLA included "Kachak gangs"[22] (the Kachak were rebel bands that consisted mainly of Kosovar Albanians and regularly challenged Serb rule from the early days of the first Yugoslavia around 1918), "primitive Albanian hordes," and "vicious and bloody mercenaries and murderers" (Rusi 2003: 105), while the Macedonian security forces were described as "defenders of the fatherland" (73). Conversely, the Albanian-language media referred to the NLA insurgents as "fighters" against the Macedonian security forces and paramilitary groups, allegedly assisted by "foreign mercenaries." Use of such loaded language helped focus attention on the insurgency as a foreboding event, and produce insecurity and danger (see also Weldes et al. 1999). Importantly, it helped produce competing and mutually exclusive bodies of knowledge about the insurgency and also about the organization of the social world along ethnonational lines, whereby the Albanian NLA was either the menacing enemy attacking the Macedonian state and its institutions with the help of Albanians from Kosovo; or, the defender of Albanian rights interests that the Macedonian state had failed to safeguard and promote since its independence in 1991.

Macedonian- and Albanian-language media, what is more, construed social reality differently (see also Daskalovski 2009: 186–90) by engaging in the process of erasure. Following Irvine and Gal (2000: 38), I use the term "erasure" to refer to "the process in which ideology, in simplifying the sociolinguistic field, renders some persons or activities (or sociolinguistic phenomena) invisible." Reporting on the anti-Muslim riots that erupted in Bitola on the evening of 6 June 2001 provides a telling example. Similar to the riots in Bitola on 28 April, the event that precipitated the violence was the killing of Macedonian soldiers (a total of five, of whom three were from Bitola) in an NLA ambush outside Tetovo. Macedonian crowds set homes and shops on fire, desecrated Muslim graves, and defaced a mosque with swastikas and anti-Albanian graffiti reading "Death to the Šiptars" (*Smrt za Šiptari*). The Albanian newspaper *Fakti* editorial described the event as "a fascist action of frenzied Macedonian crowds . . . who were hindered by almost nobody," and stated that "the truth behind all this has to do with ethnic cleansing."[23] *Flaka*'s masthead read, "The houses of Albanians were burning in front of policemen," and the paper described the Macedonian crowds as "a barbarian horde that went through the streets where Albanians are concentrated" while "the police ... not only did not stop the vandalizers, but it even protected them." Also, the burning of Albanian homes was described as "vandalism that is unprecedented and unnoticed in the twentieth-century long history of humankind" and "the biggest drama, the drama of Rome that burned because of Nero's insanity."[24] While the fact that Macedonian Muslims were among the owners of the property destroyed was generally left unnoticed by Albanian-language newspapers, some Macedonian-language newspapers included it in their own reporting. The latter media also reported differently on the role of the police, and did not provide commentary on the burnings, thus erasing the suffering caused by the riots. *Nova Makedonija*, for example, reported that, "A crowd of about five thousand people, embittered and angered by the prematurely killed young lives, last night became very furious in the streets of Bitola, setting on fire fifty shops and residences whose owners are Albanians." Also, "throughout the night, police teams mobilized, and reserve police units as well as the firefighting unit were called into service."[25] *Dnevnik* reported that "The police used tear gas to break up the angry crowd the night before yesterday, but did not succeed in deterring the crowd from setting on fire and burning the houses and shops of Albanians," and that "despite a strong security presence some houses of Albanians and Macedonian Muslims were demolished and set ablaze."[26] *Večer* also reported that owners of the destroyed property included Macedonian Muslims and Albanians.[27]

These particular discourses that were promoted through the media gradually and steadily became what Foucault calls "dominant discourses" in the sense that they helped to enunciate within each ethnonational community a social reality, a preferred social order, sustaining a certain "regime of truth" (Foucault 1980: 131). Put differently, the Macedonian- and Albanian-language media were involved in production and dissemination of claims regarding the conflict that not only were accepted and functioned as true within each community, but also contested all other truth-claims produced outside the confines of the community. Specifically, social actors tended to discuss and analyze the particularities of the armed conflict, or more aptly, media accounts of the conflict, only with co-ethnics. When in the company of the ethnographer, or family members and other co-ethnics, my research participants tended to argue forcefully that the "other" side was "abnormal" (*ne se normalni/nuk janë normalë* in Macedonian and Albanian): allegedly irrational, excessively aggressive, belligerent, and hence at fault for the continuation of the conflict. After all, as Foucault argues, discourse as an attempt to produce certain bodies of knowledge and as "a fragment of history" (Foucault 1972: 117) arising at a particular point in time regulates which particular modes of thought and conduct are defined as "normal," and which as "abnormal"— and supposedly need to be normalized (see Foucault 1978, 2003).

It is in the midst of heightened confusion and uncertainty about the present and the future that, as I show in the following three chapters, middle- and working-class Macedonians and Albanians in Skopje navigated tumultuous times and negotiated relationships of power during interpersonal and intergroup interactions.

CHAPTER 4

Performing Civility

On the Wednesday before Orthodox Easter in April 2001, my Albanian landlady Fatmira, a schoolteacher in her mid-fifties who originated from a long-established family in Skopje, called and invited me to join her and her Macedonian friend Vesna for afternoon tea in her house in Čair. The two women had known each other since the late 1960s, when Vesna, a housewife, and her husband Igor, a factory administrator, had rented the first floor in the house of Bajram, Fatmira's husband. While living under the same roof for nearly a decade, Vesna and Fatmira had come to share the joys and sorrows of daily life and had become close friends. After Vesna and Igor purchased an apartment and moved out of the house in the late 1970s, the two women had stayed in touch with phone calls and periodic visits, especially on religious holidays when it is customary for long-time friends (and also relatives) to call or pay visits and wish each other many happy returns of the day. Thus, when Easter arrived in 2001, Vesna called to say that she was planning to visit some relatives in Čair and that she wanted to make sure Bajram and Fatmira would be home when she stopped in *na gosti*, "as a guest."

Over homemade fruit preserves cooked with sugar (*ëmbëlsirë* in Albanian, *slatko* in Macedonian), store-bought juice, homemade pies, and Turkish tea, the women narrated to me, and to Bajram who was also present, in Macedonian, stories of their life together in the house, such as the occasional sharing of food, the collaborative preparation of pickled vegetables and *ajvar* (a grilled red pepper relish), baby-sitting each other's children, and the story about how Vesna's toddler son had accidentally flushed the rent money down the toilet and Bajram had waived the rent for that month. In these stories, spatial proximity was identified with harmony (see also Bahloul 1992). The women also talked wistfully about former Yugoslavia; they were especially nostalgic about the existence of a single political party and a comfortable standard of living that reportedly everyone enjoyed during Tito's rule. "What has become of us now? You, Macedonian and I, Albanian!" Fatmira exclaimed with exasperation, pointing to estrangement that can take place between people once ethnonational identity becomes the primary form of identification. Without missing a beat, Vesna replied: "But we did not do that, Ljupčo did it [Ljupčo Georgievski, Macedonian prime minister and leader of the nationalist political party VMRO-DPMNE], Thaçi [Menduh Thaçi, Albanian deputy leader of DPA/PDSH, the nationalist Albanian coalition partner] did it! Ordinary people [*obični lugje*] are not at fault!"[1] Fatmira introduced the topic of the armed conflict between the NLA and Macedonian security forces, and everyone present interpreted the conflict as *politika*. Bajram encapsulated the apparent consensus by saying that ordinary people wished to live together in peace, and the discussion then veered off into social problems, such as poverty and unemployment.

The above vignette is typical of performances of civility that occurred throughout the duration of the 2001 conflict. These performances were put forth by working- and middle-class Macedonian and Albanian men and women—mainly former and present neighbors in Čair whose social ties long predated Tito's death in 1980, and work colleagues. I use the term "civility" to describe the process whereby Macedonian and Albanian individuals, acting primarily as parties with de facto equal moral status, appeared uninterested in taking sides in, or assigning blame for, the unfolding conflict and shunned the larger question of the distribution of rights and resources. Instead, they focused attention on long-standing, interpersonal relationships and portrayed them as harmonious, reciprocal, and untainted by ethnonational prejudices.

As I explore in this chapter, through performances of civility social actors who interacted across ethnonational lines articulated subjectivities that were nonpolitical. That is, they put forth public presentations of a Self that was unaligned with political parties, did not promote any particular stance on the conflict, and viewed and treated others with courtesy and without prejudice. Such performances played a key role in sustaining and protecting a consistent sense of common sociality in the face of political turmoil. They involved the continuation of social practices and activities that occurred prior to the eruption of the insurgency, and more specifically the use of a "reverse discourse" (Foucault 1978: 101) that overturned the essentialist premises of nationalist media discourse (Macedonians versus Albanians, Self versus Other), and instead depicted differences between *politika* ("politics") and *obični lugje/njerëz të thjeshtë* ("ordinary people" in Macedonian and Albanian) and promoted a feeling of nostalgia for Tito's Yugoslavia; and the exchange of hospitality.

On Politics and Ordinary People

The distinction between politics and ordinary people has conventionally been used not only in Macedonia but also in other former Yugoslav countries (for Bosnia, see Helms 2007; Grandits 2007; Kolind 2007). In popular parlance, politics, or *politika*, is commonly defined as a "whore" (*politikata e kurva/ politika është kurvë*).[2] The practitioners of *politika* are usually depicted as amoral—greedy, corrupt, and deceitful—individuals who cultivate distrust of one's fellow citizens, aggravate animosities, manipulate people, and instigate sociopolitical disorder and instability in order to get elected and serve their private interests at the expense of the public. Such views have been reinforced by the ubiquity of political clientelism and corruption after Tito's death, the outbreak of war in Croatia and Bosnia in the early 1990s, the endorsement by the EC of Greece's refusal to extend recognition to Macedonia, and numerous scandals implicating domestic politicians in post-independence Macedonia.[3] The Macedonian daily *Nova Makedonija* eloquently captured in 1992 the strong popular sentiment against politics when it published on the front page, above the story about Macedonia's being the only former Yugoslav republic that had been denied recognition by the EC despite having met the criteria of the Badinter Commission, a photograph of a wall on which someone had written in capital letters "EVROPA KURVA."[4] The message was clear: Europe had sold itself to Greece—in other words, had made a corrupt bargain with Greece—at the expense of Macedonia for the purpose of maintaining unity and solidarity among EC members.

Generally viewed as having its own norms and set of governing principles, the domain of politics includes Macedonian and Albanian politicians and also expands to encompass all new actors assuming key roles on Macedonia's political scene at any given time. During the course of the 2001 conflict, *politika* became expansive in its inclusion of the Albanian NLA and NLA political leader Ali Ahmeti, and also foreign officials involved with the management of the crisis, such as Christopher Hill, U.S. ambassador to Macedonia in the late 1990s and architect of all major American foreign policy initiatives in Macedonia; Lord Robertson, NATO secretary general; Javier Solana, EU foreign policy chief; François Léotard, EU envoy to Macedonia; James Pardew, U.S. envoy to Macedonia; and Robert Frowick, personal representative for Macedonia of the OSCE chairman-in-office. Disparaging views about politics and politicians notwithstanding, people tend to rally behind their "own" political parties, defined along ethnonational lines, and to condemn during interactions with their co-ethnics those politicians who are considered to represent the interests of other communities as being "worse," more corrupt and deceitful, than the politicians who are viewed to represent the interests of their own (for parallels with Bosnia, see Jansen 2007: 128).

Politika has routinely been contrasted with *obični lugje/njerëz të thjeshtë* ("ordinary people"). Similar to the trope of *pošteni ljudi*, or "decent/honest people" in Bosnia, the tropes of *obični lugje* and *njerëz të thjeshtë* are used in Macedonia to refer to "an inner essence or character" (Jansen 2007: 129) of people irrespective of ethnonational affiliation. As opposed to *politika*, which is allegedly wicked, ordinary people are said to be intrinsically moral human beings, who do not share the values of politicians and act without ulterior motives and in ways that demonstrate kindness, fairness, respect, sociability, and consideration toward everyone. Jansen's definition of "decent people" in Bosnia aptly illuminates the particularities of ordinary people in Macedonia (129): "To behave decently is to be able to provide for oneself and one's family, to be honest and hard-working, to be self-sacrificing, to be considerate to others and to pay visits to them, and also to remain the same no matter what pressures or temptations to which one is exposed." Additionally, ordinary people are allegedly disinterested in *politika* and bear no responsibility for the state of affairs in the country.

The Work of *Politika*

It should be noted that invocation of the conventional terms *politika* and *obični lugje/njerëz të thjeshtë* throughout the 2001 crisis occurred in parallel with political mobilization, carrying the threat of imminent harm to people from different ethnonational backgrounds. As fighting intensified and the number of internally displaced persons increased, members of the Macedonian community participated in riots and protests against the perceived pro-Albanian and anti-Macedonian Western involvement, and also against what they viewed as the government's lenience toward the NLA and inability to protect Macedonia's national interests.[5] The demonstrations in Skopje on 25 June provide a telling case in point. Immediately after NLA insurgents were bused out of the village of Aračinovo, fully armed and under NATO escort, thousands of enraged demonstrators in the streets of Skopje fired guns in the air and besieged the Macedonian Parliament building. Moreover, the self-proclaimed group "Macedonian Paramilitary 2000" (Makedonska Paravojska 2000) issued a leaflet warning Albanian shopkeepers and market stall-holders in the Skopje district of Madžari to close shop and leave. The leaflet also warned that so-called Šiptari who had no Macedonian citizenship or received it after 1994 (that is to say, Albanians who had arrived in Macedonia from Kosovo after the uprising of 1981, when in the aftermath of Tito's death the situation in Kosovo became increasingly difficult for many Albanians) would be killed if they remained in the country past midnight of 25 June.

Despite, or perhaps because of, such sociopolitical volatility, performances of civility revolving around the interpretation of the conflict as *politika* persisted (although, as I discuss in the following chapters, they did not always punctuate daily life) in Skopje. To give credence to such interpretations, my research participants looked to Macedonia's distinctly tumultuous history from the late nineteenth century on. They often referred to the wars, occupations, persecution, and partitions that have characterized Macedonian history (see, for example, Brown 2003; Rossos 2008; Roudometof 2000) and referred to Macedonia as politically weak, a small piece of land that had served as a pawn in the political machinations of the great powers in the Balkans and had never managed to stand strong against threats to its national sovereignty and territorial integrity. They also articulated how Macedonia's ambiguity, understood as "continual and contingent indeterminacy" (Green 2005: 12) and comparable to the ambiguities of the Balkans as "a crossroads on the way to somewhere else" (127), defined an age-old and unchangeable tradition, whereby politically powerful outsiders were really always the ones to control political developments affecting Macedonia.

Additionally, the people with whom I worked in Skopje often explained the outbreak of violence in terms of American strategic interests and the involvement of the CIA.[6] According to these assessments, Washington wished to gain control of the Trans-Balkan pipeline carrying crude oil from the Bulgarian port of Bourgas in the Black Sea to the Albanian port of Vlora in the Adriatic Sea. The CIA allegedly conspired to undermine Macedonian stability in hopes of turning Macedonia into a NATO protectorate and consolidating its presence in the region. Such judgments gained credence in light of the operation of Camp Bondsteel in neighboring Kosovo, the largest and most expensive U.S. military base constructed since the end of the Vietnam War (Johnson 2004: 143), and of NATO's announcement in May 1998 of upgrading (to use the term in the announcement) a Partnership for Peace (PfP) exercise in Macedonia in September 1998 and considering establishment of a PfP training center in the Macedonian army training area Krivolak (see NATO press release in Krieger 2001: 288).[7] While it is difficult to assess the accuracy of these judgments, it is perhaps worth noting that conspiracy theories in the Balkans have in general been a familiar framework for making sense of political turmoil—as Crnobrnja argues (1994: 125–26), the popularity of conspiracies in the region lies with uncompromising fanatics and also with the stubborn prominence of old Stalinist ideas regarding behind-the-scenes machinations.

In creating the appearance of submission to larger historical and eco-nomicopolitical forces, which allegedly shaped the domain of *politika* and were exogenous to the community of ordinary people, people portrayed these forces as so excessively powerful and destructive that any attempt at regulating them was pointless. Many Macedonians and Albanians oftentimes remarked that they did not have the ability, power, and privilege to influence the course of events. As a Macedonian friend told me stoically, alluding to the historic power of the oil industry, "I am not Rockefeller. If Rockefeller there [in the U.S.] says that there is not going to be war in Macedonia, there will not be war." Additionally, appeals to *politika*, especially when articulated during social exchanges across ethnonational borders, enabled social actors to deny personal responsibility for all material, physical, and emotional harm done against members of the other community and to signal that they re-fused to attribute to others responsibility for harm exacted on members of their own community. Macedonians and Albanians with whom I worked, in other words, evacuated of all content the monolithic categories "aggressors" and "victims" of violence that were increasingly strongly promoted by politi-cians and journalists as the explanatory framework for understanding the conflict. They reinterpreted violence in an alternative framework that under-lined collective suffering (see also Young 1996: 245) and victimhood, thereby strengthening social bonds—a process that Sara Cobb (1997) describes as "the domestication of violence." What is more, as Chuengsatiansup (2001: 34–35) notes, "the intersubjectivity of social suffering, by virtue of being rooted in a shared historical and structural predicament, constitutes a sphere of shared cognizance and shared practices which together forge a collective political consciousness of an imagined community of dissenters." Appeals to *politika*, then, were by no means an expression of resignation from the political arena or of debilitating passivity in the face of adversity; rather, they revealed the careful management of the crisis at hand. While they did not directly address political grievances, social actors nonetheless fostered a sense of community and delegitimized in the name of the broader collective, construed by both parties to the social interaction as nonpolitical (harmonious, cohesive, and independent of *politika*), the use of armed force.

When used within the boundaries of one's ethnonational community, invocations of *politika* also undermined progressive ethnonational and religious polarization and allowed people to create a wider collectivity of like-minded individuals adhering to humanistic values. On one occasion, for instance, while Marina, a Macedonian woman in her late fifties, was sitting with me on her balcony chatting over coffee and enjoying the late afternoon summer sun, her sister Gordana stopped by to show us a bracelet that she had just purchased as a bridal gift for an upcoming wedding in the family. Marina admired the bracelet—shiny yellow gold studded with white stones that sparkled in the sunlight—and asked Gordana where she had purchased it and how much it cost. Her sister responded that she had bought it from a jewelry store in the old Turkish bazaar (Turska or Stara Čaršija), where Albanian- (and also Turkish-) owned jewelry stores in Skopje are primarily located, and that the Albanian owner, whom she had just met that day, had sold it to her even though she did not have the entire amount of payment at that time. Gordana added that the shopkeeper was fine with her bringing him the remainder next time she was in the area. On hearing the story, Marina was fairly surprised, not least because in summer 2001 many Macedonians grew fearful of the strong Albanian presence in the Čaršija, where the well-attended Sultan Murat mosque and a large number of Albanian-owned stores and businesses are located, but also because, as on previous occasions when there was a crisis (Brown 2009: 207), some Macedonians boycotted Albanian businesses—and vice versa. "Is there such trust between Macedonians and Albanians in these times?" Marina asked, raising her eyebrows in disbelief. "Well, do you think that *they* [Albanians] like *politika*? They don't!" Gordana responded assertively.

On another occasion, Florin, a single Albanian man in his mid-twenties who lived in the apartment building next to mine, told me when I ran into him on the street that his mother was suffering a bout of back pain. With the rest of his family, namely his older brother and pregnant wife, having left for Kosovo to escape the volatile situation in Macedonia, Florin was the only one left to look after his mother, who was determined to stay home in Skopje and, like many other Albanians I knew in the neighborhood, protect her home if need be. Florin also said half-jokingly that the brunt of the housework had all of a sudden fallen on him, and that running a household was a lot of hard work. Pointing at his crisply ironed shirt, I complimented him on his ironing skills, and Florin told me that an elderly Macedonian neighbor (*komšija*) was ironing his shirts until his mother's back pain got better. "Well [*A be*], *politika* has no relation with ordinary people!" Florin said and waved his hand in the air dismissively.

Mutual appeals to *politika* became less frequent as fighting drew closer

Figure 6. Old Turkish Bazaar in Skopje. Photo by author.

to the capital and the political climate became increasingly divisive. On 14 May a government of national unity was established comprising the main Macedonian (VMRO-DPMNE and SDSM) and Albanian (DPA/PDSH and PDP/PPD) parties. But on 3 June Prime Minister Georgievski announced in a television interview that the government of national unity was barely functioning. A few days later government spokesperson Antonio Milošoski stated that Macedonia had to declare a state of war and enact nationwide mobilization without delay, and urged intellectuals, academics, and journalists to become sensible and realize that Macedonia was at war.[8] During this time of heightened uncertainty and insecurity, when official discussion of the possibility of war was taking place and no one really knew what to expect, appeals to *politika* gave way to discussions of fate and predetermination (*sudbina/fati*) as a single, all-powerful, inescapable force in the universe, allegedly charting the trajectory of every person and of the country as a whole. Similar to Catholic and Muslim Bosnians (Bringa 1995: 240–41n19), Macedonians and Albanians alike routinely appealed to the trope of fate as a way of understanding why armed violence had erupted. They thus drew on and reinforced a cultural value that is shared among Christians and Muslims in Macedonia: the inevitability of human fate. Comments such as "This is fate," "That's how it has been written," "If that's how it has been written," and "Only God knows what will happen," proliferated when appeals to *politika* lost currency, and helped underline a greater sense of togetherness and belonging to the same social world. Far from reading such comments as deterministic or fatalistic, that is, indicative of submission to inevitability or external forces, I suggest, then, that they are telling of the ways in which local actors introduced an element of coherence into the chaotic political context in which they lived and, importantly, mutually protected everyday relationships against a background of escalating events in the country.

Nostalgia for Tito's Yugoslavia

In addition to mutually condemning the deteriorating situation in Macedonia as *politika*, many Macedonians and Albanians who came of age in the 1970s and 1980s and participated in intergroup, interpersonal interactions during the conflict also drew on personal experiences of everyday life in Tito's Yugoslavia and produced nostalgic accounts of the socialist period. Indeed, nostalgia, as Kathleen Stewart states (1988: 227), rises to importance as a cultural practice when our present becomes fragmented and ambiguous. For example, when my landlady Fatmira visited me at home on the morning of 30 May to collect my rent money for the next month, she suggested we pay a coffee visit to the next-door Macedonian neighbors Zare and Violeta, a pensioner couple in their late sixties. Fatmira had known the couple since the late 1970s when she purchased the apartment I had rented, and visited them to say hello when she stopped by the apartment from time to time. Excited to see us, and with a smile of appreciation on her face when Fatmira gave her a small bag of coffee, Mare welcomed us in her living room, where Zare was seated reading a newspaper. He immediately closed the paper, placed it next to him on the sofa, and stood up to greet us. After a brief exchange of pleasantries, Fatmira commented on the heavy rain falling under pitch-black skies in Skopje that day: "Who knows what the politicians have been up to today for rain to fall like that!" "Politicians are good for nothing [*za nikade se*]!" Mare remarked with a note of annoyance in her voice, and Zare added that politicians were the ones to blame for the deteriorating situation in the country while ordinary people wished to live, in his words, "normally, like before [*normalno, kako porano*]." Fatmira eagerly supported Zare's views, and they both described comfortable, middle-class living conditions as "normal life" (*normalen život/jetë normale*; see also Thiessen 2007), while reminiscing about steady salaries, paid vacations, and financial freedom to purchase consumer commodities and to travel outside Macedonian borders. Nostalgic stories about shopping trips to Salonika and road trips across former Yugoslavia filled the air of Mare's living room until Fatmira commented aphoristically, "after socialism, there is theft!" (*posle socializam, ima kradizam!*). Mare went on to say that after Tito's death, when ethnonationalist ideologies rose to prominence, the ideology of "brotherhood and unity" had been replaced by a new one of "brotherhood and murder" (*bratstvo i ubistvo*, Macedonian wordplay on Tito's governing ideology of *bratsvo i edinstvo* or "brotherhood and unity").

Such accounts, whereby *politika* was nonexistent in Tito's single-party state and people were ordinary, that is to say, untainted by political considerations and nationalistic zeal, are part of a wider phenomenon of nostalgia for socialism in post-independence Macedonia—and other former Yugoslav republics (see, for example, Lindstrom 2005; Volčic 2007) and the so-called postsocialist world, more generally (see, among others, Berdahl 1999, 2010; Todorova and Gille 2010). Socialist nostalgia exists in the context of feelings of "profound loss, longing and displacement in a period of intense social discord" (Berdahl 2010: 131) following the collapse of socialism. The trappings of this phenomenon include pictures of Tito in private and public settings, and coffee shops and restaurants called Tito throughout Macedonia—and in other parts of the former Yugoslavia, as it happens (see, for example, Velikonja 2008). Socialist nostalgia occurs against the background of efforts by politicians to deride the memory of Tito and the Yugoslav past as "Yugo-nostalgia" and present it directly or indirectly through speeches, writings, and other acts such as renaming streets and other public spaces, as the lack of love for one's country and unpatriotic betrayal (see also Bringa 2004; Petrović 2010).[9]

Nostalgic accounts for Tito's Yugoslavia, as is the case with any nostalgia (see Boym 2001: 38), have a utopian character: they include selected, harmonious and idealistic, portrayals of individual experience and everyday life in the former Yugoslavia, and do not address grievances that many, notably Albanians in Macedonia (similar to Albanians in Kosovo; see Schwandner-Sievers 2010: 102), tend to voice only in the company of trusted friends and close relatives. Examples of such grievances include the necessity for personal connections (*vrski*), the persecution of the Albanian population during the pre-1966, Ranković period, the lack of opportunities for the promotion of Albanian state employees into senior managerial or administrative positions, and the sociopolitical unrest following Tito's death in 1980 (see also Dimova 2010).[10]

Against a background of escalating political turbulence and confusion, nostalgia, as both a rhetorical trope and a mnemonic practice, acquired widespread public appeal. The exchange of nostalgic stories about daily life in the former Yugoslavia enabled people in Skopje to situate themselves and others in an alternative time and place whereby everyday life was predictable, coherent, and unambiguous in all its expressions. In Stewart's words (1988: 277), "nostalgia takes on the generalized function to provide some kind (any kind) of cultural form. In positing a 'once was' in relation to a 'now' it creates a frame for meaning, a means of dramatizing aspects of an increasingly fluid and unnamed social life." The strategic mobilization of nostalgia helped fashion a kind of counter-present, a corrective to an insecure present, in which everyone participated.

Enacting Civility

Performances of civility across ethnonational borders did not only center on sharing nostalgia for everyday life in Tito's Yugoslavia and deploying the distinction between *politika* and *obični lugje/njerëz të thjeshtë*; they also involved the practice of hospitality.

As in other countries in the region, such as Bosnia (see Bringa 1995) and Greece (see Herzfeld 1987), hospitality in Macedonia is intimately connected to honor. In the colloquial Macedonian of Skopje and other northern dialects the verb used to denote the offering of hospitality, *časti* (standard Macedonian *čest i*), has the same origin as the noun *čast* (standard Macedonian *čest*), which means "honor" (see also Bringa 1995: 69). The forms with *a* are generally associated with the Serbian standard language but are frequently used in contemporary Skopje colloquial Macedonian.[11] Within the Albanian community, hospitality occupies a central place in the system of moral norms regulating social relations, and its dictates have been codified in the *Kanun* of Lekë Dukagjini, a widely practiced customary law covering in one its twelve books the subject of *nder*, or "honor" (see Young 2000: 41–54).[12] Macedonian and Albanian households gain honor when the hosts treat guests well and make them feel comfortable. Offering food and drink is a key part of hospitality. During 2001, anytime when the topic of the conflict seeped into conversations, offering a humanistic and nonpolitical view of the world became an equally important element. In the vignette featuring Fatmira, Vesna, and Bajram at the beginning of the chapter, for instance, the serving of Turkish tea, and homemade food and sweets was coupled with casual conversation (*muhabet*), including storytelling and gossip. The pleasant passage of time indicated social intimacy and commitment to preserving an amicable relationship in spite of political upheaval.[13] The practice of receiving and entertaining guests at home in Macedonia, as is the case elsewhere in the world (see Meneley 1996), carried the expectation of ensuing reciprocity because it was morally binding on the guests and created a sense of continuity in daily life.

Hospitality also pertains to interactions on special social occasions when people pay their respects (*pravaat čest/bëjnë nder*) and strengthen social relations. Such occasions include Christian and Muslim religious holidays and observances (Christmas, Easter, Kurban Bajram, and the Islamic holy month of Ramadan), lifecycle events (births, baptisms, marriages, and deaths), the celebration of newlyweds (*mladenci*) on 22 March, and name days (*imenden*). Exchanges of hospitality continued to take place across ethnonational borders among long-standing friends in Skopje during the period of armed hostilities. Even as turmoil extended well into summer, people navigated the landscape of the conflict and maintained social bonds. For instance, when my Albanian friends Besa, a twenty-five-year-old teacher from Skopje, and Krenar, an electronics store owner of the same age, had their civil wedding ceremony and wedding reception in the groom's southern hometown of Struga in early July, concerns arose among Macedonian and Albanian wedding guests (family, friends, and colleagues) living in Skopje regarding the safety of travel to Struga and back. Although a ceasefire was arranged under UN auspices on July 5, armed fighting persisted in northwestern Macedonia, where the NLA continued to expand the territory under its control. Stories about NLA checkpoints on the edge of Tetovo, reported in the media later that month, already circulated among people. The prospect of driving through Tetovo and being stopped at roadblocks possibly manned by the NLA was thus especially daunting to the Macedonian guests. For their part, Albanian guests were particularly apprehensive about the prospect of taking the alternate route and traveling through Bitola due to the anti-Muslim riots in the city in late April and early June.

To address these concerns, wedding guests decided that the wedding procession should be split into two: a column of cars with Macedonians traveling to Struga (and back to Skopje) via Veles, Prilep, and Bitola (and back); and a column of cars with Albanians traveling via Tetovo, Gostivar, and Kičevo (and back). In accordance with traditional Albanian wedding customs, the mothers of the bride and groom gave the drivers small white towels to tuck under the windshield wipers, indicating to people who saw the passing vehicles that the passengers were part of a wedding party. I rode on a car in the Albanian column and, before we approached Tetovo, we made a short stop to make sure that the towels were safely tucked under the wiper blades. If the insurgents were watching us from the surrounding hills, they could thus understand that we were on our way to an Albanian wedding. This act seemed to make many people more relaxed although others pointed out the threat of reprisal in case the insurgents viewed our participation in a festive occasion as a belittling of their fight. "If nothing else," one of my co-passengers said half-jokingly after assessing the situation, "the fact that the towel is white [resembling a white flag of truce] should keep us out of trouble!" The cars sped up as we drove through the city. By the time we reached Struga and met up with the rest of the party, most of the towels were blown away. There was no sign of the towels on the windshields of the cars transporting the Macedonian guests—passengers had placed them inside the vehicles. In the course of the trip, friends riding in the two separate columns frequently used their cell phones to call and ask about the whereabouts and safety of each other.

Social ties across ethnonational borders were also preserved and protected through social exchange related to hospitality. Men who engaged in business transactions (for example, owned currency exchange shops and traded foreign currencies) and adjacent shop owners continued to stop by each other's homes or shops and drink Turkish coffee or tea together while chatting in Macedonian. In ethnically mixed workplaces, such as the hospital in Čair and elementary schools, colleagues sustained communal coffee breaks during which they exchanged cigarettes. Also, female neighbors kept exchanging coffee-visits, mostly when men were at work and the children or grandchildren they looked after were at school. In my apartment building, Macedonian and Albanian women, especially those who lived right next door to each other and often ran into each other in the hallways outside their apartments, extended impromptu invitations to coffee. Their conversations unfolded in Macedonian, but also in Serbian at times when Albanian women who originated from Kosovo could not converse in Macedonian and Macedonian women who had grown up in the former Yugoslavia spoke Serbian.

An important part in the maintenance of congeniality during such interactions, and performances of civility more generally, was the ostentatious rejection of narratives transmitted by the electronic and print media and flamboyant commentary about the effect of media exposure. Consider, for example, what happened one evening in early May 2001 when I visited with my Albanian hairdresser Luljeta, a woman in her late twenties who had just moved with her husband out of her in-laws' apartment and into an apartment a few buildings down the street. While in both the Macedonian and Albanian communities it is customary for newlyweds to move in with the groom's parents, many couples who can afford to live on their own break the pattern and tend to live in proximity to their in-laws. Luljeta and I were catching up with each other's news while, as is commonly the case in Macedonia, the television played in the background. When the evening news came on at seven o'clock, we interrupted our chat to watch on a Macedonian TV channel an interview with a man whose story seemed to catch Luljeta's interest. The man claimed in Macedonian, his head turned away from the camera, that his name was Faton (an Albanian name) and that the NLA had come to his Albanian-populated village and threatened him with torture unless he joined the fighting against Macedonian security forces. Luljeta, like many Albanians in the ensuing days, expressed in private conversations skepticism about the veracity of the man's story and wondered whether the Macedonian government, as a way of justifying collateral damage to Albanian civilians in conflict-stricken areas, had bribed the man to appear on TV and give the insurgents a bad name. Luljeta was particularly confused about the man's accent—which, according to her, sounded nothing like the way that Albanians, particularly those from villages, tended to speak Macedonian. As we were debating whether the story could be true, Luljeta, rather disturbed by the possibility of government wrongdoing—her voice raised, hands gesturing through the air—switched TV channels and suggested we watch the news on a different channel in case the story was presented differently.

Our attention was so much absorbed in the TV news that we both jumped out of our seats at the sound of the doorbell. "Listen, listen," Luljeta told me in a commanding voice, keeping her gaze fixed on the TV as she slowly got up from the sofa and walked toward the door. Before she answered the bell, she paused for a moment and strained her ears to listen to the TV anchorman just in case she had missed anything. Luljeta finally opened the door; it was Mare, her Macedonian neighbor who had stopped by on one of her regular coffee visits. Mare was in her late twenties, held a college degree from Skopje University, and had a full-time job. The women were married to Albanian and Macedonian men, respectively, who had become close friends while attending Skopje's technical high school Nikola Karev. Joint business ventures between Macedonians and Albanians are rather uncommon in Macedonia, but the two men had decided to set up a small computer software firm a few years after their high school graduation. With their husbands working long hours or frequenting downtown cafés most evenings, and without children and elderly parents at home to look after, Luljeta and Mare often spent time together at home sharing food snacks, drinking Turkish coffee, and engaging in casual conversation in Macedonian. As the two women were settling into their seats, Luljeta picked up the remote control from the coffee table in front of her, ostensibly exasperated. "Newscasts, newscasts! My head will explode!" (*glavata kje mi pukne!*) she exclaimed and pushed a button on the remote.

Just like that, all talk about the conflict and a man reportedly called Faton that had filled the room prior to Mare's arrival ceased. Commercials about detergents, banks, and juice and coffee brands became the background noise against which the two women exchanged their news in Macedonian—the clothing sale downtown, the meal they had cooked that day, the whereabouts of their husbands. For Luljeta to have kept the news broadcast on would have been a blatant transgression of civility, as it would have left open the possibilities for disagreement or hostility in case one of the people present (including the ethnographer) inadvertently made a divisive comment on the reported developments regarding the conflict. By changing the TV channel she showed she took issue with the media content. The very expression she used, *glavata kje mi pukne* (*do të më plas koka* in Albanian), is commonly used in Macedonia to register frustration and exasperation in a confident and animated manner. During the conflict people frequently summoned it to underline how incomprehensible and overwhelming the daily news reporting of the conflict was. Like many who partook in performances of civility, Luljeta extended to her interlocutors an indirect invitation to elude the potentially polarizing topics of the NLA insurgency and media coverage of unfolding events and refocused attention on manageable aspects of everyday life.

In Perfect Harmony?

Performances of civility were not always clear-cut and straightforward, whereby both parties to the interaction exhibited spirited eagerness and determination to articulate explicit interpretations of the armed conflict as *politika*. They were often rife with uncertainty, especially when they involved intergroup interactions between business associates or professional peers. I became acutely aware of such complexities one spring evening in May 2001 when my neighbor Nikola, a single Macedonian man in his late twenties who held a Bachelor of Science in biochemistry from the University of Skopje, introduced me to an Albanian friend of his who also lived in the neighborhood.

I had agreed to meet Nikola for coffee after his shift in one of the small convenience stores in downtown Skopje to discuss his questions regarding graduate school in the United States—applying to graduate school abroad is one of the avenues commonly explored by young people wishing to emigrate.[14] As we were strolling around the central square, Nikola and I decided to look for a table at Blue Café, one of the most popular outdoor cafés at the time. Due to a widespread sense of uncertainty and danger, people in the capital tended not to go out in the evening as much as prior to the eruption of hostilities; instead, they stayed home and watched television to keep abreast of the latest news. Cafés downtown were thus not too crowded in the evenings and it was fairly easy to get a table. "There," Nikola said and gestured with his head to a table. "Do you want me to introduce you to an Albanian (Albanec) from the neighborhood?" he asked on an impulse, knowing my interest in expanding my network of social contacts in the Albanian community in Skopje. We walked over to the table, where two men were seated, leaning over scattered pieces of paper and writing intently. Nikola placed his hand on the shoulder of one of the men, who immediately looked up, straightened his back, and extended his hand for a handshake. A calculator, a glass of beer, and a cup of espresso could now be discerned amid the papers. "How are you? Come on [*Ajde*], sit down for coffee; sit here," the man said and gestured us to the adjoining table, "Just a little bit [longer] and we will finish [our work]."

Shortly afterward, we pulled the two tables together. As we settled into our seats, Nikola made the introductions—"Vasiliki, Damian, Amir." I explained that I was an ethnographer, and Nikola quickly added that I could speak Albanian. "Speak to her in Albanian so that we see if she is telling the truth!" Nikola told Amir in his usual teasing manner. Straightaway, Amir exploded into such a roaring and hard laughter that his face started sweating. "I cannot do it now, it feels funny to me! [*smešno mi doagja*]" he said in Macedonian in the midst of his laughter, when, all of sudden, he stopped, fell silent, and reached for the cup of espresso in front of him.

As I learned that evening, Damian and Amir, both in their mid-thirties, had been business partners for the past eight years and run a profit-making enterprise. Damian owned a small factory that raised chickens, and Amir worked at Bit Pazar selling the eggs. Both men were married. Damian lived with his wife and two children in a house in the upscale suburb of Radišani on the outskirts of Skopje, and Amir lived with his wife, three children, elderly parents, and the family of his brother in a house in Čair. After we all chatted about the business, I asked the two men about their thoughts on the outbreak of the insurgency—a question that, in retrospect, was perhaps too straightforward given that the insurgency was a politically sensitive topic. Signaling his willingness to create a pleasant atmosphere conducive to a relaxed discussion, Damian picked up his pack of cigarettes and offered cigarettes to everyone at the table before lighting one for himself. He leaned farther back in his chair, lifted his eyebrows slightly, and said the following:

> There have never been problems between Macedonians and Albanians, this conflict now is something artificial [*veštačko*]. I work more with Albanians than I do with Macedonians. I do not see him [Damian points at Amir] as an Albanian but as an ordinary man [*običen čovek*]. Money and interest: this is all that matters. [He quickly adds] Well . . . we are together not only for money but also for the company [*druženie*]. We go out to lunch or dinner and we take turns paying, he will pay the bill one time, next time I will pay! He has been to my house, I have been to his house. People [*narodot*] are not at fault. Politics has done all this! What is happening right now is only politics [*samo politika*]!

He stopped to take a deep puff on his cigarette and then asked Amir, "Isn't that right?"

Startled by the direct question, Amir hesitated, unsure what to say. "What can I say?" he uttered in Macedonian, shrugging his shoulders. "There is war for money. Only politicians..." and before he could finish his sentence he burst forth into the same forced laughter as before, beads of sweat reappearing on his brow. Quick to finish Amir's sentence, Damian looked at me and broke in, "Eh! It goes without saying [*se razbira*], only politicians are to blame, ordinary people [*obični lugje*] are not at fault. Politics is a whore!" and went on to recount some positive social interactions he had had with people of Albanian background. Meantime, Amir and Nikola started conversing separately. With no other customers sitting nearby, I could not help but overhear that Nikola was still trying to convince Amir to speak Albanian with me when Amir replied, "I am a bit tense [*stegnat*] now, I need to relax to speak Albanian." His light tone was now at variance with the seriousness in his voice. Indeed, the only time Amir used Albanian was at the end of the meeting, after he asked the waitress for the bill and I insisted that I pay for my coffee. With a serene expression on his face he told me while shaking his head in negation, "No, no, out of the question! [*Jo, jo, s' mundet!*]"

A closer look at the awkwardness in interpersonal, intergroup interactions (consider Amir's sweating, minimal articulateness, and gales of affected laughter in the above vignette) sheds valuable light on the intricacies of performances of civility. Such awkwardness reveals how participants in the social exchange perceived a disconnect between themselves and their interlocutors. Although I did not meet Amir again, many Albanians in private conversations with me intimately associated their discomfort with ambiguity and uncertainty regarding the intentions of their Macedonian interlocutors. Some Albanians with whom I worked told me that statements about *politika* were possibly a show of power, whereby Macedonians condescendingly dismissed any attempt to improve the status of the Albanian population in Macedonia. Others were not sure whether Macedonians intentionally eschewed the topic of the conflict and resorted to the popular truism about *politika* as a way of verbally signaling their unwillingness to engage in confrontation and eagerness to protect the social relationship. Yet others, especially as the armed conflict drew nearer to the capital, argued that statements about *politika* were perhaps indicative of internal constraints, notably fear of potential retribution from the NLA, preventing Macedonian individuals from speaking frankly about the deteriorating political situation in the country.

Such plurality of readings and possible meanings was also a key part of the meaning-making process in which many Macedonians participating in performances of civility engaged privately. Some Macedonians, supported by accounts of the insurgency in the Macedonian-language media (such as the previously mentioned story about an Albanian man who was reportedly blackmailed into joining the NLA), told me that Albanians who did not outrightly state that the conflict was *politika* were probably too intimidated to express openly their opinions about the unfolding events. People also suggested that Albanians' awkward reactions were perhaps a tactic to steer clear of the topic of the conflict and signal unwillingness to enter into open confrontation. Against the background of escalating violence and the departure of Albanian women and children from Macedonia, Macedonians tended to consider the possibility that such reactions indicated endorsement of the NLA insurgency and were subtle and indirect attempts to undermine any attempt at solidarity.

Inconclusive discussions, then, regarding possible intentions and objectives in interactions frequently took place within each community. During such deliberations, people raised questions about truth and reality and maintained the undecidability of the social. Outside the confines of their communities, they evaded determinate meaning and undercut any attempt at a definitive sociopolitical arrangement. And while this ambiguity opened up the possibility of a violent confrontation, aimed to gain clarity about the viewpoints of those who partook in social exchange and achieve closure of meaning, at the same time it left ample room for the avoidance of interpersonal friction and the safeguarding of the integrity of social bonds—a path that people frequently chose to take. Similar to Damian and Amir in the vignette above, social actors reined in the possibility for an unfavorable turn of events. By deftly navigating the social world under unstable and perilous conditions, they also generated the possibility for explicit and direct articulation, and perhaps resolution, of larger ethnonational grievances some other time.

CHAPTER 5

When the Going Gets Tough

As fighting spread steadily in northwestern areas of the country, a strong sense of vulnerability and insecurity increasingly permeated everyday life in Skopje. To navigate through their environment, Macedonian men and women during interpersonal interactions across ethnonational lines tended to engage in efforts to create and sustain a stable and predictable socio-political order where they and members of the Albanian collectivity had distinct roles to play and definitive positions to occupy. In this chapter, I analyze these efforts and their political implications. My aim is to show the impossibilities of attaching definitive meaning to social reality, as construed by members of the Macedonian collectivity, and of establishing a fixed set of relationships of power despite urgent and compelling efforts to do so. When I speak of relationships of power among social actors, I draw upon the work of Foucault and describe relations whereby, as will become clear in what follows, "one person tries to control the conduct of the other" (1997: 291–92), "a mode of action which does not act directly and immediately on others [but] instead acts upon their actions: an action upon an action, on existing actions or on those which may arise in the present or the future" (1983: 219–20).

Performances of Manhood

Throughout the conflict, especially from late spring onward as the Mace-donian government forces seemed unable to contain the insurgency and the NLA gained increasing control over Macedonian territory, some of my young Macedonian research participants (in their twenties and early thir-ties) told me spiritedly that if things were to spin completely out of control, and the threat of full-scale war materialized in the country, Macedonians would demonstrate that they were "worse" (*ploši*) than Serbs in terms of doing harm to Šiptari—the derogatory term for Albanians. Those who engaged in interlingual wordplay and used the Turkism *beter*, which sounds like the English "better" but in fact in Turkish means "worse," occasionally made similarly belligerent comments, arguing with suggestive sarcasm and wit that in the eventuality of war Macedonians would prove to be *beter* than Serbs.[1] In these claims, Serbian militarism and combative aggression, exemplified in anti-Albanian Serbian government policies in the course of the twentieth century and most recently during the Kosovo war in 1999, emerged as the standard of comparison for assessing Macedonian masculine and national value and virtue. The alleged possession of the skills required to inflict on Albanians greater damage and cause them greater suffering than the Serbs had done in the past was a key component of claims to manhood which were put forward by some Macedonian men with whom I spoke in the field. Real manhood, more specifically, was equated with soldiering and, what is more, with the particular skills that a Macedonian man/soldier needed, and allegedly intrinsically possessed, to show that he was not just good at but rather (to paraphrase Herzfeld 1985: 16) "*better* at being a man"—better than the Albanian adversary, and also better than the Serb ex-combatant who had fought against the Albanian enemy without eradicating it in the past. These skills included professed prowess in battle and determination to establish once and for all conclusive supremacy over the Albanian Other.

While highly affective statements comparing the malevolence of Macedonian and Serbian men were not very common within the Macedonian community, such statements nonetheless reveal how palpable the possibility of civil war during the 2001 conflict was. In the following pages, I explore how claims to belligerent, competitive, and self-assured Macedonian manhood were played out during interpersonal, intergroup interactions, and the implications of such enactments for meaning-making against a volatile political background. The performances of manhood that concern me here are an eloquent, and perhaps a most extreme, example of what Sherry Ortner (1996: 12–13) calls "serious games." That is to say, similar to games, they featured actors, rules, and goals and provided a forum for multiple subject positions that interrelated and interacted, and actors played with skill, intention, wit, and knowledge. At the same time, the performances were serious because they were pervaded by power and inequality and played with intensity and in earnest, and the stakes involved, as I show below, were high.

Throwing Down the Gauntlet

To the best of my knowledge, Macedonian men of all ages (not Macedonian women or members of the Albanian community) tended to bring up the subject of the NLA insurgency in a direct and confrontational manner during interpersonal exchanges with Albanian men. People who participated in such interactions and were personally acquainted did not have long-standing social ties to each other, and also the Albanian parties to the exchange usually occupied lower socioeconomic positions.

Consider, for example, the following vignette that took place in Bit Pazar between Gazmend, an Albanian seller of women's shoes and slippers, and Igor, a Macedonian retail tax collector. Gazmend, a man in his early forties, had moved in the late 1970s together with his wife from a village in the vicinity of Skopje to a small apartment in Čair. I met the family through my Albanian-language tutor, who taught their youngest son in her elementary school class. Eager to help me connect with more people from all walks of life, Gazmend offered to introduce me to some of the Albanian vendors in Bit Pazar, and so one day in March 2001 I went to see him. The market bustled with sellers shouting out their wares and buyers perusing the aisles. Gazmend was busy attending to a small group of women in Islamic dress (headscarves and long over-garments resembling coatdresses) when I arrived, but left his two brothers, with whom he operated the business, in charge, and exited his market stall to greet me and shake hands. We stood and chatted for a short while, and before too long Igor emerged from the crowd and advanced toward us. The two men briefly exchanged pleasantries in Macedonian as I listened to their conversation, and then Igor put on a solemn expression on his face, pulled his head back, and said in a slightly raised voice: "Well [*A be*], Gazmend, what's going to happen [*što ḱe bide*] with you Albanians? What do you lack? . . . You lack nothing." He pensively yet confidently looked Gazmend straight in the eye and waited for a response. "Well, this is *politika*, the interests of the great powers are in question," responded Gazmend without missing a beat. Igor lifted his right arm, his face breaking into a smile, as he patted Gazmend on the shoulder and said, "I am joking!" He then greeted his interlocutor goodbye, turned away, and disappeared into the market crowd.

During intergroup interactions, Macedonian men, similar to Igor, tended to act as self-proclaimed representatives of the Macedonian collectivity and treat Albanian men not as self-propelled individuals, but rather as members of a single and undifferentiated group who supported the NLA insurgency. They thus appeared insulted, adopting a fairly confrontational and imperious approach toward their interlocutors and condemning as unjustified the NLA undertaking. These performances of male Macedonians revolved around the issuance of a challenge to verbal combat, whereby the status of the Albanian community in Macedonia would be debated, and involved the peremptory request for Albanian men to accept the challenge and account for the (assumedly wrong-) doings of the NLA and the Albanian community. Such agonistic conduct, meant to control the actions of Albanian men, underlined confidence in one's argumentative skills and the ability to "out-man" (outperform and overpower—and consequently prove that one was better at being a man than) their Albanian assumed opponent. The presumed triumphant victory of the Macedonian side by means of discursive reason and rational reflection implied Macedonian male and national supremacy and the symbolic degradation of the Albanian enemy. It is in this sense that verbal combats became metaphorical battlegrounds on which larger ethnonational antagonisms were to be fought and scores were to be settled—assumedly, to the advantage of Macedonians and the detriment of Albanians. Macedonian men established in action their claim to manhood, and superior manhood at that: they proclaimed personal excellence and national supremacy over Albanian men and the Albanian collectivity, displayed forthright belligerence and self-assurance, and spoke fluently without any sign of fear or concern about giving offense.

Male contests were directly geared toward achieving two complementary and mutually reinforcing objectives: first, the successful performance of manhood—a performance hinging on the social actor's "ability to identify the self with larger categories of identity" (Herzfeld 1985: 10), Macedonian ethnonational identity in particular; and second, the unambiguous definition of social reality in terms of Macedonian male and ethnonational dominance. This intimate connection between manhood and nationhood can be understood in the context of the project of nation building, whereby gender and nation are intertwined to give social reality specific meaning, form, and order. "Constructions of nationhood," Yuval-Davis remarks (1997: 1), "usually involve specific notions of both manhood and womanhood." The nation, conceived as an absolute mono-ethnic entity, is thereby symbolically equated with the patriarchal family in which heterosexual men, portrayed as fathers and brothers, and women, portrayed as mothers and sisters, have very specific places to occupy and distinctive gender roles to fulfill. Men are expected to fight and defend the nation's territorial borders and interests against all enemies and also protect the women within the family of the nation, while women are expected to reproduce an ethnically pure nation (see, among others, Connell 1990; Stychin 1998). Such associations are key to understanding

how during full-scale war in the Balkans rape has served as a means of communication among warring groups of men. As many scholars have shown
(see, among others, Bracewell 2000; Gal and Kligman 2000: 15–36; Seifert
1994; Žarkov 2007), by raping women of the enemy side, men act as national
warriors who mar the purity of the women and, by extension, the purity of
the nation to which the women belong. This is how they humiliate and thus
prevail over enemy males and rival ethnonational groups, who prove unable
to protect their female "kin" and safeguard the purity of their nation.[2] Cultural ideals that are conventionally construed and promoted as masculine,
such as honor, competitiveness, fearlessness, risk-taking, bravery, and hero-
ism, have become inextricably intertwined with nationalist politics in the
modern nation-state (see Nagel 1998). It is against this background, whereby
"the 'microculture' of masculinity in everyday life articulates very well with
the demands of nationalism" (252), that male antagonisms in the arena of
everyday affairs cannot be separated from larger competitions in the arena of
ethnonationalist politics.

Beyond promoting such gendered and sexualized understandings of
the nation, the modern project of nation-building in post-independence
Macedonia, and indeed elsewhere in Europe, has borrowed the rhetoric of
ethnicity (see Royce 1982: 84) and has in turn been accompanied by ethnonational state-building and concomitant hierarchical definitions of the
state as the homeland of one people. Ideas of the state and the nation are
so inseparable (state-sponsored commemorations of national events provide
eloquent evidence) that any threat to the integrity of the state is viewed as a
threat to national integrity and is hence regarded as posing the greatest risk
to the integrity of Macedonian masculinity. Thus, when the NLA insurgency
threatened to eliminate the essential elements of the ideological construction
of the Macedonian state, and subvert the pre-2001 sociopolitical order and
everyone's distinctive positions within it, Macedonian masculinity also came
under attack. The NLA's expansion of control over Macedonian territory set
the stage for "a spectacle of injured masculinities" (see Ismail 2006: xiiv),
whereby Macedonian men sought to heal their injured sense of masculinity
and wounded sense of ethnonational pride by enacting control over the behavior and actions of Albanian men in public. In this context, performances
of manhood acquired a heightened sense of urgency: for those involved, the
stakes were high.

What transpired during interpersonal interactions between Macedonian
and Albanian men nonetheless complicated the efforts of Macedonian men
to restore the old order of things that had been disturbed by the insurgency.

In response to challenges to partake in exchanges of rhetorical blows, male members of the Albanian community, similar to Gazmend in the foregoing vignette, usually kept to themselves their opinions regarding the issues of the NLA insurgency and Albanians' status in the country and resorted to the popular truism about *politika*, which as discussed in Chapter 4 was also an integral part of performances of civility. The use of the truism in situations of outright confrontation between men opened up room for various interpretations, thereby revealing how Albanian men trod an ambiguous line between disrupting and validating the rules of "a serious game" (Ortner 1996: 12–13) that was explicitly geared toward foregrounding Macedonian masculine and ethnonational honor and dominance by controlling the conduct of Albanian individuals. To name but a couple of interpretations, in eschewing the topics of the NLA insurgency and the Albanian community's status in the country, Albanian men perhaps tactfully denied the legitimacy of their self-proclaimed opponents and their endeavor to fix absolute meaning, and thus perhaps outflanked Macedonian men. Then again, deployment of clichés could signal lack of both wit and courage to take up the gauntlet, and hence could point to the uncontested establishment of the version of social reality that was promoted by Macedonian men, whereby the positions of power and authority that members of the Macedonian and Albanian groups occupied in relation to each other and within the state structure prior to the NLA insurgency were fixed and not open to dispute.

Once they had heard from the Albanian party to the exchange, Macedonian men tended to frame their agonistic conduct as play, as something that should not be taken for real. After Gazmend, for instance, had evaded the question regarding the allocation of rights and privileges to Albanians in Macedonian society, Igor readily dismissed as a joke the verbal challenge that he had issued in the first place. Such communication about communication—what Gregory Bateson defines as "metacommunication" (1951: 209) and links with play ([1955] 1972)—was nonetheless fraught with ambiguity, and left ample room for at least a couple of interpretations. The representation of agonistic rhetoric as play could signal that Macedonian men, after having suffered defeat in their endeavor, changed their game plan to soften the blow and save face: specifically, to give their predicament an appearance of frivolity and make-believe that Macedonian masculine and ethnonational honor and dominance were under no threat whatsoever. An alternative reading of their comportment concerns the possible demonstration of an implicit understanding with Albanian men to avoid outright conflict.

These alternative interpretations lent an aura of ambivalence to male exchanges across ethnonational lines in the sense that the true nature of these exchanges could not be discerned with certainty (were they amicable, hostile, defensive, offensive, or a combination thereof?). Beyond pointing to the ambivalence of language and human communication, however, interactions between men reveal ambiguity surrounding the positions of dominance social actors occupied in the social structure, as delineated by Macedonian men. Inconclusive struggles over legitimacy, over who has the authority to direct the conduct of others in the first place and what counts as legitimate order, are also important in this regard. Efforts to affirm Macedonian manhood and restore the Macedonian national collectivity to its original position in the old, pre-insurgency order of things, where everyone occupied distinctive positions, were thus indeterminate. The specificity of sociopolitical power and the nature and meaning of social reality, despite efforts to the contrary, remained unsettled in the everyday public domain of interpersonal communication between Macedonian and Albanian men throughout the armed conflict.

Roughing Things Up

This ambiguity concerning relationships of power and their structuring was also at the core of forceful interpersonal interactions in the public arena, that is, interactions that did not involve at least some minimal degree of apparent congeniality and revolved around mutual attempts to exercise power over others. Such interactions featured Macedonian and Albanian men in their twenties and thirties who either were not personally acquainted or shared loose friendship bonds. They also took place more and more frequently in the context of the continuously deteriorating and fragile political situation in the country, as some men's interests to assign ethnonational groups to structural positions within the nation-state's symbolic order—that is to say, the social order cast in symbolic terms based on male gender—became increasingly compelling.

Consider the following vignette. One May morning in 2001, at his request, I accompanied my neighbor Blerim—an Albanian man in his early thirties who worked as a salesclerk at a shoe store in the small shopping center Mavrovka—to the German embassy in downtown Skopje. Blerim, like many other Albanians at the time of the conflict, had decided to make the best of the situation by applying for political asylum in Germany, one of the popular European destinations for Albanian asylum seekers from Kosovo in 1985–1990 and during the end of the 1990s (see Stacher 2000: 127). His choice, as is often the case with people navigating the postsocialist landscape (see, for example, Silverman

2000; Zanca 2000), involved the role of supporter for me, the Western ethnographer, and I eagerly stepped into this role when Blerim asked. While standing outside the embassy, Blerim and I were trying to figure out the best way to proceed. Suddenly, a nearby man in his late twenties who was also waiting and had apparently heard us converse in Albanian addressed the following question in Macedonian to Blerim: "Do you perhaps want to go to Germany and finance the [Albanian] terrorists?" Taken aback, and obviously irritated by the remark, Blerim responded in Macedonian, "What terrorists? We have nothing to do with [the Basque organization] ETA or [the Irish] IRA!" Unwilling to withdraw from the confrontation, the Macedonian man gave a loud, sarcastic laugh and went on to say, "How [come] you have nothing? You are all the same!" Blerim was getting increasingly upset and his face was flushed red as he retorted, "Come on, get out of here!" [*A be, begaj tamu!*] Who addressed you? Get out!" The Macedonian man shook his head mockingly while Blerim scornfully waved his hand in the air. The tension was palpable, and the rest of the people waiting looked on while the interaction unfolded. Seemingly irritated, both men took a few steps away and turned their backs on each other.

Let me briefly mention one additional story that occurred against the background of the escalating armed conflict. Driton, an Albanian clothing merchant in his mid-twenties whom I met through mutual friends, described to me one afternoon in early June 2001 the following forceful exchange with one of his Macedonian peers. Driton and the man in question socialized from time to time in the same circle of friends, consisting of a Macedonian neighbor of Driton and some of the neighbor's Macedonian friends.

> As we were walking, a Macedonian friend [*shok*] turned to me and said, "Abe, Driton, what do you Albanians want?"[3] I took my wallet out of my pocket, showed him my ID card and responded, "Here: do you see this [the ID card]? I want it printed in both Macedonian and Albanian!" "But it cannot be like that!" he cut me off. "Why can't it?" I replied in surprise and he repeated, "Out of the question! [*ne može!*]" "It is better not to say anything further," I said. I put my wallet back in my pocket, and we all kept walking.

Driton stopped for a moment to take a breath and continued, his voice quivering with agitation: "[He is a] Friend and [yet] he talked like that! He did not say 'everyone [in the country] should be happy, we will see.' No, [he said] 'it cannot!'"

I present to the reader these two ethnographic vignettes because they shed additional light on the nuances of power relations informing performances of manhood. These vignettes show that Albanian men opted to undertake, in a reactive mode to Macedonian men's performances, competing efforts to establish their manhood and lay claim to a superior form of masculinity when they saw fit. Integral to these efforts was the expression of fearless readiness to engage in verbal combat or articulate lingering Albanian grievances against the Macedonian state. The concept of "hegemonic masculinity" (see, among others, Connell 1987; Whitehead 2002) is an effective theoretical tool for a better understanding of such competing efforts. According to Caroline and Filippo Osella (2006: 49), "hegemonic masculinity is an idea, a style, a set of practices of dominance, which coalesce around an idealized type of masculinity as the desirable goal. Those few who manage to achieve the goal will become the dominant man—the hegemonic males." Dominance, in other words, is of key concern. As the above stories make clear, hegemonic masculinity is not a fixed category but a process of intense negotiation and mutual contestation, which is aimed at exercising power and asserting control over other, subordinate (and hence emasculated; see Brandes 1980) masculinities—subordinate in terms of ethnonational identity. Forceful exchanges between Macedonian and Albanian men in the public arena, then, provided a distinct forum for the practicing of cultural ideals of masculinity, and firmly set the stage for the potential emergence of a hierarchy of masculinities and the hierarchical ordering of society at large—and, as I have explored in greater detail elsewhere (see Neofotistos 2010), mutual competitions for the prize of the "greater" man in terms of both masculinity and ethnonational strength permeate sexual relationships with women from different ethnoreligious backgrounds.

Sharp competition over dominance in the context of a rapidly and unpredictably changing political environment illuminated what Jeganathan in his study of masculinity in Sri Lanka calls (2000: 61) a "space for violence," a space within which the possibility of violence arises. Nonetheless, the possibility of the escalation of male contests into physical violence did not materialize—at least, not always. This, of course, raises the general question of how to make sense of the lack or, perhaps more accurately, the nonescalation to higher levels of violence in instances of intense male sociality. A categorical answer is impossible because it would deny the significance of acknowledging cultural specificity and context, yet any attempt at an answer cannot afford to overlook the cultivation of inconclusiveness that occupies the space for violence. In Macedonia, the negotiation of competing masculinities during the 2001 conflict more often than not was unfinished and open-ended, leaving unsettled in the domain of everyday life the question of male control over others and the larger issue of ethnonational dominance in society. I do not intend to imply that physical violence between Macedonian and Albanian men never takes place. For, pub or coffee-shop brawls and student fights between youth occasionally occur in post-independence Macedonia. Rather, I am suggesting that the public performances examined here offer a more comprehensive view of the space for violence, and illuminate how social actors gauge the social world and navigate the contingency of social interaction in unstable times.

Expressing Vulnerability

Efforts to produce a fixed and well-defined social and political order and delineate everyone's respective positions and roles within it were undertaken not only by Macedonian men but also by some Macedonian women, mothers in particular, during interactions with male Albanian acquaintances, young men in their twenties and thirties. In the remainder of this chapter, I explore these efforts. While male intergroup interactions were geared toward the demonstration and establishment of Macedonian male and ethnonational dominance, the social exchanges below were initiated for the proclaimed purpose of satisfying personal concerns relating to the protection of women's children from potentially imminent danger. Yet again, as I show below, attempts to establish fixed relationships of power were made and challenged, this time through a shared language of moral discourse.

I often witnessed interactions between Macedonian women and Albanian men in one of my neighborhood's grocery stores. The store attracted a large and, importantly for my discussion here, ethnically mixed clientele not just because it had fresh produce every day and the widest range of merchandise one could find in the neighborhood. It was popular also because, unlike other neighborhood stores, it employed both Macedonian-language speakers (members of a Bosnian Muslim family, who owned the store) and a couple of Albanian men who could speak Macedonian and could cater to both the Macedonian- and Albanian-speaking clientele, as was the norm during the Yugoslav period. Indeed, the practices of multilingual communication (see, for example, Cowan 1997; Irvine and Gal 2000) and codeswitching (see Friedman 1995b) were the norm in nineteenth-century Macedonia and continued to permeate social life in Yugoslavia, notably in urban centers, until language gradually became linked to ethnic identity. In Macedonia, Skopje in particular, these practices further diminished due to demographic changes after World War II. Many Muslims immigrated to Turkey in the 1950s, and from the late 1960s onward people in large numbers increasingly migrated from rural areas and Kosovo to the Macedonian capital in order to take advantage of the opportunities generated by industrialization. The ruralization of Skopje, aptly described by the phrase *golemo selo*, or "big village," in turn undermined the practice of multilingualism, customarily performed among long-established urbanites.

Consider, for example, the following interaction. One morning in May 2001, I stopped at the store to purchase some groceries.Nothing seemed out of the ordinary. Outside the store, the three brothers who owned the business received fruit and vegetable shipments while an Albanian worker in his mid-twenties, Mustafa, diligently arranged the merchandise on the crates and attended to customers. Inside the store, the wives of the owners took turns working behind the counter, weighing groceries on a scale, handling money, or writing in a thick notebook (*tefter*) the names of customers who, due to financial difficulties, had no money to pay for the goods purchased but promised to pay at a later date. Even though the store was buzzing with customers shopping for groceries and items of daily use, such as coffee, cigarettes, peanuts, canned tomatoes, and bars of soap, Mustafa took the time, as he usually did, to make small talk about my research, his plans to take English language classes in the near future, the unfolding armed conflict, the fresh fruit delivered that day.

Suddenly, a female customer who was leaving the store took Mustafa by his right arm gently, yet with a sense of determination and urgency. She spoke Macedonian in a subdued, imperative tone, but every word she uttered was distinct, unmistakable and carefully selected: "Tell me," she said, "if anything is to happen, for my child's sake, so that I save the child!" The customer's intense face did not change when she finished her sentence. "Neighbor [*Komšija*], how should *I* know what will happen?" Mustafa gasped, surprise and wonder written all over his face. The customer persisted, keeping her eyes fixed on his face, not at all distracted by my presence or by hurried customers reaching for the apples in the crates beside us. "You *will tell* me, right? For the child!" Mustafa said nothing; a deep, contemplative silence fell over him before he nodded in appeasement. With a slight smile, aimed at inspiring confidence, he replied, "Well, all right [*Ajde*], I will tell you." Mustafa's response bore witness to the futility of alternative responses, especially in view of the woman's firm persistence. "Fine; OK then [*Ajde*], ciao," the woman said; she looked into the distance and waved a casual goodbye, raising her right hand slightly in the air before she disappeared.

In Anticipation of War

Macedonian women who felt that their personal stakes in the outcome of the insurgency were so high that they needed to take direct, personal action, like the woman in the above vignette, employed practices in anticipation of war—what Jeganathan (1998) in his study of violence in southern Sri Lanka calls "tactics of anticipation." These practices centered on mobilization of social capital and instrumentalization of motherhood, and were geared toward constructing an orderly social world and establishing a particular set of relationships of power.

More specifically, some Macedonian women in Skopje mobilized social capital that was embedded in their network of Albanian acquaintances. My use of the term "social capital" draws on the work of James Coleman, who defines the term as follows (1990: 302):[4]

> Social capital is defined by its function. It is not a single entity, but a variety of different entities having two characteristics in common: They all consist of some aspect of a social structure, and they facilitate certain actions of individuals who are within the structure. Like other forms of capital [namely, physical and human capital], social capital is productive, making possible the achievement of certain ends that would not be attainable in its absence. Like physical capital and human capital, social capital is not completely fungible, but is fungible with respect to specific activities. A given form of social capital that is valuable in facilitating certain actions may be useless or even harmful for others. Unlike other forms of capital, social capital inheres in the structure of relations between persons and among persons. It is lodged neither in individuals nor in physical implements of production.

Coleman's line of thought underlines that one may exercise control over some resources (for example, private goods and skills) and may also be interested in resources, controlled by other actors, that can fully or partially determine the outcome of events in which one is interested. Social actors thus often-times engage in social relationships while nurturing an understanding of the resources that others control and with a view to acquiring control, or the right to exercise control, over resources of particular interest to them in a specific social context (1990: 33–34).

This conceptual scheme of social action helps us to better understand how some Macedonian women in Skopje navigated their way through highly uncertain and unstable times.

Specifically, they delineated coherent constellations of power within the interpretive framework promulgated by the Macedonian-language media, whereby Macedonian personal safety and national security were put in grave jeopardy by the NLA and the Macedonian state was unmistakably threatened with utter collapse. In their accounts, Macedonian women represented the Macedonian individual and collective self as weak and powerless (as opposed to strong and powerful); at the same time, the NLA's increased control over Macedonian territory became the criterion to define members of the Albanian community as dangerously powerful. An integral element of the process through which Macedonian women made sense of their new circumstances was the redefinition of relationships with male Albanian acquaintances as relationships with people who, because of their common ethnonational background with the insurgents and their male role as defenders of Albanian national interests, allegedly had unique access to and control over an especially valuable and desirable resource, namely information regarding the plans of the NLA and the unfolding of the conflict.

When delineating such social and political arrangements during interactions with Albanian men, Macedonian women also embraced prevailing values in Macedonian society regarding women's role as mothers. They instrumentalized this role and used the idiom of motherhood as a mode of political action, postulating that antagonists in politics nonetheless do share certain cultural assumptions. It is in their role as mothers that they appealed for compassion toward their children and families. In so doing, they lent credibility and moral legitimacy to their requests for information about the conflict and its outcome. They conducted themselves above reproach and potentially made it morally difficult for Albanians to deny sharing any insights that they might have had into the situation in the country. Unlike mothers navigating political turmoil elsewhere (see, for example, Jetter et al. 1997), Macedonian women did not use the idiom of motherhood as the basis for collective political action. Acting as mothers, they nonetheless engaged in a form of everyday activism that directly and compellingly addressed pressing political issues. Their interactions with Albanian men occurred together with more organized forms of activism, namely, small-scale, anti-violence protests organized by various Macedonian women's organizations in Skopje and other Macedonian cities over the duration of the armed conflict.

The moral force of Macedonian women's tactics also needs to be assessed through reference to the significance of traditional values of femininity, including childbearing and mothering, particularly for Gheg-speaking Albanians of Montenegro, Kosovo, and northwestern Macedonia.[5] As Whitaker notes (1981: 149), for example, the value of women in northern Albanian society has traditionally rested in their capacity to give birth (especially to boys) and ensure the perpetuation of the patrilineal line. Such attitudes are increasingly questioned and challenged by members of the Albanian community, but still tend to have a strong hold over Albanian men irrespective of their age group and social background and, as I discuss in the next chapter, regardless of their views on the importance of women's emancipation (see also Dimova 2006). Macedonian women, acting as mothers, tapped into a reservoir of traditional values extremely cherished by many Albanian men, so their appeals took on even greater moral resonance.

Practices that were deployed in anticipation of war, then, were geared toward relieving feelings of emotional distress and anxiety in some Macedonian women and injecting an element of stability, or at least predictability, into volatile circumstances. The practices in question, what is more, helped some women (re)construct an orderly social world and render it meaningful by locating in it themselves and Albanian men whom they knew. At the core of these practices lay a form of activity whereby the moral principle of common humanity was invoked to urge Albanian men to choose to do the "right thing," namely alleviate unpredictability, notify others of potentially deleterious events, and help them survive in case of war. Assertions of confidence and trust in Albanian men's humanity were also instrumental in engendering a general sense of moral duty. A particular network of power relations was thus produced: the exercise of power was contained in the emphasis on moral duty in terms of common humanity, specifically on the moral responsibility to help mothers in need of support, and the prescription of a specific course of conduct for Albanian men to consider following. "The exercise of power," as Foucault notes (1983: 221), "consists in guiding the possibility of conduct and putting in order the possible outcome." This is not to deny traces of inflexibility, even a subtle kind of coercion, in the exercise of power over others: some Macedonian women were ill-disposed to the possibility of actions and outcomes that were alternative to the ones they designated. Remember, for example, how the Macedonian customer in the above vignette brushed aside Mustafa's question as to how he should be expected to know what the future course of events might be, and insisted that he share any information to which he might be, or become, privy regarding the plans of the NLA insurgents.

Playing the Game

The interactions under exploration here provided ground for the emergence of initiatives to challenge perspectives, put forward by Macedonian women, regarding configurations of power in Macedonian society at the time of the armed conflict and to tackle attempts to guide their conduct in specific directions. The deployment of *komšija*, the colloquial term for neighbor, was a common tactic toward that end. The term is of Turkish origin and Slavic form, and Macedonians and Albanians generally prefer it over the Slavic and Albanian terms for "neighbor"—*sosed* (m.)/*sosedka* (f.) and *fqinj* (m.)/*fqinje* (f.) respectively. *Komšija* is customarily used to describe people living in geographical proximity to each other, and connotes trust, support, reciprocity in social relationships, and solidarity. This sense of the term stems from a long, strong tradition of urban neighborliness (*komšiluk/kojshilluk*; from Turkish *komşuluk*) that emerged during the Ottoman era and survived the collapse of Ottoman rule. In particular, urbanites with different religious, social and/ or ethnic backgrounds continued to define their social identities primarily as neighbors who indulged in relaxed conversation, shared the joys and sorrows of daily life, and trusted and treated each other with utmost respect— although marriages across religious lines were and, as is the case in central Bosnia (Bringa 1995: 79–80), continue to be commonly avoided.[6] In her examination of urban sociability in *staro*, or "old," Skopje after the Ottomans departed from Macedonia in 1912, Ellis (2003: 34) mentions that neighbors were considerate at all times despite the porous boundary separating the private and public spheres—a neighbor who was en route to the baker's to have his/her bread cooked, for instance, would pick up the bread boxes neighbors had placed in front of their doors and take those boxes to the baker's, too. Even though, similar to Bosnia (see Maček 2008: 105), the social importance of neighborliness gradually declined with urbanization and the faster pace of modern life, people in Skopje still greatly value considerate and supportive neighbors, and often use the term *komšija* to evoke a greater sense of solidarity and trust, moral sameness, mutual assistance, and reciprocity. The term is also commonly used among strangers who wish to signal eagerness to participate in amicable exchanges and satisfy common interests—for example, between customers and bazaar merchants or small shopkeepers (see also Maček 2009: 105).

By invoking this widely shared system of moral and social values, intimately associated with a history of neighborly solidarity, Albanian men signaled that they played the game, which is to say that they upheld an urbane code of honorable behavior and placed value on social harmony. In this way, they adhered to a cultural logic linking conceptions of value, identity, and interpersonal conflict—what Carol Greenhouse defines as the "avoidance ethic" (1992: 248) and describes as "the nonbehavioral dimensions of avoidance... the logic of values that make [the avoidance of conflict] meaningful" (236) allowing "people an opportunity to associate themselves with a value system that is itself highly valued culturally" (235). The avoidance ethic allowed Albanian men to challenge allegations that they were privy to information regarding the course of events because they were supposedly associated with the NLA, and affirm that they were equally powerless and in exactly the same circumstances as their Macedonian interlocutors: they suffered the same agonies, were similarly subjected to the unpredictability of events, and had the same—no greater and no less—capability to mitigate uncertainty associated with the risk of war. In this sense, Albanian men destabilized representations of social reality and sociopolitical arrangements put forth by Macedonian women. They did not fulfill their assigned social roles as powerful protectors. Rather, they introduced a new interpretive framework for making sense of the world, whereby they stood outside the circle of NLA participants and were insiders in a unified body politic—a community of *obični lugje*, or "ordinary people" (see also Neofotistos 2009b). Indeed, "affirmations of the ethic of avoidance appear to be part of a process by which insiders"—a group of self-styled insiders, I would further add—"reaffirm their own status and identity" (Greenhouse et al. 1994: 121).

The avoidance ethic was intimately related to conflict avoidance behavior and at times used as a conflict mitigation tactic. Consider the following story from the same neighborhood grocery store. One time, as Mustafa narrated the exchange to me, a Macedonian female customer while chatting with the Albanian wife of one of the storeowners shared the news that the army unit of her husband, a reservist ordered to active duty, was stationed at a hill near Skopje. While I was not present when that exchange took place, I was shopping in the store when the same (as Mustafa later told me) Macedonian customer, after having purchased groceries, said that her husband's unit had come under attack from the NLA and accused the Albanian woman of having divulged (presumably to her husband or other male relatives) information about the location of the unit and of being responsible for what had happened. "You told!" she furiously said, castigating her for having transgressed the conventional code of female behavior whereby silence and gossip, and not the conduct of war, are female preoccupations (see also Herzfeld 1991). The Albanian woman was overcome by surprise for a brief moment. "Me, neighbor [*komšija*]?" she said in disbelief before the customer stormed out of the store, leaving everyone else present at a loss for words.

In general, in the context of confrontational interpersonal, intergroup interactions, addressing someone as *komšija* served both as a mild rebuke for improper conduct and, what is more, as a commanding moral appeal inviting, without stringent remarks or severe reprimands, the other party to the exchange to adhere to a set of highly regarded values and conduct themselves as a *komšija* should and would: namely, in solidarity and in accordance with the principles of respect and consideration toward others. The exercise of power was yet again contained in the emphasis on moral duty in terms of shared humanity, and also in the prescription of a course of conduct for others to consider following. After all, as Foucault notes (1988: 19), "power is strategic games between liberties [that is to say,] strategic games that result in the fact that some people try to determine the conduct of others."

This, then, is how male Albanian social actors undercut Macedonian women's understandings and representations of the sociopolitical order and efforts to guide the way in which men behaved in the context of escalating armed hostilities and political turmoil. While the initiatives they chose to undertake did not necessarily convince women to revise their conduct, nonetheless Albanian men cultivated an aura of fluidity and inconclusiveness with regard to relations of power and introduced alternative understandings and representations in the realm of everyday sociality.

CHAPTER 6

Claiming Respect

In this chapter, I examine how in the course of the armed conflict many of my Albanian research participants engaged in performances of respectable and "modern" selfhood during encounters with Macedonian state employees in positions of authority and during outings in downtown Skopje respectively. Drawing on the work of Jean and John Comaroff (1993), I treat these performances as rituals, that is to say as "a site and a means of experimental practice, of subversive poetics, of creative tension and transformative action" (xxix), "experimental technology intended to affect the flow of power in the [social] universe" (xxx). What I find in this theorization of ritual especially appealing for the purposes of my analysis is the ritual's creative capacity, its ability to engender new, alternative possibilities for thinking about and acting in the world; in the words of the aforementioned authors (xxix): "under its [the ritual's] authorship and its authority, individual and collective aspirations weave a thread of imaginative possibilities from which may emerge, wittingly or not, new signs and meanings, conventions and intentions." The possibilities for thought and action emergent in the context of the performances explored here, subverted widespread, and made room for new social and moral arrangements and understandings in Macedonian society. Unfolding during a period of heightened political instability, these performances shed light on nonviolent tactics, alternative to the armed tactics of the NLA insurgents, to address the status of Albanians in Macedonian society.

Performing Respectability

For members of the Albanian community, the outbreak of the insurgency and the expansion of hostilities raised sharp concerns over the possibility of retaliatory action by state employees, notably university professors and bureaucrats, most of whom were Macedonian and remained in positions of authority up to the end of the insurgency (and until certain constitutional amendments after the signing of the Ohrid Framework Agreement took effect). Male and female Albanian students taking university exams in late spring 2001, for instance, were worried and indignant over the possibilities that their Macedonian professors might ask for bribes or give bad grades on inconsequential pretexts. To give another example, Albanians who interacted with bureaucrats felt disquieted at the prospect of paying bribes to get things done and also anxious about the possibility that they might be treated with disdain and abuse. To be sure, corruption has long permeated all levels of Macedonian society—so much so that former Macedonian prime minister Branko Crvenkovski during his term of office in the 1990s (1992–1998) asked for a parliamentary vote of confidence to fight corruption (see also Vankovska 2006).[1] Corruption and the disrespectful or abusive behavior of some state employees have been routine practices in independent Macedonia. Everyday interactions with people in positions of authority have been a source of anxiety and concern for members of all communities, as so often happens in bureaucratically organized societies (see, for example, Herzfeld 1992). In the Albanian community in particular, anxiety and concern have been intimately tied to what Gupta (1995) calls the "discursive construction of the state," specifically the Albanian-language media reproduction of political rhetoric throughout the 1990s concerning the critical events explored in Chapter 1 and depicting the Macedonian state as an undemocratic political entity where Albanians were treated like second-class citizens. The role of personal stories and memories of Yugoslav rule, transmitted orally through elders, also needs to be taken into account when describing the relationship between the state and the Albanian community. These narratives depict sociopolitical and economic marginalization and exclusion and stress an unbroken historical continuity between the communist regime in Belgrade and the political establishment in post-independence Macedonia. As Sutton (1998) shows, the past comes into play as social actors seek to make sense of the present and challenge (or legitimate) present-day practices. It is in this context that everyday practices of corruption and disrespectful or abusive behavior by some Macedonian state employees have become viewed by the Albanian community at large as intentionally targeting Albanians, and are especially contested.

To navigate this possibility of misconduct, which became increasingly worrisome due to heightened political volatility during the armed conflict, the working- and middle-class Albanians with whom I worked in Skopje staged performances of respectability during interactions with members of the Macedonian community whom they did not know well personally. Let me illustrate with the following vignette. One May morning in 2001, I visited the Macedonian Radio Television (MRT) building, where I had arranged to meet with Yllka, a twenty-six-year-old Albanian journalist with the Albanian Division, and discuss with her and some of her colleagues media reporting during the conflict.[2] Yllka originated from a village in the vicinity of Skopje, and, as so often happens, had used kinship connections as a means to migrate to the capital, where in the early 1990s she had pursued an undergraduate degree in Albanian Language and Literature at Skopje University.[3] Like many young Albanian women who increasingly attend state and private universities, Yllka wanted an education and a career.

The growing significance of women's education in the Albanian community needs to be understood against the background of Albanian efforts by male politicians in post-independence Macedonia to promote, both nationally and internationally, an image of the Albanian community as modern and democratic, as opposed to traditional and authoritarian, in order to make a convincing argument that the Albanian community was deserving of improved status in the newly formed state. The issue of women's emancipation indeed often lies at the core of political ideology and nationalist discourse (see, for example, Woodward 1985; Bagghi 1996). Such sentiments achieved resonance among male members of the Albanian community, in part thanks to efforts of Albanian women intellectuals and activists, who founded the first Albanian women's NGO, the Albanian Women's Alliance, in 1992 and went from door to door to encourage the education of Albanian women (see Dimova 2006: 319). As Dimova (312) eloquently notes, "sending a daughter or sister to school became a sign of loyalty to the Albanian [ethnonational] movement."

Let us return to the ethnographic vignette. As I was waiting in the lobby of MRT for Yllka to arrive, I noticed a paper sign, taped to the front side of the glassed-in reception desk, reading in scruffy, capital letters ZADOLŽITELNA KONTROLA, or OBLIGATORY INSPECTION, in Macedonian. Another handwritten paper sign reading *Prijavnica*, or *Registration*, was taped a few inches away, right above a visitors' registry that lay open on the counter. Such signs are usually found in the entrances and lobby areas of government buildings and state institutions in Skopje. Behind the reception desk sat a balding employee, his belly protruding from under his shirt. Instead of inspecting visitors' bags for potentially threatening objects or asking visitors to sign the registry, the man had his face buried in a Macedonian-language newspaper and was puffing at a cigarette. Only when he turned the pages of the paper did he look over the top of his glasses from one corner of the lobby to the other, his gaze straying past me. During those brief moments, and before he buried his face back in the newspaper, the man's look became severe—his eyebrows furrowed and his face wore a stern expression. Nobody else in the building but me, however, appeared to pay any attention to the man, and it seemed that for his part he could not be any less distressed.

About twenty minutes later, Yllka appeared cheerfully. "I am only ten minutes late!" she said with a big smile on her face as she smoothed her hair from the wind blowing outside. "Come on [Ani], let's go upstairs!" she exclaimed, eager to show me around the TV station and introduce me to some of her colleagues. As we walked toward the steps that led up to a platform, Yllka suddenly froze in her tracks—"Wait!" she exclaimed. "Let's ask if we can enter!" Taken aback by the suggestion, I told Yllka that was not necessary because everyone who had entered the building before she arrived had gone about his or her way without asking for permission. As I turned to go upstairs, Yllka took hold of my arm and said commandingly, "Wait!" nodding her head affirmatively to convince me that she knew better. To my surprise, she took out of her handbag her journalist ID card with her Albanian name written on it, walked back around to the registration desk, and bent down slightly to speak into a round hole in the glass. She firmly held up her ID for the employee to see, and asked in a loud voice that carried an impeccable Macedonian accent and a slight hint of irony, "May we enter?" The man slowly raised his head and looked at Yllka. Seemingly irritated by the interruption, he took a big puff from his cigarette while staring the young woman in the face. He narrowed his eyes, blew the smoke out through his nostrils and, without uttering a single word, gave Yllka a slight nod. The young woman put her ID back in the handbag and walked toward me as the man's gaze followed her. "It is better this way, more certain [më sigurtë]!" she said, and added:

> Maybe he would have asked us to return to the lobby because he knows that I am Albanian; he might have asked to see my ID card just like that, for personal amusement [për qejf], for maltreatment.[4] Or, he might have asked us to return because I am bringing into the building someone whom he has not seen before and he thought that you, too, are Albanian and wanted to ask where we were going. In any case, it is better like this. Now he can't say anything! We can go upstairs freely.

Having worked with MRT for six years, Yllka was familiar with the lax visitor registration procedures in the building. The armed conflict, however, lent an air of distrust to the practice of the ordinary. Suspicious that the Macedonian employee's indifference in reality masked intentionality, Yllka identified the possibility that the man might have requested that we, out of all the visitors to the building and because we were speaking in Albanian, follow his command and write our names in the visitors' registry. This, according to Yllka, would have been a malevolent—carefully calculated, deliberate, and egotistical—act in which the Macedonian public servant would be selectively exercising his authority against individuals he identified as Albanian (Yllka and I) and flexing his muscle, so to speak, on behalf of the Macedonian collectivity. According to this figuration of social relations, past and present ethnonational tensions would be seeping into the encounter. From Yllka's viewpoint, her personal and moral integrity, together with the integrity of Albanian ethnonational identity itself, would be compromised if such an eventuality were to materialize: she would be left with no alternative except to do as the employee had requested and would be forced to participate in the man's presumed show of power, allegedly meant to assert Macedonian supremacy.

To prevent this scenario from occurring, Yllka presented herself as a respectable individual, a morally upright member of Macedonian society who was ready to follow social conventions promoting smooth functioning of daily life and governing "appropriate" social conduct—in this particular case, show her ID card and request from the Macedonian employee permission to enter the building. The spontaneous and ostentatious theatricality of Yllka's performance, meant to distinguish her strikingly from other visitors and capture the full attention of her interactant, is noteworthy here: whereas one might expect that Yllka would act like other visitors and ignore the presence of the employee, she made a point of letting him know that she was, and the only one at that, observing conventional regularities of her own will, even (or especially) when nobody was looking, and was thus fully and justifiably deserving of respect.

The Politics of Respectability

Like Yllka, many Albanians with whom I worked in Skopje expressed the wish to prevent the satisfaction of the assumed desire of Macedonians in positions of authority—namely, to establish in everyday contexts the supremacy of the Macedonian Self over the Albanian Other. Such remarks shed light on the ways members of the Albanian community created meaning and afford us an understanding of the affective underpinnings of performances of respectability. That is to say, social actors refigured individual emotions in collective terms as "political affect," as "a resource emanating from and giving meaning to shifting political situations and asymmetries" (George 1996: 104), asymmetries of power in particular. These representations of social life were not without consequences; they gave rise to orientations of action.

Indeed, Yllka's performance is representative of the ways Albanians in Skopje tended to navigate the social world and their positions in it during the period of the NLA insurgency—that is, with heightened suspicion that Macedonian salaried employees in positions of authority would aggress on them and with a quick readiness to redress hostility and forestall presumed adversaries by initiating the attack. Male and female Albanian students majoring in subjects other than Albanology at Skopje University (and hence taking exams in the Macedonian language) often recounted that they did their best to avoid inaccuracies in grammar and vocabulary and excel in written exams, or converse in Macedonian in the best accent possible during oral exams, to avoid providing their professors with "ammunition" they could use to establish relations of domination. Along somewhat similar lines, Albanian clients of public service bureaucracies often mentioned that they were very careful to use correct Macedonian when filling out forms or interacting with Macedonian bureaucrats, and sometimes enlisted the help of relatives to perform these tasks on their behalf, to avoid being controlled.

In enacting respectability, Albanians crafted a public persona that countered widespread stereotypes of Albanians as rebellious, dangerous, untrustworthy, dishonest, and so on (see Neofotistos 2004). They underlined conformity with social conventions and moral norms and upheld fragile sociopolitical arrangements. At the same time, they kept in check Macedonian individuals in positions of authority and deprived them of the possibility of gaining personal and ethnonational group advantage over Albanian individuals and their community. In this sense, respectability acquired a political dimension: its performance was the contestation, disguised under the cloak of proper public behavior, but poignant in view of the NLA territorial alliances of the distribution of power and the fundamentals of privilege within the larger Macedonian society.

Through their behavior and actions, many Albanians asserted not only that they were masters of their existence but also that they controlled the process or outcome of communication during everyday encounters—indeed, exercised control in social relations. And this is exactly where the ritualistic character of performances of respectability lay: in the destabilization of systems of power and control prior to the NLA insurgency and in the crafting of imaginative possibilities for new arrangements and understandings, whereby members of the Macedonian community were left with no choice but to give respect to Albanian individuals and meet them on an equal footing. Similar to ritual (see Comaroff and Comaroff 1993: xxi), and much like the enactment of "modern" selfhood I explore in the second half of the chapter, enactment of respectable selfhood existed in an antagonistic relationship to routine modes of action and meaning-production in the social world, and at the same time "(re-)makes social predicaments" (xxx).

Postsocialist Transformations

Throughout the conflict, many young Albanians (in their twenties and thirties) with aspirations for socioeconomic mobility tended in public to enact social performances of "modern" selfhood with the explicit intent, they told me, of attracting the attention of Macedonian passersby and influencing their assumed views concerning the presence of the Albanian population in the country. These public performances, which were common but were not distinctly articulated as such prior to the NLA insurgency, took place in downtown Skopje and involved shopping or window-shopping for Western consumer goods at the main shopping mall, called City Commercial Center (Gradski Trgovski Centar), drinking coffee at trendy coffee shops in the vicinity of the mall, or walking about the main city square, conversing emphatically in Albanian.

Before I delve into the particularities of such performances, I will take a detour to discuss, first, the larger context of postsocialist transformation in which strong anti-Albanian prejudice together with common understandings of the "modern" have emerged in post-independence Macedonia, and second, the sociopolitical significance of being "modern" in today's Macedonia. Addressing these issues goes hand in hand with my treatment of the public enactment of "modern" Albanian selfhood as a form of ritual. For, as Jean and John Comaroff (1993: xxx) suggest, ritual "is an especially likely response to contradictions created and (literally) engendered by processes of social, material, and cultural transformation, processes re-presented, rationalized, and authorized in the name of modernity and its various alibis ('civilization,' 'social progress,' 'economic development,' 'conversion,' and the like)." Let me then explain the context of the emergence of contradictions in response to which Albanians tended to stage performances of "modern" self-hood throughout the conflict.

A good place to start is the current global abjection of Macedonia, set in motion by the disintegration of Yugoslavia and unfolding in the wider context of postsocialist transformation (see Burawoy and Verdery 1999). I borrow the term "abjection" from James Ferguson to refer to "a process of being thrown aside, expelled, or discarded. But its literal meaning also implies not just being thrown out but being thrown *down*—thus expulsion but also debasement and humiliation" (1999: 236, emphasis original). To explain, Macedonia enjoyed official recognition as a republic in socialist Yugoslavia and shared in the international prestige Yugoslavia enjoyed under Tito's rule. After its emergence as an independent nation-state in 1991, however, its very existence, as already mentioned, has been disputed more forcefully than ever before by Bulgaria, Serbia, and especially Greece. Post-independence Macedonia has repeatedly been refused entry to NATO and the EU, and significant constraints have been placed on freedom of movement (until very recently, non-foreign passport holders needed visas to travel abroad) and freedom to trade.[5] In their conversations with me, many people articulated a sense of exclusion from the world outside the borders of Macedonia and of an irrevocable loss of standing in international society.

For my Macedonian research participants the experience of abjection is aggravated by financial degradation and sharp economic inequalities between members of the Macedonian and Albanian communities. Having been heavily reliant on the socialist state, many Macedonians lost their jobs and the privileges of state employment, such as steady salaries and paid vacations, when the socialist system collapsed.[6] Albanians, who had been much less dependent on the socialist state and keener to pursue entrepreneurial opportunities abroad (mainly in Germany and Switzerland), had accumulated economic capital and were able to send remittances and provide support for their families back home. Such practices were common among Albanians during socialism, but they have made socioeconomic inequalities between the two ethnonational communities more visible and pronounced in the postsocialist period. Many Macedonians view Albanians who currently are in a comparatively stronger financial position as reminders of a lost and better world. Dimova (2010) shows how widespread feelings of loss have provided a breeding ground for strong anti-Albanian prejudice in Macedonian society. Macedonians with whom I worked often also told me that Albanians owed their allegedly newfound economic strength to illegal activities, such as trafficking in women, guns, and drugs.

Equally important, the dissolution of the former Yugoslavia was accompanied by a massive import of foreign media images, communicating representations of the "West." Even though Western print media were available in limited quantities in Macedonia in the 1970s, the flood of foreign newspapers and magazines was unlike anything to be found prior to independence. In addition, Latin American soap operas with intriguing plots and popular American series like *Judging Amy* and *Desperate Housewives*, which mark a notable difference from 1950s reruns like the *Cisco Kid* in the 1970s or shows like *Dallas* in the 1980s, introduced on a massive scale media images that celebrated the cultural and economic values of Western capitalist society.[7] In this framework values such as consumerism, material wealth, privacy, individualism, and the nuclear (as opposed to extended) family, became perceived in Macedonia as "Western."

Wider geopolitical changes in the former Yugoslavia and the concomitant large influx of foreigners are additional important factors to be considered in understandings of the larger context in which Albanian performances of "modern" selfhood were enacted. Specifically, while during socialist rule Skopje was an important enough provincial capital to have a Turkish consulate, a Greek consulate, and an American Information Center that functioned as a de facto (but not a de jure) consulate, Skopje's importance to regional stability and security increased after the eruption of the Yugoslav wars of succession. In the 1990s the city experienced the arrival of a very large number of Western foreigners who worked with UNPROFOR, UNPREDEP, and other international NGOs to avert the spillover of the Yugoslav wars into independent Macedonia. These foreigners had greater access to things and activities that became commonly associated in Macedonia with "modern" life, such as going out to restaurants, traveling abroad for work or vacation, and having access to material goods produced and sold abroad.

The embracing of consumerism and other Western capitalist values, projected by the mass media and introduced into post-1991 Macedonia by foreigners, has signaled the emergence of new constellations of individual and social worth—that is to say, larger systems of meaning concerning who and what is valued in Macedonian society. As a single Albanian man who had a university degree and a high-paying job in a German-owned firm in Skopje told me once while bragging about the numerous women with whom he had been going out, the more keys men have on their keychain, the greater the social worth attributed to them and the more popular they thus become: a large number of keys indicates individualism, material success and prosperity, and, more generally, adoption of the basic tenets of western capitalism.

Irrespective of their ethnic backgrounds, men and women whose lifestyles meet imagined Western standards tend to be viewed as "modern," "worldly," "European," "urban," "cultured/civilized," "refined," "human" and so on, and thus enjoy high social prestige—unless they are believed to have attained such lifestyles through criminal and immoral means.[8] Conversely, those who do not embrace Western values and lifestyles are commonly referred to as "left living in the past," "Balkan," "peasant," "uncultured/uncivilized," "backward," and so forth, are considered "less than human," and tend to have low social prestige. Members of both communities under examination here, in other words, articulate socioeconomic divisions in terms of who is "modern" and who is not—and, as I have discussed elsewhere (Neofotistos 2010), Albanian men tend to reappropriate the ethnic slur Šiptar to assess and make claims about their worth and that of other Albanians.

Local people also interact within socioeconomic networks that cut across ethnonational lines. Many Macedonians in Skopje tend to describe as "modern" and "European" Albanian individuals with whom they are personally acquainted (for instance, neighbors, co-workers, professional colleagues, social acquaintances) and who engage in social practices and uphold values that conform to "Western" standards of life. To give but one example, a Macedonian woman who lived in a relatively upscale suburb of Skopje once told me while boastfully describing her mono-ethnic neighborhood that only one Albanian (Albanec) lived on her street. She went on to add emphatically, "*but he is modern*," and describe the man as a university professor with two children and a wife who did not wear a headscarf—a potent symbol, against the background of contemporary global debates on the place of Islam in Europe (see, for example, Bowen 2007), of Islamic threat to Western values.

Such remarks remain fairly common to this day and point to the porousness of ethnonational boundaries, especially as pertaining to Albanian old-dwellers (*starosedelci*) who lived in Skopje before the city absorbed successive waves of newcomers (*novodojdeni*), including Macedonian and Albanian immigrants, from villages in Macedonia and Kosovo (see Neofotistos 2004). At the same time, remarks about men and women who are nonetheless "modern" for being Albanian reveal the generalized negative view of Albanians as adherents of allegedly outdated and backward social practices, including strong patriarchal control, extended families, multiple offspring, and the wearing of headscarves in public space. These practices, what is more, are widely viewed in the Macedonian community as reminders of the country's Ottoman history and rural past. While anti-Albanian prejudice certainly existed in socialist Yugoslavia (see, for example, Allcock 2000: 168), it has become more acute in the postsocialist period due to widespread concerns regarding the international image of Macedonia, specifically concerns over projecting the image of a country that is "modern" and good enough to be on a par with other European countries (see also Graan 2010, Neofotistos 2012). Practices that do not conform to "modern" standards are thus believed to send a negative message to powerful outsiders abroad—that Macedonia is riddled with Oriental backwardness, Islamic religious dogmatism, and outdated, rural traditionalism—and to eliminate the possibility of ever ameliorating Macedonia's standing in the international arena (see also Neofotistos 2008).

Consumerism and "Modern" Identity

Downtown Skopje is the primary locality where many city (and some non-city) residents construct "modern" identity in post-independence Macedonia.[9] Such constructions are intimately bound with consumerism. Two factors are of key importance in this respect: the acquisition of Western consumer goods and the practice of shopping in retail stores in downtown Skopje (see also Thiessen 2007).

With regard to the first factor, unlike the socialist period, especially in its latter phase, when many Western products were only readily available abroad and people traveled to Germany, England, Italy, or Spain to purchase them, one can nowadays find an abundance of retail stores carrying expensive by local standards, and highly desired, foreign brand apparel.[10] During my field research, I spent endless hours at the shopping mall with my male and female friends admiring in store windows, among other items, Benetton sweaters, Lacoste polo shirts, Swatch watches, Salvatore Ferragamo shoes, and designer sunglasses. Those among my friends who were unmarried or married without children and lived in households that enjoyed relatively comfortable economic circumstances tended to spend a large part of their job earnings, or of cash gifts and other funds from parents or other relatives at home or abroad, on goods such as those mentioned above; they also kept an eye out for Western brand-name clothing and accessories that went on sale, and purchased such goods at a discount. People who cannot afford to purchase Western brand goods in downtown stores tend to travel by bus to Turkey and neighboring Bulgaria (more frequently prior to Bulgaria's EU accession in 2007, when no visa was required to cross the border between Macedonia and Bulgaria) and purchase, usually for a fraction of the price, counterfeits—or purchase counterfeits from friends or neighbors who travel abroad.

Figure 7. Skopje's main square, circa 2004. Photo credit: Ahmet Bekir.

In addition, shopping in downtown stores occupies a central position in the construction of "modern" identity. The importance attributed to this practice cannot be understood outside the context of choice of shopping destinations in Skopje and of the valuation of these destinations in the postsocialist context. Shopping at the Gradski Trgovski Centar—and at the more recently constructed Ramstore mall, as well as at the smaller malls Bunjakovec and Beverly Hills, all in the same part of town and a few minutes' walk from the main square—involves interacting with smartly dressed and (often annoyingly) attentive shop assistants and having the option of trying on clothes in dressing rooms. The shopping experience is different across the Stone Bridge (Kamen Most), which connects the older Ottoman part with the historically newer part of Skopje. Here, the city's largest open-air market (Bit Pazar) bustles with people buying and selling anything from fresh produce and toilet paper to shoes and clothes, displayed in market stalls or hanging from awnings. The vendors, most dressed in shabby clothes, tend to customers quickly while yelling out their merchandise to attract the attention of prospective buyers. The stores beyond the immediate Bit Pazar area and inside the old Turkish bazaar (Turska or Stara Čaršija) offer merchandise that includes, among other items, low-end apparel, Islamic clothing for women, jewelry, loom-woven rugs, and tourist souvenirs.

For many people in postsocialist Macedonia, shopping at the downtown mall and the acquisition of Western material goods (or of counterfeit products imitating Western brand names) create an intimate sense of partaking in the lifestyles of people who reside in the "West." The notion of the "West" is not usually associated in Macedonia with a particular physical location (although Albanians and Macedonians generally tend to use the term to refer to the United States and European countries with strong economies and stable political systems by comparison, notably England, France, Germany, and Switzerland); rather, it indicates an imagined and, in the light of Macedonia's global abjection, desired state of being. Far from suggesting a disjuncture between the so-called "real" and the so-called "unreal/false," I borrow the term "imagined" from Arjun Appadurai: "The image, the imagined, the imaginary—these are all terms that direct us to something critical and new in global cultural processes: the imagination as a social practice" (1996: 31; emphasis removed). Understood as such, imagination is "a form of negotiation between sites of agency (individuals) and globally defined fields of possibility." As Thiessen argues in her ethnographic study of a group of Macedonian female engineers (2007), the practice of shopping and the acquisition of foreign goods at the shopping mall downtown are not so much about emulating a Western lifestyle. Rather, they are about constructing social identities *in relation to* values and attitudes that have come to be viewed as "Western." It is through such practices that Macedonian and also Albanian social actors symbolically transcend the economic and political boundaries between post-independence Macedonia and the rest of the world, remedy the global disconnect (see Ferguson 1999), and create a sense of connection to the "West."

Enacting "Modern" Albanian Selfhood

It is in this wider sociopolitical context, where anti-Albanian prejudice has taken deep root and the endorsement of Western values and ideals provides a sense of belonging to the wider world, that many of my young male and female Albanian research participants with middle-class aspirations enacted "modern" selfhood in the downtown area of Skopje throughout the armed conflict. There was nothing understated about such performances. They were vigorous and emphatic, full of confidence and purpose. Those who put them forth aimed, they told me, to draw attention to their presence downtown and, important, demonstrate to random Macedonian passersby that the Albanian collectivity was "modern" and "European." One day in spring 2001, for instance, as the conflict was raging some forty kilometers north of Skopje, Nuri, a single Albanian man in his mid-twenties who worked in a mini-market in Čair and whose parents I had met through networking in the Albanian community, turned up fifteen minutes late for a coffee meeting in one of the coffee shops in the central square of downtown Skopje. Nuri apologized profusely and explained that the reason for the delay was that he had been waiting for his mother to iron his shirt. "I want to look good when I come to this part [of the city]" he said with a serious face, while adjusting the collar of his black Lacoste polo shirt around his neck.

To be sure, the desire to appear well groomed, that is to say, dressed in well pressed, Western-style, Western brand-name clothing when headed downtown, is shared among many young people not only from Albanian but also from Macedonian ethnonational backgrounds. It was common practice among many of my young Macedonian female friends, for example, to spend hours at home trying to decide what to wear, putting on make-up, ironing clothes, and washing and styling their hair before they met friends for coffee at downtown cafés, shopped for Western consumer goods (or window-shopped, thereby still showing dispositions toward consumerism and materialism), or leisurely strolled the streets around the central city square. Following the latest trends in Western fashion and taking care to appear well groomed in public indicate "modern" and "European" selfhood.

Such practices are an integral part of sociality and at the same time they were laden with additional significance to many of the young Albanians with whom I interacted. This significance is intimately bound up with what sociologist Rob Shields (1997: 188) terms "social spatialisation," namely "the ongoing social construction of the spatial at the level of the social imaginary (collective mythologies, presuppositions) as well as interventions in the landscape (for example, the built environment)." I am mainly interested here in geographical understandings of Skopje that are widespread in the Macedonian community and depict the southeastern, historically newer, mainly Macedonian-populated part as "modern" and "European," and the northwestern, mostly older and predominantly Albanian-populated part as "backward" and "Balkan." The underlying assumptions in the social production of space concern the mapping of ethnonational alterity onto the city's landscape and the definition of imagined boundaries. Macedonians and Albanians are thus considered to "belong" to certain parts of Skopje as the city landscape becomes imbued with symbolic meaning and value.

It is against this background of a rigid and compartmentalized Macedonian view of the world that looking one's "best" in downtown Skopje had political significance: it was a means for many Albanians with whom I worked to blur the imagined boundaries drawn by members of the Macedonian community, and confront and redress anti-Albanian prejudice in Macedonian society. What is more, Albanians in Skopje tended to promulgate forcefully alternative social and moral understandings and symbolic meanings, according to which they were "modern" and "European" and Macedonians should accept the Albanian collectivity as such. The performance of "modern" selfhood in the so-called Macedonian part of the city was not so much a way to assert sameness. Rather, it represented an in-your-face, simultaneously proud and celebratory, assertion of Albanian-ness: an assertion that Albanians should not and would not be excluded from, or marginalized in, Macedonian society. Indeed, as Henrietta Moore (1994: 83) notes, "Shifting the grounds of meaning, reading against the grain, is often something done through practice, that is, through the day-to-day activities that take place within symbolically structured space. This . . . can include using space in a different way or commandeering space for new uses or invading the space of others." Jean Comaroff's observation regarding ritual (1985: 119) is also equally and aptly applicable here: "Ritual is always the product of a more or less conflicted social reality; a process within which an attempt is made to impress a dominant message upon a set of paradoxical or discordant representations."

While they took place prior to the eruption of the insurgency, such ritualistic missions downtown acquired a stronger sense of urgency as the conflict intensified. I noticed, for example, how many Albanians with whom I worked conversed with me in Albanian unusually loudly and distinctly while they were downtown, window-shopping, strolling along the main shopping mall and central square, or sitting at downtown cafés. The subject of the conversation did not seem to make much difference; the extravagant prices of Western brand clothing, the rainy weather, the peace demonstrations, the food eaten at home that day—each and every topic was discussed in a loud voice in Albanian while we were downtown. Uncomfortable with the possibility that we might be drawing too much attention, especially since the sense of impending war was enfolding the capital, I once suggested to Bukuria, a hairdresser in her early twenties who lived in Skopje with her husband and his extended family and dressed in Western-style outfits that we might want to keep our voices down. Without hesitation, she responded: "I want all Macedonians to hear me speak Albanian so that they can see that we [Albanians] are human, too [*Edhe ne jemi njerëz*]!"

Albanians with aspirations for socioeconomic mobility, then, made a point of asserting their presence and demonstrating "modern" dispositions at a time when the very humanity of Albanians was openly or allusively criticized by the Macedonian-language media and a large segment of the general populace. In so doing, they blatantly refuted the construction of the Albanian community in essentialist terms, undermined Macedonian-ness as a necessary attribute of humanness, and insisted that they be respected. In view of the growing success of the NLA insurgency, members of the Macedonian collectivity were particularly commanded to accommodate Albanian ethnonational difference and insurgent demands for greater rights. The victories of the NLA and the defeats of the Macedonian security forces on the battlefront, together with the international attention paid to the insurgency, in other words, gave the assertion of Albanian-ness in downtown Skopje particular poignancy. As if to rub salt into the wound, Albanian social actors set out to emphasize that they had become a force to be reckoned with, a force that Macedonians could not afford to ignore.

Public performances of "modern" selfhood in this context cannot be separated from the mobilization of personal memories and emotions for the performative pursuit of private and collective interests. Consider the example of my neighbor Artan, who arrived in Skopje from Kosovo, together with his mother and two siblings, after his father passed away in the mid-1980s. Artan's mother was originally from a village in the vicinity of the city and wanted to return to Macedonia to be closer to some of her relatives. The family relocated to Skopje so that Artan could enroll in Zef Lush Marku, the only high school with an Albanian-language track in the city. On high school graduation and unable to continue his studies due to insufficient financial means, Artan had found a job in a mini-market and grown increasingly dissatisfied with the limited opportunities for socioeconomic advancement in Macedonia. During our conversations and downtown outings, Artan stressed that he was especially distraught over the difficulties he was experiencing in finding a higher-paying job with better working conditions because, he argued, he did not have the proper personal connections (*vrski*)—people in managerial positions who could hire or vouch for him. Artan, like many Albanians who wished to advance claims for rights and equality by inviting public scrutiny during the insurgency, recognized that Macedonians, too, encountered such difficulties, but often asserted that Albanians were in an altogether disadvantageous position because of the widespread ethnic and religious prejudice against them.

The insurgency thus provided some people with a compelling framework for making selected past experiences legible—for making the past "usable" (see Brown and Hamilakis 2003). I do not mean to exclude the possibility that young Albanians who were well integrated into Macedonian society (professionals with jobs in state institutions or high-paying jobs in private firms and organizations) and endorsed capitalist values did not engage in this process of history-making and assert in public "modern" selfhood and nationhood vis-à-vis Macedonians. I did not, however, observe such enactments during my field research in the early 2000s (or during my subsequent field trips to Macedonia), and so I cannot discuss such potential cases. At all events, performances of "modern" selfhood highlighted Albanians' insistence on confronting and redefining the negative image of the Albanian collectivity and their willingness to sustain and promote in a strong and assertive way a sense of belonging to Macedonian society in the midst of fluctuating and unpredictable circumstances. Like performances of respectable selfhood, they were meant to address the status of the Albanian collectivity in Macedonia without resorting to violence, and provide nonmilitary alternatives to armed conflict.

Epilogue

Despite a string of tit-for-tat killings in August that seriously threatened to derail international mediation efforts, the armed conflict between the Macedonian armed forces and the Albanian NLA came to an official end with the signing of the Framework Agreement in the Macedonian town of Ohrid on 13 August 2001.[1] The Agreement, brokered by the international community, was signed by late president of the Republic of Macedonia Boris Trajkovski and political leaders of the four main government and opposition Macedonian and Albanian parties—namely, Ljupčo Georgievski (VMRO-DPMNE), Branko Crvenkovski (SDSM), Arben Xhaferi (DPA/PDSH), and Imer Imeri (PDP/PPD). It served as the basis for amendments to the 1991 Founding Constitution and for legislation (on, among other issues, decentralization and the redrawing of municipal boundaries) meant to address directly Albanian grievances and improve the overall status of the Albanian community in Macedonia in exchange for the NLA's voluntary surrender of insurgent weapons to NATO and disbandment (for the full text of the Agreement, see Appendix).

NATO's thirty-day arms collection operation, officially called Operation Essential Harvest and organized in response to Boris Trajkovski's request for NATO to assist in disarmament of the NLA, was met with anger by members of the Macedonian community. On 1 September hundreds of Macedonians, mainly internally displaced persons, gathered in front of the Parliament building in Skopje to protest NATO's allegedly pro-Albanian involvement in the crisis and keep MPs from entering to initiate parliamentary procedures for the implementation of the Framework Agreement. Anger did not preclude sharp satire, articulating a bitterly comic and bleak view of the political circumstances in Macedonia. In early September, several Macedonian-language television and newspaper media groups, without participation of the Albanian-language media, organized an event inviting members of the general public to surrender their weapons voluntarily and deposit them in front of the Parliament building. The event was called Go Obravme Bostanot; the phrase translates into English as "Watermelon Harvest," thereby mocking the NATO operation, and is widely used in Macedonia to describe the unfavorable position in which one finds oneself when dealt a bad hand—"up the creek without a paddle." Two plastic dolls dressed in clothing bearing NATO insignia were placed in front of the Parliament building supposedly to oversee the disarmament process. Thousands of Macedonians (more than fifty thousand, according to newspaper estimates) participated in the event and deposited a wide variety of items, from rolling pins, watermelons, and vegetables to old TV antennas, music tapes, and plastic toy guns. After these "weapons" were collected, a delegation of Macedonian journalists who had helped organize the event met with the late Macedonian president to deliver a letter stating that the operation was a success and the weaponry would be passed to NATO for destruction. The "weapons" were piled onto tractors and unloaded in front of NATO headquarters in Skopje. The NATO officers on duty at the scene were also presented with a few watermelons—a gift they accepted at first but later, during a regular NATO press briefing, returned to the journalists.

In late September, NATO announced that it had exceeded its goal of collecting thirty three hundred insurgent weapons, and declared Operation Essential Harvest a success. NLA leader Ali Ahmeti also announced that the insurgent army had disbanded. Under international pressure, including threats to cancel an aid donors' conference for Macedonia scheduled for October, the articles in Annex A of the Agreement were converted into constitutional amendments and adopted by the Macedonian Parliament on 17 November 2001.[2] The Constitution no longer referred to Macedonia as "the national state of the Macedonian people" and instead promoted among all peoples a sense of civic belonging to the Macedonian state. Specifically, the amended Preamble read: "The citizens of the Republic of Macedonia, taking over responsibility for the present and future of their fatherland . . . have decided to establish the Republic of Macedonia as an independent, sovereign state, with the intention of establishing and consolidating rule of law, guaranteeing human rights and civil liberties, providing peace and coexistence, social justice, economic well-being and prosperity in the life of the individual and the community." Additional amendments mandated that in units of local self-government where at least 20 percent of the population spoke a language other than Macedonian that language and its alphabet become official in addition to Macedonian and the Cyrillic alphabet. Moreover, the Constitution guaranteed the equitable representation of all communities—and hence the increase in the percentage of Albanians—in public bodies at all levels and in other areas of public life (for the complete list of amendments, see Appendix).

Post-2001 Volatility

Post-2001 Macedonia has been marked by tension and uncertainty surrounding the full and fair implementation of the Framework Agreement. For the most part, Macedonians and Albanians supported the Agreement in the direct aftermath of the armed conflict and viewed it as a necessary step toward domestic stabilization.[3] At the same time, many Macedonians to this day feel that they were forced into making major concessions to the Albanian community and remain anxious that the Framework Agreement has strengthened alleged Albanian irredentist aspirations in the Balkans, including the partition of Macedonia.

In the months immediately following the end of the conflict, and with NATO peacekeepers on the ground, the issues of amnesty for former NLA insurgents and return of displaced persons and refugees generated spirited controversy in the country. After the June 2002 parliamentary elections, the formation of a new coalition government between the rather moderate Macedonian Social Democratic Union of Macedonia (SDSM) and the Albanian Democratic Union for Integration (DUI), organized by former NLA leader Ali Ahmeti, gave international observers reason to hope for the smooth implementation of the Agreement. Political tensions persisted, nonetheless, and centered on heightened disagreement between government and opposition parties regarding the extent and pace of implentation of institutional reforms. To address national security concerns, President Trajkovski asked the EU to launch its first-ever peacekeeping mission, Concordia, between March and December 2003 as a follow-up to NATO's peacekeeping operation, and the police mission Proxima, aimed at combating corruption and organized crime in the Balkan region, between December 2003 and December 2005.

When Nikola Gruevski, successor of Ljubčo Georgievski as leader of the center-right party VMRO-DPMNE, won the July 2006 parliamentary elections and chose the Democratic Party of Albanians (DPA) and three smaller parties as his coalition partners, trouble erupted. Gruevski's decision to exclude from the government coalition the Albanian party DUI, which had won the greatest number of Albanian votes, angered DUI members and supporters. Thousands of DUI activists protested in front of the Parliament building, blocked major roads, and boycotted Parliament for a couple of months. Rumors, and boastful claims made by hard-liners, that Albanians might again take up arms swirled around Skopje. DUI's return to Parliament in early September 2006 was short-lived: in January 2007 the party boycotted Parliament for four months, alleging poor implementation of the Framework Agreement. Bitter wrangling between Macedonian and Albanian, and also among Albanian parties over constitutional and institutional amendments continued after DUI's return to Parliament and in the end gave way to political stagnation.

To complicate matters farther, the Kosovo Assembly's declaration of independence from Serbia at an extraordinary meeting on 17 February 2008 generated intense anxiety among many people in Macedonia. Although Macedonia recognized the independence of Kosovo in October 2008 and the two countries established diplomatic ties a year later, fears that radical Albanian elements might provoke political turmoil, aimed at uniting the predominantly Albanian-populated parts of northwestern Macedonia with Kosovo, are still widespread. Such fears spring from Serbia's refusal to recognize Kosovo's declaration of independence and from the lingering dispute over the Kosovo-Serbia boundary. Domestic and regional volatility and fears for the future of the country have also been greatly exacerbated by Macedonia's exclusion from NATO and the EU on account of the still unresolved name dispute between Greece and Macedonia. Tensions between these two countries reached new heights after the resumption of negotiations to resolve the name dispute in early 2008. Shortly before the annual NATO summit in Bucharest in April 2008, Greek prime minister Kostas Karamanlis stated: "Without a mutually accepted solution [to the name], there cannot be a membership invitation."[4] At the same time, billboards that advertised a private art exhibit and reproduced a painting entitled *60 Years of Exodus* (*60 godini ekzodus*) appeared in Skopje featuring the Greek flag with the swastika instead of the cross; the artist placed in the middle of the main field of the flag a photograph of his grandparents and their children who, like thousands of other Macedonian-speaking families, left their homes and properties in northern Greece during the Greek Civil War (1946–49) and and fled to the Republic of Macedonia.

The association between Nazi Germany and Greece sparked Greek fury and a few days later, on 3 April 2008, Greece vetoed Macedonia's bid to join NATO, openly disregarding the significant progress Macedonia had made toward the satisfaction of the criteria for accession established in NATO's Membership Action Plan (Chivvis 2008: 156). The action also flouted Article 11,

Paragraph 1, of the 1995 Interim Accord under which Greece would not object to Macedonia's application for membership in international, multilateral, and regional organizations and institutions unless Macedonia applied using a name different from "The former Yugoslav Republic of Macedonia." Greece threatened to undertake similar action when Macedonia tries to join NATO and the EU in the future (Macedonia gained the status of EU candidate member state in 2005) unless the country changed its name.

Under such strained circumstances, Premier Gruevski called early parliamentary elections for June 2008. The election was marred by allegations of fraud and intimidation, and violence involving supporters of the two main Albanian parties DUI and DPA. One Albanian man was killed in a shootout with Macedonian police in the village of Aračinovo and several others were wounded during clashes among supporters of the two main rival Albanian groups. These events had the effect of yet another shock to the body politic. I was in Skopje when the events unfolded and witnessed how rumors of renewed armed violence circulated among the populace, spreading fear and confusion. The Macedonian government came under international criticism for ineffectiveness to organize "free and fair" elections—a designation that, as Coles (2007) notes, has become largely synonymous with democratic governance—and a repeat election was organized a couple of weeks later in areas where irregularities occurred in the first round. Appealing to a bruised sense of Macedonian national pride, the VMRO-DPMNE-led electoral block won the healthiest majority in Parliament (almost 49 percent of the vote) in over a decade and this time around Gruevski chose as its coalation partner the Albanian DUI, which secured almost 13 percent of the vote compared to the almost 8.5 percent by the Albanian DPA.[5]

The coalition came under fresh strain in September 2009 when MANU published a two-volume encyclopedia claiming, among other things, that Albanians had settled in Macedonia in the sixteenth century and referring to them as Šiptari and "highlanders" (planinci). Albanian politicians and intellectuals from Macedonia, Albania, and Kosovo condemned the publication, and Ahmeti said in a television appearance that the truce that had existed between Macedonians and Albanians since 2001 in Macedonia was broken. He also threatened to leave the coalition unless the prime minister distanced himself from the publication. Academician Blaže Ristovski was subsequently discharged from his duties as encyclopedia chief editor, and MANU announced it would replace the disputed passages with new ones. Gruevski called for dialogue, and the government continued its work. Political turmoil was renewed in 2011 by the opposition's boycott of Parliament over allegations that the government violated media freedom. Early parliamentary elections were scheduled for June 2011. VMRO-DPMNE and its partners won a decisive victory (56 seats in the 120-seat Parliament, 7 fewer than in the previous elections) and formed a government coalition with DUI (15 seats in the 120-seat Parliament, 3 fewer than in the previous elections) after Gruevski met Ahmeti's prerequisite requirements—amending the laws on language use and the use of flags, and dropping four cases of alleged crimes by the NLA in 2001.[6]

The Challenges Ahead

In 2011, more than ten years after the signing of the Ohrid Framework Agreement, uncertainty about the political future of Macedonia remains high. Undoubtedly, many of the reforms laid out in the Ohrid Framework Agreement have already been, or are in the process of being, implemented. To name but a couple, the controversial Albanian University in Mala Rečica near Tetovo was officially recognized as a state institution of higher learning in January 2004 (see Balalovska 2006; Ragaru 2008). Also, the Macedonian Parliament passed a law on the redrawing of municipal boundaries (Law on Territorial Organization of Local Self-Government) in August 2004, strengthening local self-government. Efforts continue at the national level to ensure proportional representation of all communities in state administration, enhance local self-government, implement decentralization measures, and improve the efficiency of the judicial system (see also Daftary and Friedman 2008). Nonetheless, there is an ongoing controversy over whether reforms should reflect the spirit or the letter of the Agreement (see, for example, Bieber 2008).

To exacerbate challenges relating to the implementation of the Framework Agreement and its implications for Macedonia's future, the political instrumentalization of religion contributes to an ongoing ethnoreligious polarization. In 2002, a 66-meter cross (Millennium Cross) was installed on the highest point of Mount Vodno, which overlooks Skopje, for the proclaimed purpose of celebrating 2000 years of Christianity in Macedonia and the world. When brightly lit at night, the cross can hardly escape the attention of city residents and visitors. The initiative was undertaken by the Macedonian Orthodox Church and funded in part by the VMRO-DPMNE-led government of Ljubčo Georgievski despite public controversy and objections by Macedonian opposition and Albanian leaders, over the high cost (three million Euros, reportedly) and the arrogant disregard for Macedonia's multiculturalism.[7] Georgievski's adamant endorsement of the initiative is best understood as an effort to ignite support for his party if one takes into account the crisis of legitimacy that VMRO-DPMNE suffered during the 2001 conflict. According to an opinion poll in July 2001, for example, the party's percentage of popular support plummeted from around 12 percent prior to the outbreak of violence to 7.4 percent.[8]

While it did not help boost the party's popularity (the rival SDSM won more seats in the parliamentary elections of September 2002 and, together with DUI, formed an SDSM-led government coalition), the installation of the Millennium Cross contributed to further radicalization of the Albanian population. Specifically, the rebuilding of the Aračinovo village mosque, which was destroyed by Macedonian government forces during fighting in 2001 under the pretext that NLA insurgents fired mortars from the mosque, was undertaken in 2002 largely on the initiative of DUI. The project was completed in 2008, and the mosque now has two minarets (it had one minaret before it was destroyed) and stands 76 meters high—taller than the Millennium Cross. Equally noteworthy, and indicative of ethnoreligious antagonism in post-2001 Macedonia, DUI inaugurated in 2006 on Albanian Flag Day (28 November) an equestrian statue of Gjergj Kastrioti, widely known as Skanderbeg and regarded as an Albanian national hero.[9] The statue in Skopje depicts Skanderbeg holding the rein of his horse in his left hand, while extending his right arm forward at chest level and holding the palm of his hand open. The statue is strategically placed in the south entrance to the Turska Čaršija opposite Vodno and is facing the Millennium Cross (see Figure 8).[10] More recently in February 2011, eight people were injured when Macedonian and Albanian groups clashed over building a church-looking structure on the hill where an Ottoman fortress stands overlooking the old Stone Bridge in downtown Skopje (Skopsko Kale). The structure is built atop the foundations of a thirteenth-century church discovered during recent excavations and, according to the Cultural Heritage Protection Office, will house an archaeological museum featuring artifacts unearthed in the hill area.

Besides such controversial and divisive initiatives, an antiquitization movement that seeks to lay claim to the cultural heritage of ancient Macedonia also contributes to ethnoreligious polarization and further exacerbates the already strenuous political relations with Greece. A brainchild of Macedonian radicals, who aim to increase their popularity in post-independence Macedonia by engaging Greek attacks against Macedonian identity, the antiquitization movement gained momentum in the aftermath of the 2001 crisis. Manifestations of this movement include decisions by the VMRO-

Figure 8. Statue of Skanderbeg in Skopje. Photo by author.

DPMNE-led government and Prime Minister Gruevski to rename the capital's airport "Skopje International Alexander the Great Airport," Skopje's stadium "Philip II Arena," and the main highway E75, which cuts across the country from Serbia to Greece, "Alexander of Macedon." Also notable in this regard are private yet government-endorsed initiatives to establish kin ties with the Hunzukuts, a tribal group in Pakistan that claims descent from

Alexander the Great (comparable initiatives are undertaken in Greece; see
Neofotistos 2012). The movement reached a new level with the purported
discovery by MANU member Tome Boševski and Professor Aristotel Tentov
that the Rosetta Stone was written in ancient Macedonian, a language allegedly closely related to modern Macedonian (cf. Ilievski 2006).

A physical and most recent example of the antiquitization movement is
the so-called Skopje 2014 project. This multimillion-Euro urban project, first
made known in 2009 and managed by the Macedonian Ministry of Culture
and the Municipality of Centar, includes among other tasks the building of
an Orthodox church (Sts. Constantine and Helena church), and the erection
of a monument depicting Alexander the Great on his horse and at least a
dozen tall statues of other historical figures, whom the government claims
as Macedonian, in and around the central square of the capital.[11] Albanian
and Macedonian opposition parties demanded for over six months that the
project be discussed in Parliament, arguing that the project was exceedingly
costly, obliterated the historical presence and contributions of non-Ortho-
dox and non-Macedonian communities in Macedonia, and thus provided
a breeding ground for economic, social, and political destabilization in the
country. Protests by Macedonian groups (mainly student activists) Prva Arhi
Brigada, or "First Archi-Brigade," and Progresiven Mlad Sindikat, or "Progressive Youth Syndicate," also took place in downtown Skopje. Despite these
reactions, three bronze statues were already erected by June 2010. In June
2011 a 14.5-meter, 30-ton bronze statue of Alexander the Great was installed
atop a high pedestal, generating new concerns about possible Greek retalia-
tion despite the statue's official name "Warrior on a Horse" (*Voin na Konj*).[12]
The statue is surrounded by eight bronze lions and soldiers, carrying shields
bearing the 14-ray variant of the so-called sun/star of Vergina (or "sun/star of
Kutleš," as the symbol is known in today's Macedonia)—a variant of the symbol on which Greece, as of this writing, does not hold a registered trademark.
As of this writing, plans to carry out the project remain in effect and more
than half a dozen statues have been erected.

The political situation in post-independence Kosovo, as mentioned earlier, continues to cast a long shadow over Macedonia and has become an ar-
row in DUI's political quiver, raising uncertainty as to whether the potential
for war in Macedonia and the region has completely disappeared. Uncertainty came to a head in late July 2011 when Kosovo Albanian authorities in
Prishtina sent special police units to take control of northern border crossings
from the European Union Rule of Law Mission in Kosovo (EULEX Kosovo),
and enforce a block on imports from Serbia in retribution for Serbia's ban

on Kosovo's exports since 2008. A group of Serb hard-liners attacked and set ablaze the Jarinje border post, killing one Albanian policeman, and local Serbs set up barricades and blocked road traffic. KFOR declared the area a military zone, and KFOR troops came under attack by machine guns and rockets before taking control of Kosovo's border crossings. Commenting on the events, as the ten-year anniversary of the signing of the Ohrid Framework Agreement was approaching, Ali Ahmeti stated the following in a TV interview: "If there are pretensions to change [Kosovo's] borders, I do not take any responsibility whatsoever to become the guardian of peace in Macedonia because a situation might arise whereby people self-organize in the same way as in 1990, 1999, and 2001." Ahmeti added, "If the situation gets out of control no one can take responsibility or guarantee that Albanians do not organize a common front."[13]

Last, but certainly not least, the name dispute with Greece continues to compound uncertainty over Macedonia's political future and exacerbate social tensions, economic hardship, and ethnonational rivalries. Shortly after Greece successfully blocked Macedonia's entry to NATO in 2008, Macedonia filed a lawsuit at the International Court of Justice in The Hague against Greece, accusing it of violating the 1995 Interim Accord. Greece claims that Macedonia violated the Accord by usurping Greek heritage and harboring territorial aspirations. As of this writing, a decision is expected in fall 2011. Negotiations between the two sides on the name issue have not yielded any positive results and, as this book was going to press, no solution appeared in sight.

Perseverance in the Face of Volatility

As we have seen, the 2001 armed conflict is symptomatic of persistent struggles over the sociopolitical order in post-1991 Macedonia. The eruption and unfolding of the NLA insurgency created renewed uncertainty and anxiety about the future of the country and its people, compounded by the security situation in neighboring Kosovo at that time. To position themselves in the midst of extremely unpredictable and dangerously unstable circumstances, Macedonian and Albanian social actors in Skopje during interpersonal, intergroup interactions engaged in a multiplicity of practices and performances that were united in the eschewal of one single and absolute meaning—eschewal, that is, of any suggestion of definitive truth about the nature of social reality and the configuration of everyday life. People who enjoyed professional or long-standing social ties claimed to rationalize armed hostilities as *politika* and often discussed positive memories of the socialist period, mutually creating a harmonious, uncontested social order. Efforts by male and female Macedonians to define the sociopolitical order based on their own terms were wittingly undercut by members of the Albanian community. Moreover, social performances of "modern" and respectable Albanian selfhood were attempts to confront negative assumptions regarding the position of Albanians in Macedonian society and without resort to arms opened up the possibility of a new social and moral order. The social performances and practices of everyday sociality analyzed in this book did not, of course, completely eliminate the risk of war; they nonetheless helped to highlight and promote indeterminacy at the level of everyday life and ward off war.

My ethnographic account of the 2001 political crisis then reveals how an end to the violence that threatened to engulf Macedonia was by no means in the hands of the international community alone. Far from being passive onlookers, members of the Macedonian and Albanian communities navigated their way through turbulent and uncertain times and helped to counter the threat of the spread of armed violence throughout the whole country. Their resilience and inventiveness can help us to better understand how post-independence Macedonia has thus far persevered, perhaps against all odds, in the face of extreme volatility and external pressures. The interpersonal exchanges and negotiations through which they produced meaning in the midst of crisis offer a more comprehensive picture of the dynamics that shape violence and peace in the contemporary world.

Ohrid Framework Agreement
and the 2001 Constitutional Amendments

The following points comprise an agreed framework for securing the future of Macedonia's democracy and permitting the development of closer and more integrated relations between the Republic of Macedonia and the Euro-Atlantic community. This Framework will promote the peaceful and harmonious development of civil society while respecting the ethnic identity and the interests of all Macedonian citizens.

1. Basic Principles

1.1. The use of violence in pursuit of political aims is rejected completely and unconditionally. Only peaceful political solutions can assure a stable and democratic future for Macedonia.

1.2. Macedonia's sovereignty and territorial integrity, and the unitary character of the State are inviolable and must be preserved. There are no territorial solutions to ethnic issues.

1.3. The multi-ethnic character of Macedonia's society must be preserved and reflected in public life.

1.4. A modern democratic state in its natural course of development and maturation must continually ensure that its Constitution fully meets the needs of all its citizens and comports with the highest international standards, which themselves continue to evolve.

The full text of the Agreement can be found on the official website of the Secretariat for the Implementation of the Framework Agreement: http://siofa.gov.mk/mk/. The Constitution of the Republic of Macedonia can be found on the official website of the Macedonian Parliament: http://www.sobranie.mk/en/default-en.asp?ItemID=9F7452BF44EE814B8DB897C18 58B71FF.

1.5. The development of local self-government is essential for encouraging the participation of citizens in democratic life, and for promoting respect for the identity of communities.

2. Cessation of Hostilities

2.1. The parties underline the importance of the commitments of July 5, 2001. There shall be a complete cessation of hostilities, complete voluntary disarmament of the ethnic Albanian armed groups and their complete voluntary disbandment. They acknowledge that a decision by NATO to assist in this context will require the establishment of a general, unconditional and open-ended cease-fire, agreement on a political solution to the problems of this country, a clear commitment by the armed groups to voluntarily disarm, and acceptance by all the parties of the conditions and limitations under which the NATO forces will operate.

3. Development of Decentralized Government

3.1. A revised Law on Local Self-Government will be adopted that reinforces the powers of elected local officials and enlarges substantially their competencies in conformity with the Constitution (as amended in accordance with Annex A) and the European Charter on Local Self-Government, and reflecting the principle of subsidiarity in effect in the European Union. Enhanced competencies will relate principally to the areas of public services, urban and rural planning, environmental protection, local economic development, culture, local finances, education, social welfare, and health care. A law on financing of local self-government will be adopted to ensure an adequate system of financing to enable local governments to fulfill all of their responsibilities.

3.2. Boundaries of municipalities will be revised within one year of the completion of a new census, which will be conducted under international supervision by the end of 2001. The revision of the municipal boundaries will be effectuated by the local and national authorities with international participation.

3.3. In order to ensure that police are aware of and responsive to the needs and interests of the local population, local heads of police will be selected by municipal councils from lists of candidates proposed by the Ministry of Interior, and will communicate regularly with the councils. The Ministry of Interior will retain the authority to remove local heads of police in accordance with the law.

4. Non-Discrimination and Equitable Representation

4.1. The principle of non-discrimination and equal treatment of all under the law will be respected completely. This principle will be applied in particular with respect to employment in public administration and public enterprises, and access to public financing for business development.

4.2. Laws regulating employment in public administration will include measures to assure equitable representation of communities in all central and local public bodies and at all levels of employment within such bodies, while respecting the rules concerning competence and integrity that govern public administration. The authorities will take action to correct present imbalances in the composition of the public administration, in particular through the recruitment of members of under-represented communities. Particular attention will be given to ensuring as rapidly as possible that the police services will generally reflect the composition and distribution of the population of Macedonia, as specified in Annex C.

4.3. For the Constitutional Court, one-third of the judges will be chosen by the Assembly by a majority of the total number of Representatives that includes a majority of the total number of Representatives claiming to belong to the communities not in the majority in the population of Macedonia. This procedure also will apply to the election of the Ombudsman (Public Attorney) and the election of three of the members of the Judicial Council.

5. Special Parliamentary Procedures

5.1. On the central level, certain Constitutional amendments in accordance with Annex A and the Law on Local Self-Government cannot be approved without a qualified majority of two-thirds of votes, within which there must be a majority of the votes of Representatives claiming to belong to the communities not in the majority in the population of Macedonia.

5.2. Laws that directly affect culture, use of language, education, personal documentation, and use of symbols, as well as laws on local finances, local elections, the city of Skopje, and boundaries of municipalities must receive a majority of votes, within which there must be a majority of the votes of the Representatives claiming to belong to the communities not in the majority in the population of Macedonia.

6. Education and Use of Languages

6.1. With respect to primary and secondary education, instruction will be provided in the students' native languages, while at the same time uniform standards for academic programs will be applied throughout Macedonia.

6.2. State funding will be provided for university level education in languages spoken by at least 20 percent of the population of Macedonia, on the basis of specific agreements.

6.3. The principle of positive discrimination will be applied in the enrolment in State universities of candidates belonging to communities not in the majority in the population of Macedonia until the enrolment reflects equitably the composition of the population of Macedonia.

6.4. The official language throughout Macedonia and in the international relations of Macedonia is the Macedonian language.

6.5. Any other language spoken by at least 20 percent of the population is also an official language, as set forth herein. In the organs of the Republic of Macedonia, any official language other than Macedonian may be used in accordance with the law, as further elaborated in Annex B. Any person living in a unit of local self-government in which at least 20 percent of the population speaks an official language other than Macedonian may use any official language to communicate with the regional office of the central government with responsibility for that municipality; such an office will reply in that language in addition to Macedonian. Any person may use any official language to communicate with a main office of the central government, which will reply in that language in addition to Macedonian.

6.6. With respect to local self-government, in municipalities where a community comprises at least 20 percent of the population of the municipality, the language of that community will be used as an official language in addition to Macedonian. With respect to languages spoken by less than 20 percent of the population of the municipality, the local authorities will decide democratically on their use in public bodies.

6.7. In criminal and civil judicial proceedings at any level, an accused person or any party will have the right to translation at State expense of all proceedings as well as documents in accordance with relevant Council of Europe documents.

6.8. Any official personal documents of citizens speaking an official language other than Macedonian will also be issued in that language, in addition to the Macedonian language, in accordance with the law.

7. Expression of Identity

7.1. With respect to emblems, next to the emblem of the Republic of Macedonia, local authorities will be free to place on front of local public buildings emblems marking the identity of the community in the majority in the municipality, respecting international rules and usages.

8. Implementation

8.1. The Constitutional amendments attached at Annex A will be presented to the Assembly immediately. The parties will take all measures to assure adoption of these amendments within 45 days of signature of this Framework Agreement.

8.2. The legislative modifications identified in Annex B will be adopted in accordance with the timetables specified therein.

8.3. The parties invite the international community to convene at the

language other than Macedonian shall also be issued in that language, in addition to the Macedonian language, in accordance with the law.

(4) Any person living in a unit of local self-government in which at least 20 percent of the population speaks an official language other than Macedonian may use that official language to communicate with the regional office of the central government with responsibility for that municipality; such an office shall reply in that language in addition to Macedonian. Any person may use any official language to communicate with a main office of the central government, which shall reply in that language in addition to Macedonian.

(5) In the organs of the Republic of Macedonia, any official language other than Macedonian may be used in accordance with the law.

(6) In the units of local self-government where at least 20 percent of the population speaks a particular language, that language and its alphabet shall be used as an official language in addition to the Macedonian language and the Cyrillic alphabet. With respect to languages spoken by less than 20 percent of the population of a unit of local self-government, the local authorities shall decide on their use in public bodies.

[*Before the article was converted into an amendment and adopted by Parliament (Amendment V, which replaced Article 7), Article 7 of the Macedonian Constitution read:*

The Macedonian language, written using its Cyrillic alphabet, is the official language in the Republic of Macedonia. In the units of local self-government where the majority of the inhabitants belong to a nationality, in addition to the Macedonian language and Cyrillic alphabet, their language and alphabet are also in official use, in a manner determined by law. In the units of local self-government where there is a considerable number of inhabitants belonging to a nationality, their language and alphabet are also in official use, in addition to the Macedonian language and Cyrillic alphabet, under conditions and in a manner determined by law.]

Article 8

(1) The fundamental values of the constitutional order of the Republic of Macedonia are

• the basic freedoms and rights of the individual and citizen, recognized in international law and set down in the Constitution;

• equitable representation of persons belonging to all communities in public bodies at all levels and in other areas of public life; . . . .

[*Before the article was converted into an amendment and adopted by Par-*

liament (Amendment VI, which is an addition to line 2 of Article 8), Article 8 of the Macedonian Constitution read:

The fundamental values of the constitutional order of the Republic of Macedonia are:

• the basic freedoms and rights of the individual and citizen, recognized in international law and set down in the Constitution;

• the basic freedoms and rights of the individual and citizen, recognized in international law and set down in the Constitution;

• the free expression of national identity;

• the rule of law;

• the division of state powers into legislative, executive and judicial;

• political pluralism and free, direct and democratic elections;

• the legal protection of property;

• the freedom of the market and entrepreneurship;

• humanism, social justice and solidarity;

• local self-government;

• proper urban and rural planning to promote a congenial human environment, as well as ecological protection and development; and

• respect for the generally accepted norms of international law.]

Article 19

(1) The freedom of religious confession is guaranteed.

(2) The right to express one's faith freely and publicly, individually or with others is guaranteed.

(3) The Macedonian Orthodox Church, the Islamic Religious Community in Macedonia, the Catholic Church, and other Religious communities and groups are separate from the state and equal before the law.

(4) The Macedonian Orthodox Church, the Islamic Religious Community in Macedonia, the Catholic Church, and other Religious communities and groups are free to establish schools and other social and charitable institutions, by ways of a procedure regulated by law.

[After Article 19 of Annex A of the Agreement was converted into a amendment and adopted by Parliament, the Amendment (Amendment VII, whose Items 1 and 2 replaced paragraphs 3 and 4 respectively of Article 19 of the Constitution) read:

1. The Macedonian Orthodox Church, as well as the Islamic Religious Community in Macedonia, the Catholic Church, Evangelical Methodist Church, the Jewish Community and other Religious communities and groups are separate from the state and equal before the law.

2. The Macedonian Orthodox Church, as well as the Islamic Religious Community in Macedonia, the Catholic Church, Evangelical Methodist Church, the Jewish Community and other Religious communities and groups are free to establish schools and other social and charitable institutions, by way of a procedure regulated by law.

Prior to the adoption of the amendment, Article 19 of the Macedonian Constitution read:

The freedom of religious confession is guaranteed. The right to express one's faith freely and publicly, individually or with others is guaranteed. The Macedonian Orthodox Church and other religious communities and groups are separate from the state and equal before the law. The Macedonian Orthodox Church and other religious communities and groups are free to establish schools and other social and charitable institutions, by way of a procedure regulated by law.]

Article 48

(1) Members of communities have a right freely to express, foster and develop their identity and community attributes, and to use their community symbols.

(2) The Republic guarantees the protection of the ethnic, cultural, linguistic and religious identity of all communities.

(3) Members of communities have the right to establish institutions for culture, art, science and education, as well as scholarly and other associations for the expression, fostering and development of their identity.

(4) Members of communities have the right to instruction in their language in primary and secondary education, as determined by law. In schools where education is carried out in another language, the Macedonian language is also studied.

[*Before the article was converted into an amendment and adopted by Parliament (Amendment VIII, which replaced Article 48), Article 48 of the Macedonian Constitution read:*

Members of nationalities have a right freely to express, foster and develop their identity and national attributes. The Republic guarantees the protection of the ethnic, cultural, linguistic and religious identity of the nationalities. Members of the nationalities have the right to establish institutions for culture and art, as well as scholarly and other associations for the expression, fostering and development of their identity. Members of the nationalities have the right to instruction in their language in primary and secondary education, as determined by law. In schools where education is carried out in the language of a nationality, the Macedonian language is also studied.]

Article 56

(2) The Republic guarantees the protection, promotion and enhancement of the historical and artistic heritage of Macedonia and all communities in Macedonia and the treasures of which it is composed, regardless of their legal status. The law regulates the mode and conditions under which specific items of general interest for the Republic can be ceded for use.

[*Before the article was converted into an amendment and adopted by Parliament (Amendment IX, which replaced paragraph 2 of Article 56), Article 56 of the Macedonian Constitution read:*

All the natural resources of the Republic of Macedonia, the flora and fauna, amenities in common use, as well as the objects and buildings of particular cultural and historical value determined by law, are amenities of common interest for the Republic and enjoy particular protection. The Republic guarantees the protection, promotion and enhancement of the historical and artistic heritage of the Macedonian people and of the nationalities and the treasures of which it is composed regardless of their legal status. The law regulates the mode and conditions under which specific items of general interest for the Republic can be ceded for use.]

Article 69

....

(2) For laws that directly affect culture, use of language, education, personal documentation, and use of symbols, the Assembly makes decisions by a majority vote of the Representatives attending, within which there must be a majority of the votes of the Representatives attending who belong to communities not in the majority in the population of Macedonia. In the event of a dispute within the Assembly regarding the application of this provision, the Committee on Inter-Community Relations shall resolve the dispute.

[*After Article 69 of Annex A of the Agreement was converted into an amendment and adopted by Parliament, the Amendment (Amendment X, which replaced Article 69 of the Constitution) read:*

1. The Assembly can take a decision if its meeting is attended by a majority of the total number of Representatives. The assembly makes decisions by a majority vote of the Representatives attending, but no less than one-third of the total number of Representatives, in so far as the Constitution does not provide for a qualified majority.

2. For laws that directly affect culture, use of language, education, personal documentation, and use of symbols, the Assembly makes decisions by a majority vote of the Representatives attending, within which there must be

a majority of the votes of the Representatives attending who belong to communities not in the majority in the population of Macedonia. In the event of a dispute within the Assembly regarding the application of this provision, the Committee on Inter-Community Relations shall resolve the dispute.

Prior to the adoption of the amendment (Amendment X, which replaced Article 69), Article 69 of the Macedonian Constitution read:

The Assembly may work if its meeting is attended by a majority of the total number of Representatives. The Assembly makes decisions by a majority vote of the Representatives attending, but no less than one-third of the total number of Representatives, in so far as the Constitution does not provide for a qualified majority.]

Article 77

(1) The Assembly elects the Public Attorney by a majority vote of the total number of Representatives, within which there must be a majority of the votes of the total number of Representatives claiming to belong to the communities not in the majority in the population of Macedonia.

(2) The Public Attorney protects the constitutional rights and legal rights of citizens when violated by bodies of state administration and by other bodies and organizations with public mandates. The Public Attorney shall give particular attention to safeguarding the principles of non-discrimination and equitable representation of communities in public bodies at all levels and in other areas of public life.

[*Before the article was converted into an amendment and adopted by Parliament (Amendment XI, whose Item 1 replaced paragraph 1 of Article 77 and Item 2 was added to paragraph 2 of Article 77), Article 77 of the Macedonian Constitution read:*

The Assembly elects the Public Attorney. The Public Attorney protects the constitutional and legal rights of citizens when violated by bodies of state administration and by other bodies and organizations with public mandates. The Public Attorney is elected for a term of eight years, with the right to one reelection. The conditions for election and dismissal, the sphere of competence and the mode of work of the Public Attorney are regulated by law.]

Article 78

(1) The Assembly shall establish a Committee for Inter-Community Relations.

(2) The Committee consists of seven members each from the ranks of the Macedonians and Albanians within the Assembly, and five members

from among the Turks, Vlahs, Romanies and two other communities. The five members each shall be from a different community; if fewer than five other communities are represented in the Assembly, the Public Attorney, after consultation with relevant community leaders, shall propose the remaining members from outside the Assembly.

(3) The Assembly elects the members of the Committee.

(4) The Committee considers issues of inter-community relations in the Republic and makes appraisals and proposals for their solution.

(5) The Assembly is obliged to take into consideration the appraisals and proposals of the Committee and to make decisions regarding them.

(6) In the event of a dispute among members of the Assembly regarding the application of the voting procedure specified in Article 69(2), the Committee shall decide by majority vote whether the procedure applies

[*After Article 78 of Annex A of the Agreement was converted into an amendment and adopted by Parliament, the Amendment (Amendment XII, whose Item 1 replaced Article 78; also, line 7 of Article 84 was deleted) read:*

1. The Assembly shall establish a Committee for Inter-Community Relations.

The Committee consists of 19 members of whom 7 members each are from the ranks of the Macedonians and Albanians within the Assembly, and a member each from among the Turks, Vlahs, Romas, Serbs, and Bosniaks. If one of the communities does not have representatives, the Public Attorney, after consultation with relevant representatives of those communities, shall propose the remaining members of the Committee."

Prior to the amendment, Article 78 of the Macedonian Constitution read:

The Assembly establishes a Council for Inter-Ethnic Relations. The Council consists of the President of the Assembly and two members each from the ranks of the Macedonians, Albanians, Turks, Vlahs and Romanies, as well as two members from the ranks of other nationalities in Macedonia. The President of the Assembly is President of the Council. The Assembly elects the members of the Council. The Council considers issues of inter-ethnic relations in the Republic and makes appraisals and proposals for their solution. The Assembly is obliged to take into consideration the appraisals and proposals of the Council and to make decisions regarding them.

Prior to the amendment, Article 84 of the Macedonian Constitution read:

The President of the Republic of Macedonia

• nominates a mandator to constitute the Government of the Republic of Macedonia;

• appoints and dismisses by decree ambassadors and other diplomatic representatives of the Republic of Macedonia abroad;

• accepts the credentials and letters of recall of foreign diplomatic representatives;

• proposes two judges to sit on the Constitutional Court of the Republic of Macedonia;

• proposes two members of the Republican Judicial Council;

• appoints three members to the Security Council of the Republic of Macedonia;

• proposes the members of the Council for Inter-Ethnic Relations;

• appoints and dismisses other holders of state and public office determined by the Constitution and the law;

• grants decorations and honours in accordance with the law;

• grants pardons in accordance with the law; and

• performs other duties determined by the Constitution.]

Article 84

The President of the Republic of Macedonia

• proposes the members of the Council for Inter-Ethnic Relations; (to be deleted) . . . .

[*On how Article 84 of the Macedonian Constitution read prior to the amendment (Amendment XII), see above.*]

Article 86

(1) The President of the Republic is President of the Security Council of the Republic of Macedonia.

(2) The Security Council of the Republic is composed of the President of the Republic, the President of the Assembly, the Prime Minister, the Ministers heading the bodies of state administration in the fields of security, defence and foreign affairs and three members appointed by the President of the Republic. In appointing the three members, the President shall ensure that the Security Council as a whole equitably reflects the composition of the population of Macedonia [added to paragraph 2 of Article 86 upon ratification]

(3) The Council considers issues relating to the security and defence of the Republic and makes policy proposals to the Assembly and the Government.

[*Before the article was converted into an amendment and adopted by Parliament (Amendment XIII, whose Item 1 was added to paragraph 2 of Article 86), Article 86 of the Macedonian Constitution read:*

The President of the Republic is President of the Security Council of the Republic of Macedonia. The Security Council of the Republic is composed of the President of the Republic, the President of the Assembly, the Prime Minister, the Ministers heading the bodies of state administration in the fields of security, defense and foreign affairs and three members appointed by the President of the Republic. The Council considers issues relating to the security and defense of the Republic and makes policy proposals to the Assembly and the Government.]

Article 104

(1) The Republican Judicial Council is composed of seven members.

(2) The Assembly elects the members of the Council. Three of the members shall be elected by a majority vote of the total number of Representatives, within which there must be a majority of the votes of the total number of Representatives claiming to belong to the communities not in the majority in the population of Macedonia [added to paragraph 2 of Article 104 upon ratification]

[*Before the article was converted into an amendment and adopted by Parliament (Amendment XIV, which was added to paragraph 2 of Article 104), Article 104 of the Macedonian Constitution read:*

The Republican Judicial Council is composed of seven members. The Assembly elects the members of the Council. The members of the Council are elected from the ranks of outstanding members of the legal profession for a term of six years with the right to one reelection. Members of the Republican Judicial Council are granted immunity. The Assembly decides on their immunity. The office of a member of the Republican Judicial Council is incompatible with the performance of other public offices, professions or membership in political parties.]

Article 109

(1) The Constitutional Court of Macedonia is composed of nine judges.

(2) The Assembly elects six of the judges to the Constitutional Court by a majority vote of the total number of Representatives. The Assembly elects three of the judges by a majority vote of the total number of Representatives, within which there must be a majority of the votes of the total number of Representatives claiming to belong to the communities not in the majority in the population of Macedonia

[*Before the article was converted into an amendment and adopted by Par-*

liament (Amendment XV, which replaced paragraph 2 of Article 109), Article 109 of the Macedonian Constitution read:

The Constitutional Court of the Republic of Macedonia is composed of nine judges. The Assembly elects the judges to the Constitutional Court by a majority vote of the total number of Representatives. The term of office of the judges is nine years without the right to reelection. The Constitutional Court elects a President from its own ranks for a term of three years without the right to reelection. Judges of the Constitutional Court are elected from the ranks of outstanding members of the legal profession.]

Article 114

(5) Local self-government is regulated by a law adopted by a two-thirds majority vote of the total number of Representatives, within which there must be a majority of the votes of the total number of Representatives claiming to belong to the communities not in the majority in the population of Macedonia. The laws on local finances, local elections, boundaries of municipalities, and the city of Skopje shall be adopted by a majority vote of the Representatives attending, within which there must be a majority of the votes of the Representatives attending who claim to belong to the communities not in the majority in the population of Macedonia

[Before the article was converted into an amendment and adopted by Parliament (Amendment XVI, which replaced paragraph 5 of Article 114), Article 114 of the Macedonian Constitution read:

The right of citizens to local self-government is guaranteed. Municipalities are units of local self-government. Within municipalities forms of neighbourhood self-government may be established. Municipalities are financed from their own sources of income determined by law as well as by funds from the Republic. Local self-government is regulated by a law adopted by a two-thirds majority vote of the total number of Representatives.]

Article 115

(1) In units of local self-government, citizens directly and through representatives participate in decision-making on issues of local relevance particularly in the fields of public services, urban and rural planning, environmental protection, local economic development, local finances, communal activities, culture, sport, social security and child care, education, health care and other fields determined by law.

[After Article 115 of Annex A of the Agreement was converted into an

amendment and adopted by Parliament, the Amendment (Amendment XVII, whose Item 1 replaced paragraph 1 of Article 115 and Item 2 replaced paragraph 2 of Article 117) read:

1. In units of local self-government, citizens directly and through representatives participate in decision-making on issues of local relevance particularly in the fields of public services, urban and rural planning, environmental protection, local economic development, local finances, communal activities, culture, sport, social security and child care, education, health care and other fields determined by law.

2. In the city of Skopje the citizens directly and through representatives participate in decision-making on issues of relevance to the city of Skopje, particularly in the fields of public services, urban and rural planning, environmental protection, local economic development, local finances, communal activities, culture, sport, social security and child care, education, health care and other fields determined by law.

Prior to the adoption of the amendment, Article 115 of the Macedonian Constitution read:

In units of local self-government, citizens directly and through representatives participate in decision-making on issues of local relevance particularly in the fields of urban planning, communal activities, culture, sport, social security and child care, preschool education, primary education, basic health care and other fields determined by law. The municipality is autonomous in the execution of its constitutionally and legally determined spheres of competence; supervision of the legality of its work is carried out by the Republic. The carrying out of specified matters can by law be entrusted to the municipality by the Republic.

Prior to the adoption of the amendment, Article 117 of the Macedonian Constitution read:

The City of Skopje is a particular unit of local self-government the organization of which is regulated by law. In the City of Skopje, citizens directly and through representatives participate in decision-making on issues of relevance for the City of Skopje particularly in the filed of urban planning, communal activities, culture, sport, social security and child care, preschool education, primary education, basic health care and other fields determined by law. The City of Skopje is financed from its own sources of income determined by law, as well as by funds from the Republic. The City is autonomous in the execution of its constitutionally and legally determined spheres of competence; supervision of the legality of its work is carried out by the Republic. By law, the Republic can entrust the carrying out of specified matters to the City.]

Article 131

(1) The decision to initiate a change in the Constitution is made by the Assembly by a two-thirds majority vote of the total number of Representatives.

(2) The draft amendment to the Constitution is confirmed by the Assembly by a majority vote of the total number of Representatives and then submitted to public debate.

(3) The decision to change the Constitution is made by the Assembly by a two-thirds majority vote of the total number of Representatives.

(4) A decision to amend the Preamble, the articles on local self-government, Article 131, any provision relating to the rights of members of communities, including in particular Articles 7, 8, 9, 19, 48, 56, 69, 77, 78, 86, 104, and 109, as well as a decision to add any new provision relating to the subject-matter of such provisions and articles, shall require a two-thirds majority vote of the total number of Representatives, within which there must be a majority of the votes of the total number of Representatives claiming to belong to the communities not in the majority in the population of Macedonia

(5) The change in the Constitution is declared by the Assembly.

[*Before the article was converted into an amendment and adopted by Parliament (Amendment XVIII, with which a new paragraph was added to paragraph 4 of Article 131), Article 131 of the Macedonian Constitution read:*

The decision to initiate a change in the Constitution is made by the Assembly by a two-thirds majority vote of the total number of Representatives. The draft amendment to the Constitution is confirmed by the Assembly by a majority vote of the total number of Representatives and then submitted to public debate. The decision to change the Constitution is made by the Assembly by a two-thirds majority vote of the total number of Representatives. The change in the Constitution is declared by the Assembly.]

ANNEX B: LEGISLATIVE MODIFICATIONS

The parties will take all necessary measures to ensure the adoption of the legislative changes set forth hereafter within the time limits specified.

1. Law on Local Self-Government

The Assembly shall adopt within 45 days from the signing of the Framework Agreement a revised Law on Local Self-Government. This revised Law shall in no respect be less favorable to the units of local self-government and their autonomy than the draft Law proposed by the Government of the Republic of Macedonia in March 2001. The Law shall include competencies relating to the subject matters set forth in Section 3.1 of the Framework Agreement as additional independent competencies of the units of local self-government, and shall conform to Section 6.6 of the Framework Agreement. In addition, the Law shall provide that any State standards or procedures established in any laws concerning areas in which municipalities have independent competencies shall be limited to those which cannot be established as effectively at the local level; such laws shall further promote the municipalities' independent exercise of their competencies.

2. Law on Local Finance

The Assembly shall adopt by the end of the term of the present Assembly a law on local self-government finance to ensure that the units of local self-government have sufficient resources to carry out their tasks under the revised Law on Local Self-Government. In particular, the law shall:

• Enable and make responsible units of local self-government for raising a substantial amount of tax revenue;

• Provide for the transfer to the units of local self-government of a part of centrally raised taxes that corresponds to the functions of the units of local self-government and that takes account of the collection of taxes on their territories; and

• Ensure the budgetary autonomy and responsibility of the units of local self-government within their areas of competence.

3. Law on Municipal Boundaries

The Assembly shall adopt by the end of 2002 a revised law on municipal boundaries, taking into account the results of the census and the relevant guidelines set forth in the Law on Local Self-Government.

4. Laws Pertaining to Police Located in the Municipalities

The Assembly shall adopt before the end of the term of the present Assembly provisions ensuring:

• That each local head of the police is selected by the council of the municipality concerned from a list of not fewer than three candidates proposed by the Ministry of the Interior, among whom at least one candidate shall belong to the community in the majority in the municipality. In the event the municipal council fails to select any of the candidates proposed within 15 days, the Ministry of the Interior shall propose a second list of not fewer than three new candidates, among whom at least one candidate shall belong to the community in the majority in the municipality. If the municipal council again fails to select any of the candidates proposed within 15 days, the Minister of the Interior, after consultation with the Government, shall select the local head of police from among the two lists of candidates proposed by the Ministry of the Interior as well as three additional candidates proposed by the municipal council;

> • That each local head of the police informs regularly and upon request the council of the municipality concerned;

> • That a municipal council may make recommendations to the local head of police in areas including public security and traffic safety; and

> • That a municipal council may adopt annually a report regarding matters of public safety, which shall be addressed to the Minister of the Interior and the Public Attorney (Ombudsman).

5. Laws on the Civil Service and Public Administration

The Assembly shall adopt by the end of the term of the present Assembly amendments to the laws on the civil service and public administration to ensure equitable representation of communities in accordance with Section 4.2 of the Framework Agreement.

6. Law on Electoral Districts

The Assembly shall adopt by the end of 2002 a revised Law on Electoral Districts, taking into account the results of the census and the principles set forth in the Law on the Election of Members for the Parliament of the Republic of Macedonia.

7. Rules of the Assembly

The Assembly shall amend by the end of the term of the present Assembly its Rules of Procedure to enable the use of the Albanian language in accordance with Section 6.5 of the Framework Agreement, paragraph 8 below, and the relevant amendments to the Constitution set forth in Annex A.

8. Laws Pertinent to the Use of Languages

The Assembly shall adopt by the end of the term of the present Assembly new legislation regulating the use of languages in the organs of the Republic of Macedonia. This legislation shall provide that:

> • Representatives may address plenary sessions and working bodies of the Assembly in languages referred to in Article 7, paragraphs 1 and 2 of the Constitution (as amended in accordance with Annex A);

> • Laws shall be published in the languages referred to in Article 7, paragraphs 1 and 2 of the Constitution (as amended in accordance with Annex A); and

> • All public officials may write their names in the alphabet of any language referred to in Article 7, paragraphs 1 and 2 of the Constitution (as amended in accordance with Annex A) on any official documents.

The Assembly also shall adopt by the end of the term of the present Assembly new legislation on the issuance of personal documents.

The Assembly shall amend by the end of the term of the present Assembly all relevant laws to make their provisions on the use of languages fully compatible with Section 6 of the Framework Agreement.

9. Law on the Public Attorney

The Assembly shall amend by the end of 2002 the Law on the Public Attorney as well as the other relevant laws to ensure:

• That the Public Attorney shall undertake actions to safeguard the principles of non-discrimination and equitable representation of communities in public bodies at all levels and in other areas of public life, and that there are adequate resources and personnel within his office to enable him to carry out this function;

• That the Public Attorney establishes decentralized offices;

• That the budget of the Public Attorney is voted separately by the Assembly;

• That the Public Attorney shall present an annual report to the Assembly and, where appropriate, may upon request present reports to the councils of municipalities in which decentralized offices are established; and

• That the powers of the Public Attorney are enlarged:

• To grant to him access to and the opportunity to examine all official documents, it being understood that the Public Attorney and his staff will not disclose confidential information;

• To enable the Public Attorney to suspend, pending a decision of the competent court, the execution of an administrative act, if he determines that the act may result in an irreparable prejudice to the rights of the interested person; and

• To give to the Public Attorney the right to contest the conformity of laws with the Constitution before the Constitutional Court.

10. Other Laws

The Assembly shall enact all legislative provisions that may be necessary to give full effect to the Framework Agreement and amend or abrogate all provisions incompatible with the Framework Agreement.

ANNEX C: IMPLEMENTATION AND CONFIDENCE-BUILDING MEASURES

1. International Support

1.1. The parties invite the international community to facilitate, monitor and assist in the implementation of the provisions of the Framework Agreement and its Annexes, and request such efforts to be coordinated by the EU in cooperation with the Stabilization and Association Council.

2. Census and Elections

2.1. The parties confirm the request for international supervision by the Council of Europe and the European Commission of a census to be conducted in October 2001.

2.2. Parliamentary elections will be held by 27 January 2002. International organizations, including the OSCE, will be invited to observe these elections.

3. Refugee Return, Rehabilitation and Reconstruction

3.1. All parties will work to ensure the return of refugees who are citizens or legal residents of Macedonia and displaced persons to their homes within the shortest possible timeframe, and invite the international community and in particular UNHCR to assist in these efforts.

3.2. The Government with the participation of the parties will complete an action plan within 30 days after the signature of the Framework Agreement for rehabilitation of and reconstruction in areas affected by the hostilities. The parties invite the international community to assist in the formulation and implementation of this plan.

3.3. The parties invite the European Commission and the World Bank to rapidly convene a meeting of international donors after adoption in the Assembly of the Constitutional amendments in Annex A and the revised Law on Local Self-Government to support the financing of measures to be undertaken for the purpose of implementing the Framework Agreement and its Annexes, including measures to strengthen local self-government and reform the police services, to address macro-financial assistance to the Republic of Macedonia, and to support the rehabilitation and reconstruction measures identified in the action plan identified in paragraph 3.2.

4. Development of Decentralized Government

4.1. The parties invite the international community to assist in the process of strengthening local self-government. The international community should in particular assist in preparing the necessary legal amendments related to financing mechanisms for strengthening the financial basis of municipalities and building their financial management capabilities, and in amending the law on the boundaries of municipalities.

5. Non-Discrimination and Equitable Representation

5.1. Taking into account i.a. the recommendations of the already established governmental commission, the parties will take concrete action to increase the representation of members of communities not in the majority in Macedonia in public administration, the military, and public enterprises, as well as to improve their access to public financing for business development.

5.2. The parties commit themselves to ensuring that the police services will by 2004 generally reflect the composition and distribution of the population of Macedonia. As initial steps toward this end, the parties commit to ensuring that 500 new police officers from communities not in the majority in the population of Macedonia will be hired and trained by July 2002, and that these officers will be deployed to the areas where such communities live. The parties further commit that 500 additional such officers will be hired and trained by July 2003, and that these officers will be deployed on a priority basis to the areas throughout Macedonia where such communities live. The parties invite the international community to support and assist with the implementation of these commitments, in particular through screening and selection of candidates and their training. The parties invite the OSCE, the European Union, and the United States to send an expert team as quickly as possible in order to assess how best to achieve these objectives.

5.3. The parties also invite the OSCE, the European Union, and the United States to increase training and assistance programs for police, including:

• professional, human rights, and other training;

• technical assistance for police reform, including assistance in screening, selection and promotion processes;

• development of a code of police conduct;

• cooperation with respect to transition planning for hiring and deployment of police officers from communities not in the majority in Macedonia; and

• deployment as soon as possible of international monitors and police advisors in sensitive areas, under appropriate arrangements with relevant authorities.

5.4. The parties invite the international community to assist in the training of lawyers, judges and prosecutors from members of communities not in the majority in Macedonia in order to be able to increase their representation in the judicial system.

6. Culture, Education, and Use of Languages

6.1. The parties invite the international community, including the OSCE, to increase its assistance for projects in the area of media in order to further strengthen radio, TV and print media, including Albanian language and multiethnic media. The parties also invite the international community to increase professional media training programs for members of communities not in the majority in Macedonia. The parties also invite the OSCE to continue its efforts on projects designed to improve inter-ethnic relations.

6.2. The parties invite the international community to provide assistance for the implementation of the Framework Agreement in the area of higher education.

ARM: Armija na Republika Makedonija, or Army of the Republic of Macedonia

BDI: Albanian acronym for Bashkimi Demokratik për Integrim, or Democratic Union for Integration (Albanian party)

DA: Macedonian acronym for Demokratska Alternativa, or Democratic Alternative (Macedonian party)

DPA: Macedonian acronym for Demokratska Partija na Albancite, or Democratic Party of Albanians (Albanian party)

DUI: Macedonian acronym for Demokratska Unija za Integracija, or Democratic Union for Integration (Albanian party)

EULEX Kosovo: European Union Rule of Law Mission in Kosovo

ICG: International Crisis Group

ICOM: International Census Observation Mission

ICTY: International Criminal Tribunal for the former Yugoslavia

IMF: International Monetary Fund

IWPR: Institute for War and Peace Reporting

KFOR: Kosovo Force

KLA: Kosovo Liberation Army

LPM: Macedonian acronym for Liberalna Partija na Makedonija, or Liberal Party of Macedonia (Macedonian party)

MANU: Macedonian acronym for Makedonska Akademija na Naukite i Umetnostite, or Macedonian Academy of Sciences and Arts

MTA: Military Technical Agreement between the International Security Force in Kosovo (KFOR) and the governments of the Federal Republic of Yugoslavia and the Republic of Serbia

MVR: Macedonian acronym for Ministerstvo za Vnatresni Raboti, or Ministry of Interior

NDP: Macedonian acronym for Nacionalna Demokratska Partija, or National Democratic Party (Albanian party)

NDP: Macedonian acronym for Narodna Demokratska Partija, or People's Democratic Party (Albanian party)

NLA: National Liberation Army

ONA: Macedonian acronym for Osloboditelna Nacionalna Armija, or National Liberation Army

OSCE: Organization for Security and Co-operation in Europe

PDK: Albanian acronym for Partia Demokratike Kombëtare, or National Democratic Party (Albanian party)

PDP: Macedonian acronym for Partija za Demokratski Prosperitet, or Party for Democratic Prosperity (Albanian party)

PDP: Albanian acronym for Partia Demokratike Popullore, or People's Democratic Party (Albanian party)

PDP-A: Macedonian acronym for Partija za Demokratski Prosperitet na Albancite, or Party for Democratic Prosperity of the Albanians (Albanian party)

PDSH: Albanian acronym for Partia Demokratike Shqiptare, or Democratic Party of Albanians (Albanian party)

PPD: Albanian acronym for Partia për Prosperitet Demokratik, or Party for Democratic Prosperity (Albanian party)

PPD-Sh: Albanian acronym for Partia për Prosperitet Demokratik të Shqiptarëve, or Party for Democratic Prosperity of the Albanians (Albanian party)

SDSM: Macedonian acronym for Social Democratic Union of Macedonia, or Socijaldemokratski Sojuz na Makedonija (Macedonian party)

UÇK: Albanian acronym for Ushtria Çlirimtare e Kosovës, or Kosovo Liberation Army

UÇK: Albanian acronym for Ushtria Çlirimtare Kombëtare, or National Liberation Army

UÇPMB: Albanian acronym for Ushtria Çlirimtare e Preshevës, Medvegjës dhe Bujanocit, or Liberation Army of Preševo, Medvedja, and Bujanovac

UNMIK: United Nations Interim Administration Mission in Kosovo

UNPREDEP: United Nations Preventive Deployment Mission

UNPROFOR: United Nations Protection Force

UNSCR 1244: United Nations Security Council Resolution 1244

VMRO-DPMNE: Macedonian acronym for Vnatresna Makedonska Revolucionerna Organizacija-Demokratska Partija za Makedonsko Nacionalno Edinstvo, or Internal Macedonian Revolutionary Organization-Democratic Party for Macedonian National Unity (Macedonian party)

WIPO: World Intellectual Property Organization

Introduction

1. I use the name Macedonia instead of FYROM, The former Yugoslav Republic of Macedonia, under which Macedonia was admitted to the United Nations on 8 April 1993 and the Council of Europe on 9 November 1995. The latter is used officially by countries that have not yet recognized the Republic under its constitutional name (Republic of Macedonia). Nonetheless, "Macedonia" is often used in unofficial correspondence, even within the UN (Victor A. Friedman, personal communication), and was once used officially when on 25 September 2007 Srgjan Asan Kerim, president of the 62nd Session of the UN General Assembly and former foreign minister of Macedonia, introduced Branko Crvenkovski as president of Macedonia, not president of FYROM, before giving him the floor to deliver an address. The United States of America officially recognized the country as "Republic of Macedonia" in November 2004. Also, unless otherwise noted, I use "Macedonians" to refer to members of the ethnic Macedonian community, rather than to citizens of the Republic of Macedonia.

2. *Dnevnik*, 17 February 2001, 2

3. The armed conflict between Serbian forces and the KLA ended with the Military Technical Agreement (MTA) between the International Security Force in Kosovo (KFOR) and the governments of the Federal Republic of Yugoslavia and the Republic of Serbia, and with UN Security Council Resolution (UNSCR) 1244. The MTA, signed 9 June 1999, and UNSCR 1244, passed 10 June 1999, established KFOR as "a legitimate security force, under international law, for the protection of the people of Kosovo," http://www.nato.int/kfor/chronicle/2003/chronicle_05/16.htm, accessed 10 April 2011. UNSCR 1244 authorized the establishment of the UN Interim Administration Mission in Kosovo (UNMIK), headed by a special representative of the secretary general, and committed UNMIK to transferring its administrative responsibilities to provisional institutions of self-government pending a political settlement. Kosovo was administered by the UN until the Assembly of Kosovo (part of the provisional institutions of self-government, and the main legislative body) approved the Kosovo Declaration of Independence on 17 February 2008.

4. As I mention in Chapter 2, former director of the Intelligence Agency of Macedonia Aleksa Stamenkovski claimed the agency had information about the existence of the NLA prior to the eruption of the insurgency.

5. According to the latest population census, carried out in 2002, Macedonia had

2,022,547 inhabitants, of whom 1,297,981 (64.18 percent) declared themselves as Macedonians, 509,083 (25.17 percent) as Albanians, 77,959 (3.85 percent) as Turks, 53,879
(2.66 percent) as Roms, 35,939 (1.78 percent) as Serbs, 17,018 (0.84 percent) as Bosnians, 9,695 (0.48 percent) as Vlahs, and 20,993 (1.04 percent) as "other" (Census of
Population, Households and Dwellings in the Republic of Macedonia, 2002, Book I,
State Statistical Office, Republic of Macedonia, 176; population percentages are available
on the official website of the Macedonian Ministry of Foreign Affairs, http://www.mfa.
gov.mk/default1.aspx?ItemID=288, accessed 10 April 2011). A new population census
was scheduled for fall 2011 but was eventually suspended.

6. See *Dnevnik*, 31 May 2001, 1. President of the Macedonian Academy of Sciences
and Arts (MANU) Georgi Efremov denied that the plan reflected the official view of the
Academy and, after the proposal failed to gain substantial support, resigned his position. The proposal was strongly and publicly denounced by Macedonian and Albanian
politicians and foreign officials in Macedonia, the Macedonian and Albanian press, TV
news, and the general public.

7. While the term "minority" is loaded, I use it in the book strictly in a statistical
sense.

8. My use of Roms for the English plural form of Rom is intended to endorse the
position of Victor A. Friedman (see Friedman-Hancock 1995a: 6–7) that the frequently
used form Roma, the plural form of Rom in the Romani language, diverts attention from
the fact that the group in question is a distinct ethnic group. To illustrate his position,
Friedman uses the examples of the English plural form of Turk, which is Turks and not
Turkler (the transliteration into English of Türkler, the plural of Turk in the Turkish
language), and of Magyar, which is Magyars and not Magyarok (the plural of Magyar in
the Magyar language).

9. An estimated 80 percent of the Albanian Muslim population in Macedonia are
Sunni and follow the Hanbali school of Islamic jurisprudence; the remainder belong
to the Bektashi, Naqshbandi, Helveti, Rifai, Qadiri, and Melami Sufi orders (see Blumi
2006: 18). Religion plays a role in the construction of ethnonational identification in
Macedonia: Macedonian ethnonational identity is generally associated with Orthodox
Christianity, and Albanian is regarded as de facto Sunni Muslim. Also, Orthodox Albanians tend to identify culturally with Macedonians, Catholic Albanians with Albanians,
and Muslim Macedonians with Turks. The 2001 crisis contributed to an ethnoreligious
polarization that continues to this day.

10. Prior to the 2004 redrawing of municipal boundaries, Čair had a total population of 68,395: 33,238 Macedonians, 26,259 Albanians, 2,354 Bosniacs, 2,816 Turks,
1,440 Serbs, 998 Roms, 174 Vlahs, and 1,116 "other" (Census of Population, Households
and Dwellings in the Republic of Macedonia, 2002, Book I, State Statistical Office, Republic of Macedonia, 176).

11. For the embedment of the notion of "Balkan mentality" in eighteenth-century
Balkan Orthodox Christianity, see Kitromilides 1996.

12. In Albania itself, the United States is popularly perceived as having been an ally
since the end of World War I.

Chapter 1. Critical Events

1. According to Kekic (2001: 186), at the end of the 1980s Macedonia contributed a mere 5 percent toward Yugoslavia's total production of goods and services; in 1990 the country experienced a huge development gap, wider than that in the aftermath of World War II, vis-à-vis the better developed areas of Yugoslavia.

2. In 1982, Greece issued a ministerial decision whereby political refugees who fled Greece during the Civil War were allowed to return and reclaim their confiscated properties, provided that they were "Greeks by birth" (*Ellines to yenos*) (Danforth 1995: 122). This provision has thus far excluded Macedonians who were born in the geographical province of Macedonia in northern Greece (Aegean Macedonia) and live outside the borders of Greece. For comprehensive discussions of Greece's treatment of political refugees from Aegean Macedonia, and of the difficulties surrounding their relocation in Macedonia and integration into Macedonian society, see Monova 2001, 2002b, 2010. For life-history narratives of refugee children of the Greek Civil War, see Danforth and van Boeschoten 2012.

3. The following parties formed a governing coalition (see Bugajski 2002: 725): the League of Communists of Macedonia-Party of Democratic Transformation, which won 31 seats in the 120-seat Parliament and later changed its name to the Social Democratic Alliance; the Party for Democratic Prosperity, which was the largest Albanian party and gained 17 seats, and its coalition partner, the National Democratic Party, which won 5 seats; the Internal Macedonian Revolutionary Organization-Democratic Party of Macedonian National Unity (38 seats); the Alliance of Reform Forces (11 seats); the Socialist Party (4) seats; the Party for Yugoslavia (2 seats); the Party for the Complete Emancipation of Roms (1 seat); and 3 seats went to representatives of independent parties.

4. I use the Macedonian acronyms, followed by the Albanian acronyms for the Albanian parties under discussion here and throughout the book.

5. The term is formed by the conjunction of "Illyri[a]" and "Da[rdania]." Prior to the Roman conquest, Illyria was a region in the Western part of the Balkans whose borders remain unclear. Dardania was located roughly on the territory of Kosovo, southern parts of Serbia, western parts of Macedonia, and northeastern parts of Albania before the Romans conquered it in 28 B.C.

6. The English translation of the full text of the Constitution of the Republic of Macedonia can be found on the Assembly of the Republic of Macedonia website, http://www.sobranie.mk/en/default-en.asp?ItemID=9F7452BF44EE814B8DB897C1858B71FF, accessed 10 April 2011. For the original text of the 1991 Constitution, see "Ustav na Republika Makedonija," *Služben Vesnik na Republika Makedonija* 52/1991 ["Constitution of the Republic of Macedonia," *Official Gazette of the Republic of Macedonia* 52/1991].

7. In 1971, Bosnian Muslims gained status as a *narod* and numerically equal representation with the Serbian and Croatian *narodi* on governmental bodies and administrative agencies.

8. Some Bulgarian anthropologists use their disciplinary qualifications to pursue the Bulgarian state's agenda of claiming Macedonians as Bulgarians, while others criticize

the practice; see, for example, Marinov (2009). The Gorans are Slavic-speaking Muslims whose dialect is closer to neighboring Macedonian dialects than to neighboring Serbian/Croatian dialects. They live in the southwesternmost corner of Kosovo and an adjacent region in Albania in the Šar Planina mountain range. There are also two Goran villages in western Macedonia (see Friedman 2006, 2007).

9. Germany unilaterally recognized the sovereignty of Croatia and Slovenia on 23 December 1991, before the Badinter Commission rendered its opinion on 11 January 1992. Although, according to the Badinter Commission, Croatia had failed to meet the conditions for EC recognition, all EC members nonetheless followed in the wake of Germany's recognition.

10. The sun or star is a symbol of ancient Macedonian civilization, named after the village of Vergina (in today's Greece) where it was found adorning the royal tomb of Philip of Macedon—father of Alexander the Great.

11. The 1995 Interim Accord is available at http: //untreaty.un.org/unts/120001_144071/6/3/00004456.pdf, accessed 10 April 2011.

12. The same controversy surrounded the factual accuracy of the 2002 official census, showing 509,083 Albanians, 25.17 percent of the overall population. The government that took office in August 2006 announced plans to address the cases of people who have resided in the country since 1990 and do not have Macedonian citizenship. Migration Policy Institute, http: //www.migrationinformation.org/Profiles/display.cfm?ID=608, accessed 10 April 2011.

13. The sanctions were imposed to condemn the failure of federal Yugoslav (that is, Serbian and Montenegrin) authorities to bring the Bosnian War to an end.

14. The adoption of government policies in support of state higher education in Albanian, in addition to the implementation of a separate quota for each minority in 1996, helped to increase the number of Albanian students admitted to Macedonian universities. As Brunnbauer notes (2004: 588), by 1999 the percentage of Albanian students enrolled in Macedonian universities had more than doubled since the early 1990s, reaching 5.5 percent of the student body.

15. Accounts of the number of those killed and wounded during the 1997 riots in Gostivar vary. Poulton (1995: 189), for example, mentions that three people were killed and seventy people were wounded, the International Crisis Group Macedonia 1997 Report states that three civilians were killed and up to 400 were wounded (14), while Bugajski (2002: 735) mentions that two Albanians were killed and several dozen were wounded. For the Human Rights Report documenting police use of excessive force in Gostivar in 1997, see HRW 1998. According to Eran Fraenkel (2001: 268), victims of police brutality in Macedonia have included not only Albanians but also Macedonians and Roms.

16. As Lund notes (2000: 184, 283n31), in April 1996 bombs were set off near Croatian and Bosnian Serb refugee camps, and the KLA later claimed responsibility for the incident.

17. For the construction of Albanian national identity and pride concerning historical figures, see Schwandner-Sievers and Fischer 2002.

18. Vasil Tupurkovski, leader of Democratic Alternative (DA), played a key role in Macedonia's recognition of Taiwan. Tupurkovski promised during the 1998 parliamentary campaign that if elected he would bring millions of dollars in aid and investment. After his election victory, he entered the VMRO-DPMNE-led coalition government, became vice premier, and negotiated a deal whereby, according to the newspaper *Nova Makedonija*, Taipei would give Macedonia a 200 million dollar grant, 100 million dollars for state institutions, and a 700 million dollar investment in agriculture (see Tubilewicz 2007: 137) in exchange for diplomatic recognition. By mid-2000, however, Taiwan's direct financial assistance amounted to only 6.4 million dollars, and no direct investments had been made (146). On 12 June 2001, shortly after the NLA established control over the village of Aračinovo and the need for UN support became pressing in Macedonia, China and Macedonia signed a joint communiqué on restoration of diplomatic relations, while diplomatic ties between Macedonia and Taiwan were severed.

Chapter 2. The Eruption of the 2001 Conflict

1. *Dnevnik*'s daily circulation is 50,000–70,000 copies, out of a total daily newspaper circulation in the country of 90,000–120,000 copies; http://star.dnevnik.com.mk/?section=infoen, accessed 10 April 2011.

2. *Dnevnik*, 26 January 2001, 1. All translations from Macedonian or Albanian into English here and elsewhere in the book are mine unless otherwise noted.

3. Ibid., 3.

4. The buffer zone, otherwise called Ground Safety Zone (GSZ), was established as a demilitarized belt under the June 1999 Military Technical Agreement (MTA) between the International Security Force in Kosovo (KFOR) and the governments of the Federal Republic of Yugoslavia and the Republic of Serbia, but became the haven of UÇPMB guerrilla activity as early as November or December 1999 (Phillips 2004: 10).

5. In a personal interview with Evangelos Kofos in February 2000 (Kofos 2002: 158), Agim Çeku, former leader of the KLA and head of the Kosovo Protection Corps (the civilian organization created after the disbandment of the KLA to provide reconstruction and emergency response services in Kosovo), stated that the KLA had not surrendered all its arms and that Kosovar Albanians were ready to reciprocate the support they had received from their brothers in Preševo Valley during the Kosovo war; see also Judah 2002.

6. "The Tanuševci Story," *Radio Free Europe/Radio Liberty Balkan Report* 5, 18 (9 March 2001).

7. *Dnevnik*, 19 February 2001.

8. For political reactions to the border demarcation agreement between Macedonia and the Federal Republic of Yugoslavia, see ICG 2001: 5. The border remained unmarked, and talks regarding its demarcation resumed in 2008, this time between Macedonia and Kosovo, after Kosovo's independence. The Macedonia-Kosovo border demarcation agreement was ratified by the parliaments in Skopje and Prishtina in October 2009.

9. http://lists.peacelink.it/balcani/msg00619.html, accessed 10 April 2011.

10. http://www.ex-yupress.com/nin/nin83.html, accessed 10 April 2011.

11. "U.S. Troops Move in, Try to Pin Down Insurgents in Macedonia," *Stars and Stripes*, 4 March 2001, http://www.stripes.com/01/mar01/ed030601a.html, accessed 22 October 2010.

12. "NATO Confronts Albanian Rebels," http://iwpr.net/report-news/nato-con-fronts-albanian-rebels, accessed 10 April 2011.

13. "Patrolling U.S. KFOR Soldiers Were Ready for 'the Real Deal,'" *Stars and Stripes*, 9 March 2001, http://www.stripes.com/01/mar01/ed030901b.html, accessed 22 October 2010.

14. I thank Victor A. Friedman for the point about the location of the UN helicopter pad in Skopje in the 1990s.

Chapter 3. Living in a Confusing World

1. Estimates by the *International Herald Tribune* put the figure at "30,000 people, most of them ethnic Albanians." *IHT*, 14 March 2001, 5; quoted in Jeffries 2002: 258.

2. According to the International Crisis Group, approximately 5,000 demonstrators had already gathered in the square when shooting started; ICG 2001: 7.

3. *The Times*, 19 March 2001, 13; quoted in Jeffries 2002: 260.

4. *The Times*, 22 March 2001, 14; quoted in Jeffries 2002: 264.

5. *Independent*, 21 March 2001, 13; quoted in Jeffries 2002: 263.

6. *Dnevnik*, 23 March 2001, 2.

7. *Flaka*, 23 March 2001, 1–2.

8. Stabilization and Association Agreements (SAAs) were meant to help the governments of the Western Balkans focus on reforms for EU membership and were "posited on respect for the conditionality of the Stabilisation and Association process agreed by the Council [of the European Union]" (Council Report on the Review of the Stabilisation and Association Process," 11 June 2001, http://www.consilium.europa.eu/uedocs/cms_data/docs/pressdata/en/misc/09765.en1.html, accessed 10 April 2011). Besides Macedonia, Croatia, Albania, Bosnia, and Herzegovina, Montenegro and Serbia have signed SAAs with the EU. Ilirjani (2006: 25) suggests that the SAA with Macedonia on 9 April 2001 was offered by the EU as a "reward to stop fighting rather than in recognition of the success of structural reforms made by Macedonia in the process of preparation for the EU membership," while Hislope (2003: 145) argues, "Bereft of a military to force talks, EU negotiators discovered that money talks with force." The Agreement remained frozen for a few years and went into force on 1 April 2004 when the EU concluded Macedonia had made satisfactory progress toward implementing the Ohrid Framework Agreement that officially ended the armed conflict on 13 August 2001.

9. *IHT*, 31 March 2001, 2; quoted in Jeffries 2002: 270.

10. For the Macedonian paramilitary groups that were formed during the 2001 crisis, see Vankovska 2003: 16–17.

11. For Albanian mafia operations in Kosovo after the arrival of NATO forces in 1999, see Schwandner-Sievers 2001: 114–15.

12. *Start* has a circulation of 10,000 copies and is one of the three most popular weekly political magazines in the country, the other two being *Fokus* (12,000 copies) and

Denes (7,500 copies), http://www.pressreference.com/Ky-Ma/Macedonia.html, accessed 10 April 2011. The articles in question are the following: Nevenka Mitrevska, "Who Imported Hezbollah to Macedonia," *Start* 113, 23 March 2001, 6–9; and Ljubcho Palevski, "Bin Laden's Money in Macedonia," *Start* 116, 13 April 2001, 6–9.

13. On the symbolic significance of the sexual mutilation of men during the wars in former Yugoslavia, see Žarkov 2001.

14. *Kum* (m.)/*kuma* (f.) are the Macedonian terms for a marriage sponsor at a wedding (best man/maid or matron of honor) or godparent (godfather/godmother) at a christening. The Albanian term is *kumbarë* (both m. and f.). Marriage sponsorship and godparenthood are widespread forms of fictive kinship not only in the Balkans but also in Russia and the former Soviet republics and Latin America (where the fictive kinship system of godparenthood is known as *compadrazgo*), and establish strong and permanent bonds of solidarity.

15. The term *društvo*, equivalent to Greek *parea* (see Cowan 1990), is better rendered into English as "relaxed sociability" (see also Brown 1995: 201).

16. The saying is the equivalent of the English "Nero fiddles while Rome burns."

17. For the deal, obtained from one of the negotiators, see Whyte (2002: 39–41).

18. I thank Victor Friedman for this piece of information.

19. It is also estimated that approximately 26,000 Albanian refugees from Macedonia still remained in Kosovo in the fall of 2001 (Roudometof 2002: 217).

20. To the best of my knowledge, the main insurgent center, where people registered as NLA participants and received NLA ID cards, uniforms, and equipment, was set up in the town of Prizren in Kosovo. A center was also set up in Kukes (Albania). Uniforms and arms were transported across the border from Kosovo (Prizren, but also Vitina) into the Macedonian village of Tanuševci and distributed across the northewest region of the country. Insurgent centers were in turn set up in Macedonian villages, including Šipkovica, Gjermo, and Aračinovo.

21. According to data published in 2001 (see Fraenkel 2001: 265), the state owned about one third of the shares of the publishing house NIP Nova Makedonija, which produced the daily Macedonian-language newspapers *Nova Makedonija* and *Večer* and the weekly news magazine *Puls*, the daily Albanian-language newspaper *Flaka e Vëllazërimit*, and the Turkish-language newspaper *Birlik*, published three times a week. The remaining print media were privately owned. NIP Nova Makedonija was controlled by the government and promoted government interests. The publishing house was declared officially bankrupt in June 2004 and liquidated in October of that same year. Newspapers and magazines published by NIP Nova Makedonija were subsequently sold to private companies.

22. According to the New Redhouse Turkish-English dictionary (published in Istanbul in 1968), the term *kachak* derives from the Turkish verb *kachmak*, "to hide" or "to run away." On the Kachak movement, see Vickers 1998; Roudometof 2001: 188.

23. Editorial: "Ndezja ishte planifikuar më herët!" [The burning was planned ahead of time], *Fakti*, 7 June 2001, http://www.alb-net.com/pipermail/tetova-l/2001-June/000783.html, accessed 11 April 2011.

24. *Flaka*, 7 June 2001, 1–2.

25. *Nova Makedonija*, 8 June 2001, 1–3.

26. *Dnevnik*, 9 June 2001, 4.

27. *Večer*, 8 June 2001, 4.

Chapter 4. Performing Civility

1. Unlike DPA leader Arben Xhaferi, who enjoyed popularity in the Albanian community, DPA deputy leader Menduh Thaçi had a bad reputation, even among DPA supporters, for allegedly engaging in corruption and managing smuggling operations in Macedonia.

2. "Politics makes strange bedfellows" is a polite way to translate into English the saying *politikata e kurva/politika është kurvë*.

3. Examples of scandals that have stirred up public anger in post-independence Macedonia include an arms scandal involving Mithat Emini, general secretary of the Albanian party PDP, and Husein Haskaj, Albanian assistant minister of defense, in the early 1990s; an arms smuggling scandal featuring defense minister Lazar Kitanovski and foreign minister Blagoja Handjiski in the late 1990s; and, a phone-tapping scandal involving minister of interior Dosta Dimovska in January 2001.

4. Victor A. Friedman, personal communication.

5. In August and September 2001, 70,000 persons, 60 percent of them Macedonians, were registered as internally displaced (Norwegian Refugee Council 2002: 155).

6. Rumors of CIA involvement in the 2001 crisis also circulated in the international media. See "A Spooky Campaign in the Balkans?" *Radio Free Europe/Radio Liberty Balkan Report* 5, 53 (31 July 2001), http://www.rferl.org/content/article/1341146.html, accessed 10 April 2011.

7. For details on the operation of Camp Bondsteel, see Johnson 2004. For various interpretations regarding the setting up of the Camp, see Ackermann 2003: 103n 61. The military training ground Krivolak was one of the biggest shooting ranges in former Yugoslavia and is located approximately sixty miles southeast of Skopje. A NATO PfP military exercise called Cooperative Best Effort took place in Krivolak 10–18 September 1998. As of this writing, plans for a PfP regional training center in Krivolak have yet to materialize.

8. *Dnevnik*, 7 June 2001, 1. VMRO-DPMNE's call to arms was strongly denounced by SDSM (4).

9. An eloquent example of this trend is the official renaming of the main square and one of the main pedestrian streets in downtown Skopje, both formerly called Marshal Tito, Macedonia Square and Macedonia Street respectively.

10. Drakulić 1992 provides a wry and highly colored account of life in the former Yugoslavia; cf. Živković 2000.

11. At issue is the development of a strong front jer, which gives /a/ in standard Serbian but /e/ in standard Macedonian. Some Serbian dialects also have *čest* (Victor A. Friedman, personal communication). On the process of Macedonian literary language development, see Friedman 2000.

12. The *kanun*, a code of customary laws regulating everyday life among Gheg Alba-

nians, has been passed on orally from generation to generation in the form of proverbs and common sayings. There are numerous versions of the *kanun* named either after areas or after reputable agnatic clan rulers and ancestors, who have allegedly created the *kanun*. The *kanun* of Lekë Dukagjini; an affluent Albanian clan chieftain, is the best-known and most widely practiced customary law; its adherents include Albanians in the North Albanian Alps, Shkodër, Dukagjin, Western Kosovo, and Albanian popula-tions in parts of Serbia, Montenegro, and Macedonia. The *kanun* covers all aspects of everyday life such as work, marriage, gender roles, personal honor, family and economic organization, and land and livestock, and continues to regulate social status, especially with reference to blood feuds and conflict reconciliation.

13. Unlike the younger generation, the older generation of Macedonian (Thiessen 2007: 110) and Albanian women take great pride in the traditional preparation of home-made sweets.

14. Besides applying to graduate school, getting married to foreign nationals (some-times in exchange for money) and applying for au pair jobs in EU member countries are additional popular avenues for emigration from Macedonia. Additionally, many Macedonians, especially youth, instrumentalize the claims of Bulgaria (an EU member state since January 2007) on Macedonian identity, and apply for, and acquire, Bulgar-ian citizenship for purposes of geographical and occupational mobility in EU member states (see Neofotistos 2009a).

Chapter 5. When the Going Gets Tough

1. I thank Victor A. Friedman for pointing out to me the interlingual wordplay.

2. For permutations of nationalism at work in India, see Partha Chatterjee (1993).

3. The Albanian terms for "friend" are *shok* (m.)/*shoqe* (f.), and *mik* (m.)/*mikeshë* (f.). The latter connotes greater social intimacy than the former, which means "comrade" and "spouse."

4. I purposely refrain from adopting the more widely used approach to social capi-tal that has been developed by Pierre Bourdieu because Bourdieu's approach, it seems to me, emphasizes the relation between social capital and the reproduction of social stratification and inequality and, unlike Coleman's, understates the constraints social context might place on social actors (see especially Coleman 1988; for valuable insights on Bourdieu's work, see Reed-Danahay 2005). For a comparative analysis of different conceptualizations of social capital in modern sociology, see, among others, Portes 1988; Lin 2001.

5. The geographical boundary between the two main, mutually intelligible Albanian dialects, Gheg and Tosk, is roughly marked by the Shkumbin River, which cuts across Albania. Tosk was pronounced the base for the standardized literary language in 1952, but the use of Gheg remains widespread in Kosovo and Macedonia. The geographical specificities of the regions inhabited by Gheg- and Tosk-speakers (rugged mountainous regions in the north and lowland plains in the south) have informed the observance of different lifestyles between the two groups.

6. In general, marriages between Macedonian Muslims and Turks, Muslim Alba-

nians and Turks, and Vlahs and Orthodox Macedonians have been commonplace, indicating that religious more than ethnic affiliation informs marital choices in Macedonia.

Chapter 6. Claiming Respect

1. In 1999, Macedonia was ranked (with Bulgaria, Egypt, Ghana, and Romania) 63rd least corrupt of 99 countries in the Corruption Perceptions Index developed by Transparency International (TI), the Berlin-based organization that monitors corruption worldwide. In 2010, Macedonia was ranked (with Croatia, Ghana, and Samoa) 62nd of 178. For how corruption helped weaken the Macedonian state and provide fertile ground for the NLA insurgency, see Hislope 2002.

2. Macedonian Radio and Television programming includes news and entertainment in Macedonian, Albanian, Turkish, Romani, Serbian, Bosnian, and Vlah. All program divisions are in the same building, near the city center.

3. For rural-urban migration practices in the former Yugoslavia, see Denich 1970; Simić 1973.

4. Albanian *qejf* derives from Turkish *keyif* (from Arabic *kayf*), whose meanings include "health; bodily and mental condition; merriment, fun, good spirits; pleasure, amusement; inclination, whim, fancy; slight intoxication" (Alderson and Iz 1959: 188). For the related notion *kefi* in the context of communal sociability in northern Greece, see Cowan 1990.

5. Since 1 January 2010, citizens of Macedonia (and also Serbia and Montenegro) are allowed visa-free entry to Schengen countries.

6. According to the 2009 Macedonian State Statistical Office news release "Poverty Line," in 2008 the percentage of poor people was 28.7 (www.stat.gov.mk/pdf/2009/4.1.9.59.pdf, accessed 10 April 2011). As stated in the 2010 news release "Labour Market," in the second quarter of 2010 32.1 percent of the labor force were unemployed persons (www.stat.gov.mk/pdf/2010/2.1.10.28.pdf, accessed 10 April 2011).

7. Victor A. Friedman, personal communication.

8. Macedonians and Albanians generally tend to associate the emergence of the nouveaux riches in the 1990s with embezzlement of state funds and trafficking of people and goods, such as guns and cigarettes.

9. Kosovar Albanians tend to have children's birthday parties at McDonald's in Skopje—a practice commonly viewed as "modern" (as of this writing, there is no McDonald's in Kosovo).

10. Shortages of certain goods were not uncommon in Yugoslavia, especially in the south (Kosovo and Macedonia). In the 1970s, for example, people in Macedonia often traveled to Thessaloniki in northern Greece to purchase Western goods that were not available in Yugoslavia, or at least in the south. But shortages in Yugoslavia were not as severe, long-lasting, or widespread as in the rest of Eastern Europe and the USSR; moreover, their root causes were fundamentally different. The Yugoslav shortages were due to inequalities in distribution and, in the 1980s, to the drastic cut in imports required by Yugoslavia's acceptance of conditions imposed by the IMF (see Woodward 1995b; on the command economies of the Eastern Bloc, a different phenomenon, see Kornai 1980;

Verdery 1996). I am grateful to Victor A. Friedman and Susan L. Woodward (personal communications) for the information in this note.

Epilogue

1. On 7 August five alleged NLA insurgents were killed during a police raid in the Albanian-populated district of Gazi Baba in Skopje. Ten Macedonian soldiers were killed in an NLA ambush near Karpalak on the main Skopje-Tetovo highway the following day, and on 10 August eight soldiers were killed when a Macedonian military vehicle ran over a landmine north of the mainly Albanian-populated village of Ljuboten. In the immediate aftermath of the latter killing, minister of interior Ljube Boskovski ordered an intense, three-day police offensive (10–12 August) against the village; six Albanians were killed and several civilian buildings set ablaze during the offensive. Boskovski and his driver/bodyguard, Johan Tarčulovski, stood trial in April 2007 for alleged war crimes in Ljuboten at the International Criminal Tribunal for the former Yugoslavia (ICTY) in The Hague. In July 2008, Boskovski was acquitted of all charges and Tarčulovski was sentenced to 12 years in prison.

2. The aid donors' conference took place in Brussels in March 2002.

3. According to a public opinion poll conducted in September 2001, the Ohrid Framework Agreement enjoyed the approval of almost 44 percent of Macedonians and 78 percent of Albanians (*Utrinski Vesnik*, cited in Daftary and Friedman 2008: 291).

4. For Karamanlis's statement, see Greek Association for Atlantic and European Co-operation website http://www.gaaec.org/en/fyrom08, accessed 30 July 2011.

5. For the official 2008 parliamentary election results proclaimed by the Macedonian State Election Commission, see http://www.setimes.com/cocoon/setimes/xhtml/en_GB/newsbriefs/setimes/newsbriefs/2008/06/16/nb-02, accessed 10 April 2011.

6. The amended law on the use of languages, passed in an expedited procedure, stipulates that ministers and other officials (not just parliamentarians) whose mother tongue is spoken by at least 20 percent of the country's population can use their mother tongue in sessions of the Macedonian Parliament and its working bodies. The amended law on use of flags stipulates that in municipalities where over 50 percent of the population belongs to a community other than the Macedonian the members of that community can fly their national flag together with the state flag, which must be a third bigger. The four prosecutions and investigations of alleged crimes by NLA and Macedonian forces in 2001 (the "NLA Leadership" case, the "Mavrovo Road Worker" case, the "Lipkovo Water Reserve" case, and the "Neprošteno" investigation) that were dropped in July 2011 were initially brought before the ICTY and returned to Macedonian courts in 2008.

7. The reference to the cost of the Millennium Cross is from Misha Glenny, "Elections in Macedonia: Not Many Dead," http://www.opendemocracy.net/democracy-yugoslavia/article_380.jsp, accessed 10 April 2011.

8. The poll, which surveyed 835 persons from different ethnic backgrounds, was published in the Macedonian-language newspaper *Utrinski Vesnik*, 20 August 2001, 3. According to the poll, not only VMRO-DPMNE but all parties in the political arena

during the 2001 crisis suffered severe declines in popularity; SDSM from 32–34 to 17 percent; DPA/PDSH from over 10 to 6.7 percent; PDP/PPD from 5.7 to 5.1 percent. Importantly, 27.2 percent of the respondents reported that they would not vote.

9. On the construction of Skanderbeg as an Albanian national hero, see Lubonja 2002; Misha 2002. Statues of Skanderbeg have been erected in, among other locations, the Macedonian town of Debar, Tirana, Prishtina, Rome, and Geneva.

10. As Ragaru suggests (2008: 27), the inauguration of the statue can also be understood in the framework of rivalry between the Albanian parties DUI and DPA, and more specifically as DUI's attempt to attract popular support away from DPA.

11. A video visualization of the center of Skopje in 2014 can be found on the Centar municipality website, www.opstinacentar.gov.mk/video_materijali.aspx, accessed 30 July 2011.

12. For the specifics of the statue, see the Centar municipality notification, www.opstinacentar.gov.mk/page670132.aspx, accessed 30 July 2011.

13. Ali Ahmeti's TV statement can be found at http://www.youtube.com/watch?v=BTmm2LxFa_Q, accessed 6 August 2011.

GLOSSARY

A be—well; come on

Ajde—go ahead; come on; well, all right; OK then

ajvar—grilled red pepper relish

Albanec—Albanian (in Macedonian)

Ani—same as *Ajde* (in Albanian)

begaj tamu!—get out of here!

beter—worse (in Turkish)

bez vrska—irrelevant, piddling

bëj nder—honor, pay one's respects (in Albanian)

bratsvo i edinstvo—brotherhood and unity

bratstvo i ubistvo—brotherhood and murder; a wordplay on *bratsvo i edinstvo*

čest/čast—honor

česti/časti—offer hospitality

Čair—administrative district and neighborhood in Skopje (from Turkish *çayir*, "field")

čist—clean

deca begalci—refugee children

do të më plas koka—my head will burst (in Albanian)

dobro—fine

društvo—company

druženie—relaxed socializing

e jona (masculine: *i yni*)—ours (in Albanian)

ekzodus—exodus

ëmbëlsirë, def. *ëmbëlsira* (f.)—fruit preserves cooked with sugar (in Albanian)

fat, def. *fati* (m.)—fate, destiny (in Albanian)

flamur, def. *flamuri* (m.)—flag; also used as a first name (in Albanian)

fqinj, def. *fqinji* (m.)/*fqinje*, def. *fqinja* (f.)—neighbor (in Albanian)

gastarbeiter—guest workers

glavata ḱe mi pukne—my head will explode

go obravme bostanot—up the creek without a paddle

golemo selo—big village

Gradski Trgovski Centar—City Commercial Center (shopping mall in downtown Skopje)

imenden—name day

izvini—sorry, excuse me

jetë normale—normal life (in Albanian)

Kamen Most—Stone Bridge

Kasabali—Turkish-speaking Muslim urban dwellers of Macedonia

kavijar so lajno—caviar with crap (a mocking play on the name of Javier Solana)

ključ—"national key," quota system

kojshilluk—neighborliness (in Albanian)

kombi shqiptar—the Albanian nation (in Albanian)

komšija—neighbor

komšiluk—same as *kojshilluk*

komşuluk—same as *kojshilluk* (in Turkish)

kuku!—oh dear! (in Albanian)

kultura—culture

kum (m.)/*kuma* (f.)—ritual sponsor at a wedding (best man/bridesmaid)

kumbarë, def. *kumbara* (both m. and f.)—same as *kum/kuma* (in Albanian)

lele—oh dear

luftëtarë, def. *luftëtarët* (m.)—fighters (in Albanian)

mantil, def. *mantili* (sing. m.); *mantila*, def. *mantilat* (pl.)—long, loose overgarment resembling a coatdress; worn by some religiously observant Muslim women (in Albanian, also used in Macedonian as *mantil*)

mik, def. *miku* (m.)/*mikeshë*, def. *mikesha* (f.)—close friend (in Albanian)

mir—peace

Mladenci—celebration of newlyweds (on 22 March)

muhabet—casual conversation

narod—people

naselba—administrative district (also, neighborhood)

naš (m.)/*naša* (f.)—ours

nder, def. *nderi* (m.)—honor (in Albanian)

ne može—no, out of the question

ne se normalni—they are abnormal

një jetë normale—a normal life (in Albanian)

njerëz të thjeshtë—ordinary people (in Albanian)

normalen život—normal life

novodojdeni—newcomers

nuk janë normalë—they are abnormal (in Albanian)

obični lugje—ordinary people

opština—municipality

pa—well

paqe, def. *paqja* (f.)—peace (in Albanian)

për qejf—for personal amusement (in Albanian)

planinci—highlanders, mountain people

politika—politics

politikata e kurva—politics is a whore

politika është kurvë—politics is a whore (in Albanian)

pološi (pl.)—worse

posle socializam, ima kradizam—after socialism, there is theft

pravda—justice

pravi čest/čast—honor, pay one's respects

prljav—dirty

rilindje, def. *rilindja* (f.)—renaissance, rebirth; also used as a male first name, Rilind (in Albanian)

s' mundet—no, out of the question (in Albanian)

se razbira—it goes without saying

seloto gori, babata se češla—Nero fiddled while Rome burned

shami, def. *shamija* (sing. f.)/ *shamija,* def. *shamijat* (pl.)—headscarf (in Albanian, also used in Macedonian as *šamija*)

shok, def. *shoku* (m.)/*shoqe,* def. *shoqja* (f.)—friend, comrade; also, spouse (in Albanian)

slatko—fruit preserves cooked with sugar

smešno mi doagja—it feels funny

smrt za Šiptari—death to the *Šiptars*

sosed (m.)/*sosedka* (f.)—neighbor

starosedelci—old-dwellers

stegnat—tense

sudbina—fate, destiny

Şehirli—Turkish-speaking Muslim urban dwellers of Macedonia

Šiptar (m.)/Šiptarka (f.)—derogatory term for Albanian

što ḱe bide—what's going to happen

teroristi—terrorists

Turska (or Stara) Čaršija—Turkish (or Old) Bazaar

veštačko—artificial
vrski—personal connections
za nikade se—they are good for nothing
za Šiptari gasna komora—gas chambers for Šiptari
zadolžitelna kontrola—obligatory inspection

REFERENCES

Ackermann, Alice. 2000. *Making Peace Prevail: Preventing Violent Conflict in Macedonia*. Syracuse, N.Y.: Syracuse University Press.

———. 2001. "On the Razor's Edge: Is There Still a Place and Time for Long-Term Conflict Prevention in Macedonia?" Paper presented at Annual International Conference of the Centre for South East European Studies (CSEES), University of London, 14–16 June.

———. 2003. "International Intervention in Macedonia: From Preventive Engagement to Peace Implementation." In *International Intervention in the Balkans Since 1995*, ed. Peter Siani-Davies, 105-19. London: Routledge.

Alderson, Anthony Dolphin and Fahir Iz, eds. 1959. *The Concise Oxford Turkish Dictionary*. Oxford: Clarendon.

Allcock, John B. 2000. *Explaining Yugoslavia*. New York: Columbia University Press.

Anderson, Benedict. 1991. *Imagined Communities: Reflections on the Origin and Spread of Nationalism*. New York: Verso.

———. 1998. *The Specter of Comparisons: Nationalism, Southeast Asia, and the World*. New York: Verso.

Andriotes, Nikolaos. 1957. Το Ομόσπονδο Κράτος των Σκοπίων και η Γλώσσα του [*The Confederate State of Skopje and Its Language*]. Athens: [s.n.].

———. 1960. "History of the name 'Macedonia.'" *Balkan Studies* 1: 143–48.

Antonovska, Svetlana et al. 1996 [cited in Friedman 1996b]. *Broj i Struktura na Naselenieto vo Republika Makedonija po Opštini i Nacionalna Pripadnost: Sostojba 31.03.1991 godina* [*Number and Structure of the Population in the Republic of Macedonia by Communes and National Belonging: Situation 31.03.1991 year*]. Skopje: Republički Zavod za Statistika.

Aretxaga, Begoña. 1997. *Shattering Silence: Women, Nationalism, and*

Political Subjectivity in Northern Ireland. Princeton, N.J.: Princeton University Press.

———. 2005. *States of Terror: Begona Aretxaga's Essays.* Ed. Joseba Zulaika. Reno: Center for Basque Studies, University of Nevada.

Bagghi, Jasodhara. 1996. "Ethnicity and the Empowerment of Women: The Colonial Legacy." In *Embodied Violence: Communalizing Women's Sexuality in South Asia*, ed. Kumari Jayawardena and Malathi de Alwis, 113–25. London: Zed Books.

Bahloul, Joëlle. 1992. *The Architecture of Memory: A Jewish-Muslim Household in Colonial Algeria.* New York: Cambridge University Press.

Balalovska, Kristina. 2006. *Minority Politics in Southeast Europe—Macedonia 2006: Towards Stability?* Ethnobarometer Working Paper Series 11. Rome: Ethnobarometer.

Bateson, Gregory. 1951. "Information and Codification: A Philosophical Approach." In *Communication: The Social Matrix of Psychiatry*, ed. Jurgen Ruesch and Gregory Bateson, 168–211. New York: Norton.

———. [1955] 1972. "A Theory of Play and Fantasy." In *Steps to an Ecology of Mind*, ed. Gregory Bateson, 177–93. New York: Ballantine.

Berdahl, Daphne. 1999. "'(N)Ostalgie' for the Present: Memory, Longing, and East German Things." *Ethnos* 64, 2: 192–211.

———. 2010. *On the Social Life of Postsocialism: Memory, Consumption, Germany.* Ed. and intro. Matti Bunzl; foreword Michael Herzfeld. Bloomington: Indiana University Press.

Bhabha, Homi K. 1990a. "Introduction: Narrating the Nation." In *Nation and Narration*, ed. Homi K. Bhabha, 1–7. New York: Routledge.

———. 1990b. "DissemiNation: Time, Narrative, and the Margins of the Modern Nation." In *Nation and Narration,*ed. Homi K. Bhabha, 291–322. New York: Routledge.

———. 1994. *The Location of Culture.* New York : Routledge.

Bieber, Florian. 2008. "Power-Sharing and the Implementation of the Ohrid Framework Agreement." In *Power Sharing and the Implementation of the Ohrid Framework Agreement*, 7–40. Skopje: Friedrich Ebert Stiftung Office Macedonia.

Bisaku, Gjon, Shtjefën Kurti, and Luigj Gashi. 1997. "The Situation of the Albanian Minority in Yugoslavia: Memorandum Presented to the League of Nations (1930)." In *Kosovo: In the Heart of the Powder Keg*, ed. Robert Elsie, 361–99. Boulder, Colo.: East European Monographs.

Blumi, Isa. 2006. "Albania." In *Muslim Cultures Today: A Reference Guide*, ed. Kathryn M. Coughlin, 15–26. Westport, Conn.: Greenwood Press.

Bonilla, Frank and Myron Glazer. 1970. "A Note on Methodology: Field Work in a Hostile Environment: A Chapter in the Sociology of Social Research in Chile." In *Student Politics in Chile*, ed. Frank Bonilla and Myron Glazer, 313–33. New York: Basic Books.

Bowen, John R. 2007. *Why the French Don't Like Headscarves: Islam, the State, and Public Space*. Princeton, N.J.: Princeton University Press.

Boym, Svetlana. 2001. *The Future of Nostalgia*. New York: Basic Books.

Bracewell, Wendy. 2000. Rape in Kosovo: Masculinity and Serbian Nationalism. *Nations and Nationalism* 6, 4: 563–90.

Brandes, Stanley. 1980. *Metaphors of Masculinity: Sex and Status in Andalusian Folklore*. Philadelphia: University of Pennsylvania Press.

Bringa, Tone. 1995. *Being Muslim the Bosnian Way: Identity and Community in a Central Bosnian Village*. Princeton, N.J.: Princeton University Press.

———. 2004. "The Peaceful Death of Tito and the Violent End of Yugoslavia." In *Death of the Father: An Anthropology of the End in Political Authority*, ed. John Borneman, 148–99. New York: Berghahn.

Brown, Keith S. 1994. "Seeing Stars: Character and Identity in the Landscapes of Modern Macedonia." *Antiquity* 68: 784–96.

———. 1995. "Political Realities and Cultural Specificities in Contemporary Macedonian Jokes." *Western Folklore* 54, 3: 197–212.

———. 1998. "Contests of Heritage and the Politics of Preservation in the Former Yugoslav Republic of Macedonia." In *Archaeology Under Fire: Culture and Politics in the Eastern Mediterranean*, ed. Lynn Meskell, 68–86. New York: Routledge.

———. 2000. "In the Realm of the Double-Headed Eagle: Parapolitics in Macedonia 1994–9." In *Macedonia: The Politics of Identity and Difference*, ed. Jane K. Cowan, 122–39. London: Pluto Press.

———. 2001. "Beyond Ethnicity: The Politics of Urban Nostalgia in Modern Macedonia." *Journal of Mediterranean Studies* 11, 2: 417–42.

———. 2003. *The Past in Question: Modern Macedonia and the Uncertainties of Nation*. Princeton, N.J.: Princeton University Press.

———. 2009. "Sovereignty After Socialism at Europe's New Borders." In *The State of Sovereignty: Territories, Laws, Populations*, ed. Douglas Howland and Luise White, 196–221. Bloomington: Indiana University Press.

Brown, Keith S. and Yannis Hamilakis, eds. 2003. *The Usable Past: Greek Metahistories*. Lanham, Md.: Lexington Books.

Brubaker, Rogers. 1996. *Nationalism Reframed: Nationhood and the National Question in the New Europe*. Cambridge: Cambridge University Press.

Brunnbauer, Ulf. 2004. "Fertility, Families and Ethnic Conflict: Macedonians and Albanians in the Republic of Macedonia, 1944–2002." *Nationalities Papers* 32, 3: 565–98.

Bugajski, Janusz. 2002. *Political Parties of Eastern Europe: A Guide to Politics in the Post-Communist Era*. Armonk, N.Y.: M.E. Sharpe.

Bulgarian Academy of Sciences. 1980. *The Unity of the Bulgarian Language in the Past and Today*. Sofia: Publishing House of the Bulgarian Academy of Sciences.

Burawoy, Michael and Katherine Verdery. 1999. *Uncertain Transition: Ethnographies of Change in the Postsocialist World*. Lanham, Md.: Rowman and Littlefield.

Burg, Steven L. 1996. "Part II: Supporting Material." In *Toward Comprehensive Peace in Southeast Europe: Conflict Prevention in the South Balkans*, ed. Barnett R. Rubin, 27–80. New York: Twentieth Century Fund Press.

Calder, Kent E. 2008. "Critical Junctures and the Contours of Northeast Asian Regionalism." In *East Asian Multilateralism: Prospects for Regional Stability*, ed. Kent E. Calder and Francis Fukuyama, 15–39. Baltimore: Johns Hopkins University Press.

Chatterjee, Partha. 1993. *The Nation and Its Fragments: Colonial and Postcolonial Histories*. Princeton, N.J.: Princeton University Press.

Chivvis, Christopher S. 2008. The Making of Macedonia. *Survival* 50, 2: 141–62.

Christides, Christ. 1949. *The Macedonian Camouflage in the Light of Facts and Figures*. Athens: Hellenic.

Chuengsatiansup, Komatra. 2001. "Marginality, Suffering, and Community: The Politics of Collective Experience and Empowerment in Thailand." In *Remaking a World: Violence, Social Suffering, and Recovery*, ed. Veena Das, Arthur Kleinman, Margaret Lock, Mamphela Ramphele, and Pamela Reynolds, 31–75. Berkeley: University of California Press.

Churcher, Bob. 2002. "Kosovo Lindore/Preshevo 1999–2002 and the FYROM Conflict." Camberley: Conflict Studies Research Centre, Ministry of Defense UK, March.

Cobb, Sara. 1997. "The Domestication of Violence in Mediation." *Law and Society Review* 31, 3: 397–440.

Coleman, James S. 1988. "Social Capital in the Creation of Human Capital." *American Journal of Sociology* 94 Suppl.: S95–S120.

———. 1990. *Foundations of Social Theory*. Cambridge, Mass.: Harvard University Press.

Coles, Kimberley. 2007. *Democratic Designs: International Intervention and*

Electoral Practices in Postwar Bosnia-Herzegovina. Ann Arbor: University of Michigan Press.

Comaroff, Jean. 1985. *Body of Power, Spirit of Resistance: The Culture and History of a South African People*. Chicago: University of Chicago Press.

Comaroff, Jean and John Comaroff. 1993. *Modernity and its Malcontents: Ritual and Power in Postcolonial Africa*. Chicago: University of Chicago Press.

Connell, R. W. 1987. *Gender and Power: Society, the Person, and Sexual Politics*. Cambridge: Polity Press with Blackwell.

———. 1990. "The State, Gender, and Sexual Politics: Theory and Appraisal." *Theory and Society* 19, 5: 507–44.

———. 2000. *The Men and the Boys*. Berkeley: University of California Press.

Cowan, Jane K. 1990. *Dance and the Body Politic in Northern Greece*. Princeton, N.J.: Princeton University Press.

———. 1997. "Idioms of Belonging: Polyglot Articulations of Local Identity in a Greek Town." In *Ourselves and Others: The Development of a Greek Macedonian Cultural Identity*, ed. Peter Mackridge and Eleni Yannakakis, 153–71. Oxford: Berg.

———, ed. 2000. *Macedonia: The Politics of Identity and Difference*. London: Pluto Press.

Cowan, Jane K., Marie-Benedicte Dembour, and Richard A. Wilson, eds. 2001. *Culture and Rights: Anthropological Perspectives*. Cambridge: Cambridge University Press.

Crnobrnja, Mihailo. 1994. *The Yugoslav Drama*.Montreal: McGill-Queen's University Press.

Daftary, Farimah and Eben Friedman. 2008. "Power-Sharing in Macedonia?" In *Settling Self-Determination Disputes: Complex Power-sharing in Theory and Practice*, ed. Marc Weller and Barbara Metzger, 265–305. The Netherlands: Martinus Nijhoff.

Danforth, Loring M. 1995. *The Macedonian Conflict: Ethnic Nationalism in a Transnational World*. Princeton, N.J.: Princeton University Press.

Danforth, Loring M. and Riki van Boeschoten. 2012. *Children of the Greek Civil War: Refugees and the Politics of Memory*. Chicago: University of Chicago Press.

Das, Veena. 1995. *Critical Events: An Anthropological Perspective on Contemporary India*. New York: Oxford University Press.

———. 2007. *Life and Words: Violence and the Descent into the Ordinary*. Berkeley: University of California Press.

Daskalovski, Židas. 2006. *Walking on the Edge: Consolidating Multiethnic Macedonia, 1989–2004*. Chapel Hill, N.C.: Globic Press.

———. 2009. "'Spinning Out of Control': Mutual Reinforcement Discourse in Macedonia?" In *Media Discourse and the Yugoslav Conflicts: Representations of Self and Other*, ed. Pål Kolstø, 173–93. Burlington, Vt.: Ashgate.

Denich, Bette S. 1970. "Migration and Network Manipulation in Yugoslavia." In *Migration and Anthropology*, Proceedings of the 1970 Annual Spring Meeting of the American Ethnological Society, ed. Robert F. Spencer, 133–45. Seattle: University of Washington Press.

Dimova, Rozita. 2006. "'Modern' Masculinities: Ethnicity, Education, and Gender in Macedonia." *Nationalities Papers* 34, 3: 305–20.

———. 2010. Consuming Ethnicity: Loss, Commodities, and Space in Macedonia." *Slavic Review: Interdisciplinary Quarterly of Russian, Eurasian, and East European Studies* 69, 4: 859–81.

Douglas, Mary. 1966. *Purity and Danger: An Analysis of Concepts of Pollution and Taboo*. London: Routledge.

Drakulić, Slavenka. 1992. *How We Survived Communism and Even Laughed*. New York: Norton.

———. 1993. *The Balkan Express: Fragments from the Other Side of War*. New York: Norton.

Dudwick, Nora. 2000. "Postsocialism and the Fieldwork of War." In *Fieldwork Dilemmas: Anthropologists in Postsocialist States*, ed. Hermine G. De Soto and Nora Dudwick, 13–30. Madison: University of Wisconsin Press.

Ellis, Burcu Akan. 2003. *Shadow Genealogies: Memory and Identity Among Urban Muslims in Macedonia*. New York: Columbia University Press.

Elsie, Robert, ed. 1997. *Kosovo: In the Heart of the Powder Keg*. Boulder, Colo.: East European Monographs.

Feldman, Allen. 1991. *Formations of Violence: The Narrative of the Body and Political Terror in Northern Ireland*. Chicago University of Chicago Press.

———. 1995. "Ethnographic States of Emergency." In *Fieldwork Under Fire: Contemporary Studies of Violence and Survival*, ed. Carolyn Nordstrom and Antonius C. G. M. Robben, 224–52. Berkeley: University of California Press.

Ferguson, James. 1999. *Expectations of Modernity: Myths and Meanings of Urban Life on the Zambian Copperbelt*. Berkeley: University of California Press.

Foucault, Michel. 1972. *The Archaeology of Knowledge*. Trans. A. M. Sheridan Smith. New York: Pantheon.

———. 1978. *The History of Sexuality*. Vol. 1. *An Introduction*. Trans. Robert Hurley. New York: Pantheon.

———. 1980. *Power/Knowledge: Selected Interviews and Other Writings 1972–1977.* Ed. Colin Gordon, trans. Colin Gordon et al. Brighton: Harvester.

———. 1983. "The Subject and Power: Afterword." In *Michel Foucault: Beyond Structuralism and Hermeneutics*, ed. Hubert L. Dreyfus and Paul Rabinow. 2nd ed., 208–26. Chicago: University of Chicago Press.

———. 1988. *The Final Foucault*, ed. James Bernauer and David Rasmussen. Cambridge, Mass.: MIT Press.

———. 1997. *Ethics: Subjectivity and Truth.* Ed. Paul Rabinow. New York: New Press.

———. 2003. *Abnormal: Lectures at the Collège de France, 1974–1975.* Ed. Valerio Marchetti and Antonella Salomoni, trans. Graham Burchell. New York: Picador.

Fraenkel, Eran. 2001. "Macedonia." In *Nations in Transit, 2001: Civil Society, Democracy and Markets in East Central Europe and the Newly Independent States*, ed. Adrian Karatnycky, Alexander Motyl, and Amanda Schnetzer, 260–71. New Brunswick, N.J.: Transaction Publishers.

Friedman, Victor A. 1985. "The Sociolinguistics of Literary Macedonian." *International Journal of the Sociology of Language* 52: 31–57.

———. 1995a. "On the Use of the Terms 'Rom' and 'Romani'" (with Ian Hancock). *Newsletter of the Gypsy Lore Society* 18, 2: 6–7.

———. 1995b. "Persistence and Change in Ottoman Patterns of Codeswitching in the Republic of Macedonia: Nostalgia, Duress, and Language Shift in Contemporary Southeastern Europe." In *Summer School: Code-Switching and Language Contact*, ed. Durk Gorter et al., 58–67. Ljouwert: Fryske Akademy.

———. 1996 "Observing the Observers: Language, Ethnicity, and Power in the 1994 Macedonian Census and Beyond." In *Toward Comprehensive Peace in Southeastern Europe: Conflict Prevention in the South Balkans*, ed. Barnett Rubin, 81–105. New York: Council on Foreign Relations/Twentieth Century Fund.

———. 1998. "A Balkanist in Daghestan: Annotated Notes from the Field." *Anthropology of East Europe Review* 16, 2: 178–203.

———. 2000. "The Modern Macedonian Standard Language and Its Relation to Modern Macedonian Identity." In *The Macedonian Question: Culture, Historiography, Politics*, ed. Victor Roudometoff. Boulder, Colo.: East European Monographs. 173–206.

———. 2003. "Language in Macedonia as an Identity Construction Site." In *When Languages Collide: Perspectives on Language Conflict, Language Competition, and Language Coexistence*, ed. Brian D. Joseph, Johanna

DeStafano, Neil G. Jacobs, and Ilse Lehiste, 257–95. Columbus: Ohio State University Press.

———. 2006. "Determination and Doubling in Balkan Borderlands." *Harvard Ukrainian Studies* 28, 1–4: 105–16.

———. 2007. "Language Politics and Language Policies in the Contemporary Western Balkans: Infinitives, Turkisms, and Eurolinguistics." *EES News: East European Studies-Woodrow Wilson Center for Scholars* 1–4 (September–October): 10–11.

Friedman, Victor A., Susan L. Woodward, and Keith Brown, Special Section Guest Editors. 2010. "Challenging Crossroads: Macedonia in Global Perspective." *Slavic Review* 69, 4.

Gaber, Natasha and Aneta Joveska. 2004. "Macedonian Census Results: Controversy or Reality?" *South-East Europe Review for Labour and Social Affairs* 1: 99–119.

Gagnon, Valère Philip. 2004. *The Myth of Ethnic War: Serbia and Croatia in the 1990s.* Ithaca, N.Y.: Cornell University Press.

Gal, Susan and Gail Kligman. 2000. *The Politics of Gender After Socialism: A Comparative Historical Essay.* Princeton, N.J.: Princeton University Press.

Gall, Carlotta. 2001. "For Kosovars, Battle Moves to the Border of Macedonia." *New York Times*, 25 February.

George, Kenneth M. 1996. *Showing Signs of Violence: The Cultural Politics of a Twentieth-century Headhunting Ritual.* Berkeley: University of California Press.

Graan, Andrew. 2010. "On the Politics of Imidž: European Integration and the Trials of Recognition in Postconflict Macedonia." *Slavic Review: Interdisciplinary Quarterly of Russian, Eurasian, and East European Studies* 69, 4: 835–58.

Grandits, Hannes. 2007. "The Power of 'Armchair Politicians': Ethnic Loyalty and Political Factionalism Among Herzegovinian Croats." In *The New Bosnian Mosaic: Identities, Memories and Moral Claims in a Post-War Society*, ed. Xavier Bougarel, Elissa Helms, and Ger Duijzings, 101–22. Burlington, Vt.: Ashgate.

Green, Sarah F. 2005. *Notes from the Balkans: Locating Marginality and Ambiguity on the Greek-Albanian Border.* Princeton, N.J.: Princeton University Press.

Greenhouse, Carol J. 1992. "Signs of Quality: Individualism and Hierarchy in American Culture." *American Ethnologist* 19, 2: 233–54.

Greenhouse, Carol J., Elizabeth Mertz, and Kay B. Warren, eds. 2002. *Ethnography in Unstable Places: Everyday Lives in Contexts of Dramatic Political Change.* Durham, N.C.: Duke University Press.

Greenhouse, Carol J., Barbara Yngvesson, and David M. Engel. 1994. *Law and Community in Three American Towns*. Ithaca, N.Y.: Cornell University Press.

Gupta, Akhil. 1995. "Blurred Boundaries: The Discourse of Corruption, the Culture of Politics, and the Imagined State." *American Ethnologist* 22, 2: 375–402.

Halpern, Joel M. and David A. Kideckel, eds. 2000. *Neighbors at War: Anthropological Perspectives on Yugoslav Ethnicity, Culture, and History*. University Park: Pennsylvania State University Press.

Hayden, Robert M. 1992. "Constitutional Nationalism in the Formerly Yugoslav Republics." *Slavic Review* 51: 654–73.

———. 1999. *Blueprints for a House Divided: The Constitutional Logic of the Yugoslav Conflicts*. Ann Arbor: University of Michigan Press.

Helms, Elissa. 2007. "'Politics Is a Whore': Women, Morality and Victimhood in Post-War Bosnia-Herzegovina." In *The New Bosnian Mosaic: Identities, Memories and Moral Claims in a Post-War Society*, ed. Xavier Bougarel, Elissa Helms, and Ger Duijzings, 235–54. Burlington, Vt.: Ashgate.

Herzfeld, Michael. 1985. *The Poetics of Manhood: Contest and Identity in a Cretan Mountain Village*. Princeton, N.J.: Princeton University Press.

———. 1987. "'As in Your Own House': Hospitality, Ethnography, and the Stereotype of Mediterranean Society." In *Honor and Shame and the Unity of the Mediterranean*, ed. David D. Gilmore, Special Publication 22, 75–89. Washington, D.C.: American Anthropological Association.

———. 1991. "Silence, Submission, and Subversion: Toward a Poetics of Womanhood." In *Contested Identities: Gender and Kinship in Modern Greece*, ed. Peter Loizos and Evthymios Papataxiarchis, 79–97. Princeton, N.J.: Princeton University Press.

———. 1992. *The Social Production of Indifference: Exploring the Symbolic Roots of Western Bureaucracy*. Oxford: Berg.

Hislope, Robert. 2002. "Organized Crime in a Disorganized State: How Corruption Contributed to Macedonia's Mini-War." *Problems of Post-Communism* 49, 3: 33–41.

———. 2003. "Between a Bad Peace and a Good War: Insights and Lessons from the Almost-War in Macedonia." *Ethnic and Racial Studies* 26, 1: 129–51.

———. 2007. "From Expressive to Actionable Hatred: Ethnic Divisions and Riots in Macedonia." In *Identity Conflicts: Can Conflict be Regulated?*, ed. J. Craig Jenkins and Esther E. Gottlieb, 149–65. New Brunswick, N.J.: Transaction Publishers.

Human Rights Watch. 1998. *Police Violence in Macedonia: Official Thumbs Up*. New York: HRW, 1 April.

Icevska, Gordana and Ilir Ajdini. 2002. "Same World, Parallel Universes: The Role of the Media in the Macedonian Conflict." In *Ohrid and Beyond: A Cross-ethnic Investigation into the Macedonian Crisis*, 73–81. London: Institute for War and Peace Reporting.

Ilievski, Petar H. 2006. *Dva Sprotivni Prioda kon Interpretacijata na Antički Tekstovi so Antroponimicka Codržina (so Poseben Osvrt kon Antičko-makedonskata Antroponimija)*[*Two Opposite Approaches Toward Interpreting Ancient Texts with Anthroponymic Contents (with Special Regard to the Ancient Macedonian Anthroponymy)*]. http://www.manu.edu.mk/Ilievski-Dva_sprotivni_prioda.pdf, accessed April 10, 2011.

Ilirjani, Altin. 2006. *The Euro Before the EU? An Estimate of the Economic Effects of Euroization in the Western Balkans*. Chapel Hill, N.C.: Globic Press.

International Crisis Group (ICG). 1997. *Macedonia Report: The Politics of Ethnicity and Conflict*. Europe Report 26. Skopje/ Brussels: ICG, 30 October.

———. 2001. *The Macedonian Question: Reform or Rebellion*. Balkans Report 109. Brussels: ICG, 5 April.

Institute for War and Peace Reporting (IWPR). 2001. "New Balkan Conflict Brewing." 1 March. http://www.balkanpeace.org/index.php?index=article&articleid=10723, accessed 10 April 2011.

Irvine, Judith T. and Susan Gal. 2000. "Language Ideology and Linguistic Differentiation." In *Regimes of Language: Ideologies, Polities, and Identities*, ed. Paul V. Kroskrity, 35–84. Santa Fe, N.M.: School of American Research Press.

Ismail, Salwa. 2006. *Political Life in Cairo's New Quarters: Encountering the Everyday State*. Minneapolis: University of Minnesota Press.

Jansen, Stef. 2007. "Remembering with a Difference: Clashing Memories of Bosnian Conflict in Everyday Life." In *The New Bosnian Mosaic: Identities, Memories and Moral Claims in a Post-War Society*, ed. Xavier Bougarel, Elissa Helms, and Ger Duijzings, 193–210. Burlington, Vt.: Ashgate.

Jeffries, Ian. 2002. *The Former Yugoslavia at the Turn of the Twenty-First Century: A Guide to the Economies in Transition*. New York: Routledge.

Jeganathan, Pradeep. 1998. "In the Shadow of Violence: 'Tamilness' and the Anthropology of Identity in Southern Sri Lanka." In *Buddhist Fundamentalism and Minority Identities in Sri Lanka*, ed. Tessa J. Bartholomeusz and Chandra R. de Silva, 89–109. Albany: State University of New York Press.

———. 2000. "A Space for Violence: Anthropology, Politics and the Location of a Sinhala Practice of Masculinity." In *Community, Gender, and Violence*, ed. Partha Chatterjee and Pradeep Jeganathan, 37–65. New York: Columbia University Press.

Jetter, Alexis, Annelise Orleck, and Diana Taylor, eds. 1997. *The Politics of Motherhood: Activist Voices from Left to Right*. Hanover, N.H.: University Press of New England for Dartmouth College.

Johnson, Chalmers. 2004. *The Sorrows of Empire: Militarism, Secrecy, and the End of the Republic*. New York: Metropolitan Books.

Judah, Tim. 2002. *Kosovo: War and Revenge*. New Haven, Conn.: Yale University Press.

Karakasidou, Anastasia N. 1993. "Politicizing Culture: Negating Ethnic Identity in Greek Macedonia." *Journal of Modern Greek Studies* 11, 1: 1–28.

———. 1994. "Sacred Scholars, Profane Advocates Intellectuals Molding National Consciousness in Greece." *Identities* 1, 1: 35–61.

———. 1997. *Fields of Wheat, Hills of Blood: Passages to Nationhood in Greek Macedonia*. Chicago: University of Chicago Press.

Kaufman, Stuart J. 1996. "Preventive Peacekeeping, Ethnic Violence and Macedonia." *Studies in Conflict and Terrorism* 19: 229–46.

Kekic, Laza. 2001. "Former Yugoslav Republic of Macedonia (FYROM)." In *Balkan Reconstruction*, ed. Thanos Veremis and Daniel Daianu, 186–202. Portland, Ore.: Frank Cass.

Kertzer, David I. and Dominique Arel. 2002. *Census and Identity: The Politics of Race, Ethnicity, and Language in National Censuses*. New York: Cambridge University Press.

Kitromilides, Paschalis M. 1996. "'Balkan Mentality': History, Legend, Imagination." *Nations and Nationalism* 2, 2: 163–91.

Kofos, Evangelos. 1964. *Nationalism and Communism in Macedonia*. Thessaloniki: Institute for Balkan Studies.

———. 2002. "The Albanian Question in the Aftermath of the War: A Proposal to Break the Status Deadlock." In *Is Southeastern Europe Doomed to Instability? A Regional Perspective*, ed. Dimitri A. Sotiropoulos and Thanos Veremis, 151–72. London: Cass.

Kolind, Torsten. 2007. "In Search of 'Decent People': Resistance to the Ethnicization of Everyday Life Among the Muslims of Stolac." In *The New Bosnian Mosaic: Identities, Memories, and Moral Claims in a Post-War*

Society, ed. Xavier Bougarel, Elissa Helms, and Ger Duijzings, 123–38. Burlington, Vt.: Ashgate.

Kornai, Janos. 1980. *Economics of Shortage*. New York: Elsevier North-Holland.

Kostopoulos, Tasos. 2000. *I Apagorevmeni Glossa: Kratiki Katastoli ton Slavikon Dialekton stin Elliniki Makedonia* [*The Prohibited Language: State Repression of Slavic Dialects in Greek Macedonia*]. Athens: Mavri Lista.

Kostovicova, Denisa. 2005. *Kosovo: The Politics of Identity and Space*. London: Routledge.

Kovačec, August. 1992. "Languages of National Minorities and Ethnic Groups in Yugoslavia." In *Language Planning in Yugoslavia*, ed. Ranko Bugarski and Celia Hawkesworth, 43–58. Columbus, Ohio: Slavica.

Krieger, Heike, ed. 2001. *The Kosovo Conflict and International Law: An Analytical Documentation 1974–1999*. Cambridge International Documents 11. New York: Cambridge University Press.

Latifi, Veton. 2001. "Skopje Dismisses KLA Bombing Link," *Balkan Crisis Report* 218, 14 (February 2001). http://iwpr.net/report-news/skopje-dismisses-kla-bombing-link, accessed 10 April 2011

———. 2003. *Macedonian Unfinished Crisis: Challenges in the Process of Democratization and Stabilization*. Skopje: Konrad Adenauer Stiftung.

Lin, Nan. 2001. *Social Capital: A Theory of Social Structure and Action*. New York: Cambridge University Press.

Lindstrom, Nicole. 2005. "Yugonostalgia: Restorative and Reflective Nostalgia in former Yugoslavia." *East Central Europe* 32, 1–2: 7–55.

Lubonja, Fatos. 2002. "Between the Glory of a Virtual World and the Misery of a Real World." In *Albanian Identities: Myth and History*, ed. Stephanie Schwandner-Sievers and Bernd J. Fischer, 91–103. Bloomington: Indiana University Press.

Lund, Michael S. 2000. "Preventive: Diplomacy for Macedonia, 1992–1999: From Containment to Nation Building." In *Opportunities Missed, Opportunities Seized: Preventive Diplomacy in the Post-Cold War World*, ed. Bruce W. Jentleson, 173–208. Carnegie Commission on Preventing Deadly Conflict. Lanham, Md.: Rowman and Littlefield.

Mackridge, Peter and Eleni Yannakakis, eds. 1997. *Ourselves and Others: The Development of a Greek Macedonian Cultural Identity since 1912*. New York: Berg.

Maček, Ivana. 2009. *Sarajevo Under Siege: Anthropology in Wartime*. Philadelphia: University of Pennsylvania Press.

Mahon, Milena. 2004. "The Macedonian Question in Bulgaria." *Nations and Nationalism* 4, 3: 389–407.

Marinov, Čavdar. 2009. *"Kak Se Pravi Spešna Antropologija: Po Povod Kni-gata na Petăr-Emil Mitev, Antonina Željazkova i Goran Stojkovski Make-donija na krăstopăt"* [*How to Do Urgent Anthropolgy: Concerning the Book 'Macedonia at a Crossroads' by Petăr-Emil Mitev, Antonina Željazkova i Goran Stojkovski*] *Kyltyra* 3, 2530 (23 January): 14–15.

Martis, Nikolaos. 1983. *The Falsification of Macedonian History.* Athens: Graphic Arts of Athanassiades Bros.

Meneley, Anne. 1996. *Tournaments of Value: Sociability and Hierarchy in a Yemeni Town.* Toronto: University of Toronto Press.

Michas, Takis. 2002. *Unholy Alliance: Greece and Milošević's Serbia.* College Station: Texas A&M University Press.

Misha, Piro. 2002. "Invention of a Nationalism: Myth and Amnesia." In *Alba-nian Identities: Myth and History,* ed. Stephanie Schwandner-Sievers and Bernd J. Fischer, 33–48. Bloomington: Indiana University Press.

Monova, Miladina. 2001. "De l'historicité à l'ethnicité: les Égéens ou ces au-tres Macédoniens." *Balkanologie* 1–2: 179–97.

———. 2002a. "Parcours d'exil, récits de non-retour: les Égéens en République de Macédoine." Ph.D. Thesis, École des Hautes Études en Sciences Socia-les, Paris.

———. 2002b. "De la logique de retour à la logique d'établissement: le cas des réfugiés de la guerre civile grecque en République de Macédoine." *Études Balkaniques: Cahiers Pierre Belon* 9: 73–92.

———. 2010. "The Impossible Citizenship: The Case of Macedonians, Ref-ugees from the Greek Civil War in the Republic of Macedonia." In *Mi-grations from and to Southeastern Europe,* ed. Anna Krasteva, Anelia Kasabova, and Diana Karabinova, 253–66. Ravenna: Longo.

Moore, Henrietta L. 1994. *A Passion for Difference: Essays in Anthropology and Gender.* Bloomington: Indiana University Press.

Moore, Sally Falk. 1978. *Law as Process: An Anthropological Approach.* Lon-don: Routledge.

———. 1987. "Explaining the Present: Theoretical Dilemmas in Processual Ethnography." *American Ethnologist* 14, 4: 727–36.

Morris, David B. 1996. "About Suffering: Voice, Genre, and Moral Commu-nity." *Daedalus* 125, 1: 25–45.

Nagel, Joane. 1998. "Masculinity and Nationalism: Gender and Sexuality in the Making of Nations." *Ethnic and Racial Studies* 21, 2: 244.

Neofotistos, Vasiliki P. 2004. "Beyond Stereotypes: Violence and the Porous-ness of Ethnic Boundaries in the Republic of Macedonia." *History and Anthropology* 15, 1: 47–67.

———. 2008. "'The Balkans' Other Within': Imaginings of the West in the Republic of Macedonia." *History and Anthropology* 19, 1: 17–36.

———. 2009a. "Bulgarian Passports, Macedonian Identity: The Invention of EU Citizenship in the Republic of Macedonia." *Anthropology Today* 25, 4: 19–22.

———. 2009b. "Re-Thinking 'Make Do': Action 'from the Side' and the Politics of Segmentation in the Republic of Macedonia." *American Ethnologist* 36, 1: 137–48.

———. 2010. "Cultural Intimacy and Subversive Disorder: The Politics of Romance in the Republic of Macedonia." *Anthropological Quarterly* 83, 2: 279–315.

———. 2012 (forthcoming) "Going Home to Pakistan: Identity and Its Discontents in Southeastern Europe." *Identities: Global Studies in Culture and Power.*

Nikolovska, Natalija and Gordana Siljanovska-Davkova. 2001. *Makedonskata Tranzicija vo Defekt: Od Unitarna kon Binacionalna Država* [*Defect in the Macedonian Transition: From a Unitary to a Binational State*]. Skopje: Magor.

Nordstrom, Carolyn. 1997. *A Different Kind of War Story*. Philadelphia: University of Pennsylvania Press.

Norwegian Refugee Council. 2002. *Internally Displaced People: A Global Survey*. Second Edition, London: Earthscan.

Ortner, Sherry, B. 1996 *Making Gender: The Politics and Erotics of Culture*. Boston: Beacon Press.

Osborn, Michelle. 2008. "Fuelling the Flames: Rumour and Politics in Kibera." *Journal of Eastern African Studies* 2, 2: 315–27.

Osella, Caroline and Filippo Osella. 2006. *Men and Masculinities in South India*. New York: Anthem Press.

Pentassuglia, Gaetano 2002. *Minorities in International Law: An Introductory Study*. Strasbourg: Council of Europe Publishing.

Perry, Duncan. 1988. *The Politics of Terror: The Macedonian Revolutionary Movements, 1893–1903*. Durham, N.C.: Duke University Press.

Petroska-Beška, Violeta. 1996. "NGOs, Early Warning and Preventive Action: Macedonia." In *Vigilance and Vengeance: NGOs Preventing Ethnic Conflict in Divided Societies*, ed. Robert I. Rotberg, 133–44. Washington, D.C.: Brookings Institution/World Peace Foundation.

Petrović, Tanja. 2010. "Nostalgia for the JNA? Remembering the Army in the Former Yugoslavia." In *Post-Communist Nostalgia*, ed. Maria Todorova and Zsuzsa Gille, 61–81. New York: Berghahn.

Phillips, John. 2004. *Macedonia: Warlords and Rebels in the Balkans*. New Haven, Conn.: Yale University Press.

Portes, Alexander. 1988. "Social Capital: Its Origins and Applications in Modern Sociology." *Annual Review of Sociology* 24: 1–24.

Poulton, Hugh. 1995. *Who Are the Macedonians?* Bloomington: Indiana University Press.

Ragaru, Nadège. 2008. "Macedonia: Between Ohrid and Brussels." Centre d'Études et de Recherches Internationales. http:// www.ceri-sciencespo. com/cherlist/ragaru/macedonia.pdf, accessed April 10, 2011.

Ramet, Sabrina P. 2002. *Balkan Babel: The Disintegration of Yugoslavia from the Death of Tito to the Fall of Milošević*. Boulder, Colo.: Westview Press.

Reed-Danahay, Deborah E. 1997. *Auto/Ethnography: Rewriting the Self and the Social*. Oxford,: Berg.

———. 2005. *Locating Bourdieu*. Bloomington: Indiana University Press.

Reka, Armend. 2008. "The Ohrid Agreement: The Travails of Inter-Ethnic Relations in Macedonia." *Human Rights Review* 9: 55–69.

Risteski, Liupčo. 2009. "Recognition of the Independence of the Macedonian Orthodox Church (MOC) as an Issue Concerning Macedonian National Identity." *EthnoAnthropoZoom* 6: 145–85.

Rossos, Andrew. 1991. "The Macedonians of Aegean Macedonia: A British Officer's Report, 1944." *Slavonic and East European Review* 69, 2: 282–309.

———. 2008. *Macedonia and the Macedonians: A History*. Stanford, Calif.: Hoover Institution Press.

Roudometof, Victor, ed. 2000. *The Macedonian Question: Culture, Historiography, Politics*. New York: Columbia University Press.

———. 2001. *Nationalism, Globalization, and Orthodoxy: The Social Origins of Ethnic Conflict in the Balkans*. Westport, Conn.t: Greenwood Press.

———. 2002. *Collective Memory, National Identity, and Ethnic Conflict: Greece, Bulgaria and the Macedonian Question*. Westport, Connecticut: Praeger.

Royce, Anya Peterson. 1982. *Ethnic Identity: Strategies of Diversity*. Bloomington: Indiana University Press,

Royle, Nicholas. 2003. *The Uncanny: An Introduction*. New York: Routledge.

Rusi, Iso. 2002. "From Army to Party: The Politics of the NLA." In *Ohrid and Beyond: A Cross-Ethnic Investigation into the Macedonian Crisis*, 19–34. London: IWPR.

———. 2003. "Fact and Fiction: The Media's Negative Role." In *Macedonia: The Conflict and the Media*, ed. Alistair Crighton, 97–114. Skopje: Macedonian Institute for Media.

Schwandner-Sievers, Stephanie. 2001. "The Enactment of 'Tradition': Albanian Constructions of Identity, Violence and Power in Times of Crises." In *Anthropology of Violence and Conflict*, ed. Bettina E. Schmidt and Ingo W. Schröder, 97–120. New York: Routledge.

———. 2010. "Invisible-Inaudible: Albanian Memories of Socialism After the War in Kosovo." In *Post-Communist Nostalgia*, ed. Maria Todorova and Zsuzsa Gille, 96–112. New York: Berghahn.

Schwandner-Sievers, Stephanie and Bernd J. Fischer, eds. 2002. *Albanian Identities: Myth and History*. Bloomington: Indiana University Press.

Schwarz, Jonathan. 1993. "Macedonia: A Country in Quotation Marks." *Anthropology of East Europe Review* 11: 107–15.

Seifert, Ruth. 1994. "War and Rape: A Preliminary Analysis." In *Mass Rape: the War Against Women in Bosnia-Herzegovina*, ed. Alexandra Stiglmayer, 54–72. Lincoln: University of Nebraska Press.

Shea, John. 1997. *Macedonia and Greece: The Struggle to Define a New Balkan Nation*. Jefferson, N.C.: McFarland.

Shields, Rob. 1997. "Spatial Stress and Resistance: Social Meanings of Spatialization." In *Space and Social Theory: Interpreting Modernity and Postmodernity*, ed. Georges Benko and Ulf Strohmayer, 186–202. Malden, Mass.: Blackwell.

Silverman, Carol. 2000. "Researcher, Advocate, Friend: An American Fieldworker Among Balkan Roma, 1980–1996." In *Fieldwork Dilemmas: Anthropologists in Postsocialist States*, ed. Hermine G. De Soto and Nora Dudwick, 195–217. Madison: University of Wisconsin Press.

Simić, Andrei. 1973. *The Peasant Urbanites: A Study of Rural-Urban Mobility in Serbia*. New York: Seminar Press.

Simons, Anne. 1995. "The Beginning of the End." In *Fieldwork Under Fire: Contemporary Studies of Violence and Survival*, ed. Carolyn Nordstrom and Antonius C. G. M. Robben, 42–61. Berkeley: University of California Press.

Sluka, Jeffrey A. 1990. "Participant Observation in Violent Social Contexts." *Human Organization* 49, 2: 114–26.

Slyomovics, Susan. 2005. *The Performance of Human Rights in Morocco*. Philadelphia: University of Pennsylvania Press.

Sokalski, Henryk J. 2003. *An Ounce of Prevention: Macedonia and the UN Experience in Preventive Diplomacy*. Washington, D.C.: U.S. Institute of Peace.

Stacher, Irene. 2000. "Austria: Reception of Conflict Refugees." In *Kosovo's Refugees in the European Union*, ed. Joanne van Selm, 118–38. London: Pinter.

Stewart, Kathleen. 1988. "Nostalgia: A Polemic." *Cultural Anthropology* 3, 3: 227–41.

Strathern, Andrew, Pamela Stewart, and Neil Whitehead. 2005. *Terror and Violence: Imagination and the Unimaginable*. London: Pluto.

Stychin, Carl F. 1998. *A Nation by Rights: National Cultures, Sexual Identity Politics, and the Discourse of Rights*. Philadelphia: Temple University Press.

Sugarman, Jane C. 2010. "Kosova Calls for Peace: Song, Myth, and War in an Age of Global Media." In *Music and Conflict*, ed. John Morgan O'Connell and Salwa El-Shawan Castelo-Branco, 17–45. Champaign: University of Illinois Press.

Sutton, David Evan. 1998. *Memories Cast in Stone: The Relevance of the Past in Everyday Life*. Oxford: Berg.

Szajkowski, Bogdan. 2000. "Macedonia: An Unlikely Road to Democracy." In *Experimenting with Democracy: Regime Change in the Balkans*, ed. Geoffrey Pridham and Tom Gallagher, 249–72. New York: Routledge.

Taussig, Michael. 2003. *Law in a Lawless Land: Diary of a Limpieza in Colombia*. New York: New Press.

Taylor, Scott. 2002. *Diary of an Uncivil War: The Violent Aftermath of the Kosovo Conflict*. Ottawa Esprit de Corps Books.

Thiessen, Ilka. 2007. *Waiting for Macedonia: Identity in a Changing World*. Orchard Park, N.Y.: Broadview.

Todorova, Maria and Zsuzsa Gille, eds. 2010. *Post-Communist Nostalgia*. New York: Berghahn.

Trnka, Susanna. 2008. *State of Suffering: Political Violence and Community Survival in Fiji*. Ithaca, N.Y.: Cornell University Press.

Tubilewicz, Czeslaw. 2007. *Taiwan and Post-Communist Europe: Shopping for Allies*. New York: Routledge.

Vankovska, Biljana. 2003. "Security Sector Reform in Macedonia." In *Defense and Security Sector Governance and Reform in South East Europe: Insights and Perspectives*, vol. 2, *Macedonia, Moldova, Romania*, ed. Jan A. Trapans and Philipp Fluri, 21–35. Geneva: Geneva Centre for the Democratic Control of Armed Forces.

———. 2006. "The Impact of Conflict and Corruption on Macedonia's Civil-Military Relations." In *Civil-Military Relations in Europe: Learning from Crisis and Institutional Change*, ed. Hans Born, Marina Caparini, Karl W. Haltiner, and Jürgen Kuhlmann, 48–61. New York: Routledge.

———. 2007. "The Role of the Ohrid Framework Agreement and the Peace Process in Macedonia." In *Regional Cooperation, Peace Enforcement, and the Role of the Treaties in the Balkans*, ed. Stefano Bianchini, Joseph Marko, Robert Craig Nation, and Milica Uvalić, 41–63. Ravenna: Longo.

Velikonja, Mitja. 2008. *Titostalgia: A Study of Nostalgia for Josip Broz*. Ljubljana, Slovenia: Mediawatch.

Verdery, Katherine. 1993. "Nationalism and National Sentiment in Post-Socialist Romania." *Slavic Review* 52, 2: 179–203.

———. 1996. *What Was Socialism and What Comes Next?* Princeton, N.J.: Princeton University Press.

Vickers, Miranda. 1998. *Between Serb and Albanian: A History of Kosovo*. London: Hurst.

Vickers, Miranda and James Pettifer. 1997. *Albania: From Anarchy to a Balkan Identity*. New York: New York University Press.

Vlaisavljević, Ugo. 2002. "South Slav and the Ultimate War-Reality." In *Balkan as Metaphor: Between Globalization and Fragmentation*, ed. Dusan Bjelić and Obrad Savić, 191–207. Cambridge, Mass.: MIT Press.

Volčic, Zala. 2007. "Yugo-Nostalgia: Cultural Memory and Media in the Former Yugoslavia." *Critical Studies in Media Communication* 24, 1: 21–38.

von Kohl, Christine and Wolfgang Libal. 1997. "Kosovo, the Gordian Knot of the Balkans." In *Kosovo: In the Heart of the Powder Keg*, ed. Robert Elsie, 3–104. Boulder, Colo.: East European Monographs.

Vucinich, Wayne S. 1969. "Nationalism and Communism." In *Contemporary Yugoslavia: Twenty Years of Socialist Experiment*, ed. Wayne S. Vucinich, 236- 84. Berkeley: University of California Press.

Weldes, Jutta, Mark Laffey, Hugh Gusterson, and Raymond Duvall, eds. 1999. *Cultures of Insecurity: States, Communities, and the Production of Danger*. Minneapolis: University of Minnesota Press.

Weller, Marc. 1992. "The International Response to the Dissolution of the Socialist Federal Republic of Yugoslavia." *American Journal of International Law* 86, 3: 569–607.

Whitaker, Ian. 1981. "'A Sack for Carrying Things': The Traditional Role of Women in Northern Albanian Society." *Anthropological Quarterly* 54: 146–56.

Whitehead, Stephen M. 2002. *Men and Masculinities: Key Themes and New Directions*. Malden, Mass.: Blackwell.

Whyte, Nicholas. 2002. "L'heure de l'Europe: enfin arrivée?" In *Readings in European Security*, ed. Marc Houben, Klaus Becher, and Michael Emerson., vol. 1, *European Security Forum*, 33–41. Brussels: Centre for European Policy Studies.

Wilkinson, Henry R. 1951. *Maps and Politics: A Review of the Ethnographic Cartography of Macedonia*. Liverpool: University Press.

Williams, Abiodun. 2000. *Preventing War: The United Nations and Macedonia*. Lanham, Md.: Rowman & Littlefield.

Woodward, Susan L. 1985. "The Rights of Women: Ideology, Policy, and Social Change in Yugoslavia." In *Women, State, and Party in Eastern Europe*, ed. Sharon L. Wolchik and Alfred G. Meyer, 234–56. Durham, N.C.: Duke University Press.

———. 1995a. *Balkan Tragedy: Chaos and Dissolution After the Cold War*. Washington, D.C.: Brookings Institution.

———. 1995b. *Socialist Unemployment: The Political Economy of Yugoslavia, 1945–1990*. Princeton, N.J.: Princeton University Press.

Young, Antonia. 2000. *Women Who Become Men: Albanian Sworn Virgins*. New York: Berg.

Young, Allan. 1996. "Suffering and the Origins of Traumatic Memory." *Daedalus* 125, 1: 245–60.

Yuval-Davis, Nira. 1997. *Gender and Nation*. London: Sage.

Zanca, Russell. 2000. "Intruder in Uzbekistan: Walking the Line Between Community Needs and Anthropological Desiderata." In *Fieldwork Dilemmas: Anthropologists in Postsocialist States*, ed. Hermine G. De Soto and Nora Dudwick, 153–71. Madison: University of Wisconsin Press.

Žarkov, Dubravka. 2001. "The Body of the Other Man: Sexual Violence and the Construction of Masculinity, Sexuality and Ethnicity in the Croatian Media." In *Victims, Perpetrators or Actors? Gender, Armed Conflict and Political Violence*, ed. Caroline O. N. Moser and Fiona Clark, 69–82. London: Zed Books.

———. 2007. *The Body of War: Media, Ethnicity, and Gender in the Break-up of Yugoslavia*. Durham, N.C.: Duke University Press.

Živković, Marko. 2000. "Telling Stories of Serbia: Native and Other Dilemmas on the Edge of Chaos." In *Fieldwork Dilemmas: Anthropologists in Postsocialist States*, ed. Hermine G. De Soto and Nora Dudwick, 49–68. Madison: University of Wisconsin Press.

ACKNOWLEDGMENTS

The kind support and generosity of many people have made this book possible. I am grateful to members of the Albanian and Macedonian communities in Skopje who welcomed me into their lives and helped me in numerous ways, including introducing me to their friends and neighbors, graciously sharing their time with me, and checking on me throughout the period of the armed conflict to make sure that I stayed safe from harm. I am honored and privileged by their trust and friendship. I thank especially the families of my Macedonian and Albanian language tutors and of my Albanian landlady, who treated me like a family member, providing unbounded warmth and encouragement, home-cooked meals, endless amounts of Turkish tea and coffee, and always interesting stories. I have used pseudonyms to protect the privacy of all the people with whom I worked.

The research on which this work is based was supported by an International Research and Exchanges Board Individual Advanced Research Opportunities (IREX/IARO) Research Fellowship, a Research Fellowship from the Minda de Gunzburg Center for European Studies at Harvard University, and a Harvard-MIT MacArthur Transnational Security Issues research grant. This research was also aided by a Writing Fellowship in East European Studies from the American Council of Learned Societies (ACLS). A fellowship at the Harriman Institute at Columbia University provided opportunities for me to present work-in-progress and receive valuable feedback from the wider university community.

The writing of the book greatly benefited from a book manuscript workshop organized by the Baldy Center for Law and Social Policy at the State University of New York at Buffalo (UB). Time to complete the final preparation was graciously made available by UB through a Nuala McGann Drescher Leave Award. A Faculty Research Fellowship from UB Humanities Institute also greatly facilitated the final stages of the book's production, and I thank in particular Humanities Institute Director Tim Dean and Executive Director Carrie Tirado Breman. An award from the Julian Park Publication Fund in the College of Arts and Sciences at UB defrayed publication costs. The Center for East European and Russian/Eurasian Studies (CEERES) at the University of Chicago kindly supported the final stages of my book's completion by sponsoring a private manuscript consultation with the Director of CEERES, Victor A. Freedman. Vesna Markoska, working with the American Councils for International Education office in Macedonia, helped me to circumvent bureaucratic hurdles and secure permission to reproduce the map of Skopje appearing in this book. A portion of Chapter 6 appeared in "Post-Socialism, Social Value, and Identity Politics Among Albanians in Macedonia," *Slavic Review: Interdisciplinary Quarterly of Russian, Eurasian, and East European Studies* 69, 4 (2010): 882-902.

Academic colleagues and friends have offered intellectual stimulation and camaraderie at different stages of this project. I thank my fellows in the anthropology department of Harvard University, Manduhai Buyandelger, Young-a Park, Ilay Romain Ors, Michelle Tisdel, Aykan Erdemir, Tahmima Anam and Kathleen O'Connor, for their enthusiasm and conversations with me. Melissa L. Caldwell, Thomas M. Malaby, and Kimberly Hart have provided prompt and invaluable criticisms and suggestions on drafts of this work at various stages of its development. I am grateful to Lynn Mather, who in her capacity as Director of UB's Baldy Center for Law and Social Policy organized in April 2008 a workshop on my book manuscript. Susan L. Woodward and Robert M. Hayden were remarkable workshop commentators, providing constructive criticism, and generous and precious advice. I am hugely appreciative of their input and hope they find the final product to their liking. For their critical and insightful engagement with this work, I am also deeply thankful to workshop participants Lynn Mather, Barbara Tedlock, Deborah Reed-Danahay, Mateo Taussig-Rubbo, Tilman Lanz, Donald Pollock, Phillips Stevens, Kimberly Hart, and Gwynn Thomas. Biljana Vankovska and Gordana Siljanovska-Davkova helped increase my understanding of the complexities of the Ohrid Framework Agreement. My colleagues in the anthropology department have helped make UB a welcoming place for me to carry out this work. Very special thanks go to David J. Bertuca, UB's Map Librarian, who provided most generous and invaluable help with all the artwork contained in this book and responded to my many requests with immense patience, courtesy, and skill. Many thanks also go to Mislim Hasipi for his help in gathering newspaper clippings and his sharp promptness and efficiency in answering my various queries during the final stages of the manuscript's preparation. Loring M. Danforth's positive feedback and astute comments have been instrumental in bringing this work to fruition, and I am especially grateful for his unflagging support. I owe an immense and lasting intellectual debt to the Director of CEERES at the University of Chicago Victor A. Friedman, who took the time to read the penultimate draft of the manuscript with great care and unstinting attention, and provided generous commentary and key suggestions for improvement during a book consultation, sponsored by CEERES, in Chicago and thereafter. Michael Herzfeld has been a constant source of inspiration and guidance throughout the years; I owe my greatest intellectual debt to him.

At the University of Pennsylvania Press, Peter A. Agree has been enthusiastic about this project from the beginning and has offered precious encouragement at all stages. It has been a pleasure working with him. Thanks also go to Tobias Kelly, series editor for the Press series, The Ethnography of Political Violence, for his support.

None of the above-mentioned organizations and individuals are responsible for the opinions expressed in this book. I alone am responsible for any errors or shortcomings contained in the present work.

This book is dedicated to my parents, Niki and Panagioti Neofotistos. Without their love, unending and selfless support, and admirable open-mindedness this book would not have been written.